A RIDE IN MOROCCO

AMONG

BELIEVERS AND TRADERS

BY

FRANCES MACNAB

AUTHOR OF

'RELICS,' 'ON VELDT AND FARM,' 'BRITISH COLUMBIA FOR
SETTLERS,' ETC.

'Gibraltar was not the first place that England occupied
in the Mediterranean. Another place had been previously
held and abandoned—one of far greater intrinsic value,
and of incalculable commercial possibilities—Tangiers'

W. F. LORD: *England and France in the Mediterranean*

LONDON
EDWARD ARNOLD
NEW YORK
LONGMANS GREEN AND CO.
1902

PREFACE

THE following pages require no preface, but I should like to say that they are intended for readers who may feel disposed to travel in Morocco, rather than for those persons who already know the country.

My travels were confined to the beaten highway. I started with no special object. Anyone with very little experience of travelling other than by railways could do the same. But it would be desirable that they should first make themselves familiar with the general conditions of the country, and it is certainly an advantage to know something of the language.

I may add that, having had no previous relations with the near or far East, I saw Morocco entirely from a Western standpoint. To my surprise, I found this strip of Africa offered problems of great importance to the uttermost parts of our Empire; and was sufficiently attractive to the United States to furnish the occasion for a naval demonstration.

I am emboldened to write of what I saw in this coastal plain, feeling that many Westerns may be drawn there; and that to many others who may never go so far my ride in Morocco may offer somewhat special interest.

THE AUTHOR.

SOUTH WEALD,
February, 1902.

CONTENTS

CHAPTER VIII

CHAPTER IX

CHAPTER X

CHAPTER XI

CHAPTER XII

CHAPTER XIII

CHAPTER XIV

CHAPTER XV

CHAPTER XVI

CHAPTER XVII

CHAPTER XVIII

CHAPTER XIX

CHAPTER XX

CHAPTER XXI

CHAPTER XXII

CHAPTER XXIII

CONTENTS

CHAPTER XXIV

CHAPTER XXV

CHAPTER XXVI

CHAPTER XXVII

LIST OF ILLUSTRATIONS

* The above picture is a reproduction from an oil-painting in the possession of Christopher Tower, Esq., of Weald Hall, Essex. It represents the landing of Lord Sandwich in 1662 from the *Royal Charles* at Tangiers to take possession of part of the dowry of Catharine of Braganza. The date of the picture is believed to be early in the eighteenth century.

A RIDE IN :MOROCCO

AMONG BELIEVERS AND TRADERS

CHAPTER I

LANDING IN TANGIERS

It was on the first evening of the new century, just as the big gun boomed to announce that the sun had set and the faithful might eat and drink (for it was the Fast of Ramadan), that my ship dropped her anchor in the Bay of Tangiers.

The light of day had gone, but the heavens were still brilliant, and where his disc had sunk into the western sea the air was glowing on his track.

To go ashore in the dusk at an Eastern port is not the most agreeable thing to do; but so great was my desire to set foot in Africa once more, that by special favour I and my effects were taken ashore in the agent's boat, rowed by a dozen wrangling natives.

As the Moors were more interested in their disputes than in getting the Christian ashore, the boat moved leisurely, propelled by long sweeps. From the water's level Tangiers rose—a pile of square, whitewashed houses, which showed ghostly as the sky cooled. One stately palm raised its head near the centre of the town, marking the grave of a saint or the spot where some mosque had its court and fountain. The red flag of the Sultan, the minarets of several mosques,

the rounded dome of a koubah, the square, ragged outline
of the kasbah crowning the hill and overlooking the town,
added the last touches of the Orient. Yet it was Africa!

The change from day to night was effected in the time we
took in getting from the ship to the pier. The water, as
clear as glass, darkened and seemed to deepen. A pale
moon literally shone in the vault of purest azure; the
houses huddled in the old town reflected the faint rays on
their blank surface, and a hidden lantern here and there cast
its light upwards.

On the quay I found a dignified old Moor. From the
yellow slippers with no heels into which he thrust the toes
of his stockinged feet, to the transparent haik which fell
elegantly from his turbaned head, draping the dark blue
cloak, he was a handsome, well-dressed personage, and a
long white beard, kept scrupulously clean, and very fine
dark eyes assorted with an air of benevolent patronage.

After surveying me a moment and graciously inclining his
head, he sank down upon a cushion, and sat there cross-
legged. Meantime a slave accommodated me with a rickety
little stool, as a concession to my want of breeding, which
had not taught me to descend upon the floor and tuck my
legs inside my skirts.

This old gentleman was the Captain of the Port, and all
my luggage had to be passed by him. Some of the cases
caused him a flutter. ' A tent !'—a sharp glance at me, and
the mental question, ' What can a Nazarene woman want
with a tent? The hand of the Legation may be here! And
these many little cases '—as he snatched at the straps of
a camera case—' what does the woman do with these?'
The use of the camera was explained to him, and he dropped
it as if a serpent had stung him. All my things were passed.
No, there was nothing to pay. He bowed and waved, still
watching me with suspicion in the light of a solitary
candle, as I rose to depart for my hotel.

The dark forms of the Moors in their cloaks, with the tassel of the fez flying out as they gesticulated, argued, and lifted the cases, stood out in the moonlight; and I could see their dusky features in the light of the lamp—a very dingy one, which hung above the head of the old man, who might have been Father Abraham, but who was Captain of the Port. What impressed me most was their harsh, guttural voices, as they all talked together, wrangling, disputing, shouting, and vociferating from the depths of their chests. Suddenly I saw a lad, a half-clothed child, whose pale habiliments and light skin showed up against the dark cloaks and swarthy complexions of the Moors. Immediately he added his shrill piping voice to the babel, and it rang out high and sharp above the bass of the men. Two asses appeared from nowhere, as they do on the stage. Great doors banged and clattered, and my large basket trunk was to be given the post of honour; it was to lead the way. Habit has made the Moors clever at packing all manner of cases and bales on the backs of animals, but my first introduction to the surprises of Moorish transport was the silhouette of that great trunk balanced on the back of a diminutive donkey, while a Moor on either side held it in position, both shouting incessantly at each other and the donkey, which did not seem able to proceed unless urged to do so with much oratorical flourish. Not that they could by any means insure its going straight. At the first opportunity it turned aside, and I saw the outline of the old friend of my travels looking helpless and foolish as the donkey scrambled away with it up some dark alley. The Moors held on, but they screamed and yelled with such zeal that by good luck it reappeared, the donkey walking sedately with the Moors on either side. The whole thing suggested armorial bearings—and why not? What a couple of cabs could have taken easily required a long retinue of donkeys and endless Moors to wait on them. Thus I pro-

ceeded through the narrow, tortuous streets, often passing
under archways, and everywhere a crowd of human life in all
sorts of condition. Life! At every step there was a living
incident. Beggars in rags, men washing at the fountains,
the blind, the halt, the maimed, creatures deformed and
twisted out of all semblance to human beings.   Veiled
women sat with their backs to the street, with loaves of
bread laid out on the stones for sale.   A burst of barbarous
music announced the approach of a little procession of
tatterdemalions, carrying lanterns and flags, which threaded
its way through the crowd.   They were a religious sect on
their way to prayers, and their saint was in the midst.   The
rich man rode past on his fat mule, with his slave on foot
crying, 'Balaak !'* before him.   The water-carrier, with his
goatskin on his back, ran nimbly past ringing his little bell.
The Holy Fool, with his iron sceptre and dirty rags, swung
past in a lordly manner; the very poor timidly offered him
coppers, and the rich let him alone.   All the little cupboards
in the walls which answer for shops were open, and added the
colour of draperies, pottery, swords in scarlet scabbards, and
swinging brass lamps.

We passed through the city gate into the soko, or market,
where the country people dispose of their produce.   It was a
relief to be out of the narrow streets.   Flaring lights lit the
circle gathered round the seller of sweets or food-stuffs.   But
the story-teller preferred the quiet and mystery of the moonlight.   There were sellers of salt, of grain, of charcoal; there
were sheep and goats, camels and mules; women who had
walked miles with a couple of pigeons, a few eggs, or a
bundle of palmata; and nearly all the business was done
in Moorish copper coins.   But the sales were over, the
market was humming with gossip, and before rough and
tattered tents the evening meal was cooking and fires blazing.

I went down to the Hôtel Cecil after leaving some effects

* Make way !

at the Villa de France, and a good dinner and comfortable bed after a voyage are among the recognised luxuries of life. But I lay awake for hours thinking of the land and the life which stretched before me. The windows were open, and the moonlight flooded the room. A slight breath stirred the trees on the terrace, bringing at intervals the monotonous murmur of the sea.

I had come to Morocco because it was the nearest point of Africa and easiest to get at ; I fondly imagined it would be as easy to get out of. But from its bar ports, and the uncertainty and roundabout nature of its steam service, I found that this was not the case. Of interest I knew it was not lacking—this white man's Africa, which borders the land of the sons of Ham. The history of no other land records an ambition to compare with its dream of conquest, not merely by force of arms, but by culture and the deep pleasure of life ; and behind it all lay a stately background of barbaric pomp. Other empires have risen by conquest, by colonies ; Morocco alone, in the dream of Yakub El Mansûr, aspired to rule nations by the power of learning and the charm of culture. A land of palaces and shrines, of gardens, of marble hills and precious stones; a land of ruins and of hidden mineral wealth, of silence broken by the sobbing of captives and the weeping of slaves. And what strange tales were told me of the search for gold ! Each country has its own romance which hangs about the word 'gold'; but nowhere outside the 'Arabian Nights' have I heard anything to equal the tales of the Moors and their search for the precious dust. This was the land to which I had come. And as I closed my eyes, I heard above the sound of the sea and the rustle of the breeze the muezzin's midnight call. It rose and fell and rose again, that sound which once heard is never forgotten : ' Praised be God who made the world ! Prayer is better than sleep—than sleep ! Come ye to pray —come ye to pray !'

CHAPTER II

THERE is a legend which the enlightened Moors (they are
few enough) are prone to dwell upon. It runs as follows:
' When God was making the world, He paused and called the
nations to Him, and said : " Here I have made the earth,
and I have made you. Now you may each of you ask for
whatever you want in your countries, and I will give it you."
Then the nations asked for the things they most wished to
have, and whatever they asked for they received. When
it was over, they began discussing amongst themselves the
value of their requests. One had asked for a beautiful
climate; another for a handsome people and a rich soil;
a third for mineral wealth ; a fourth for rich vegetation and
beautiful scenery. " I," said the Moor, " asked for all ; and
I have got all." But the Englishman said: " I asked for
only one thing, and the rest will come. I asked for a good
government." " Ah," said the others, " we forgot that." '

Morocco is faithfully described by this story, where all
is rich and fair to the eye and sense, and where not even
utter misrule can destroy what the ancients called ' the
Garden of the Hesperides.'

The Sultan rules by right of his holy descent, and with
the sanction of the Shereef, or Saint of Wazan. Though
nominally an autocratic Sovereign, his power and influence
is jealously watched, shared, and even disputed by that of

countless shereefs, who have the royal right of collecting dues from the people, which in point of fact amount to a very burdensome taxation.

The superstitious side of the Moor comes out in his belief in saints and guardian angels. It was more than once my experience to have a Moor pointed out to me as a remarkably brave man—recklessly so. In point of fact, what made him brave was his absolute confidence in his guardian angel. He never went out on a dark night without praying fervently to this benign spirit to turn aside from him the swords and the bullets of his enemies.

It was not my good fortune to get at really close quarters with a saint. Shereefs and shereefas I met, but they were only saints by inheritance. However, a friend of mine knew a saint, and stayed with him. He lived in the hills in a remote part of the country which was very inaccessible. People came to him and brought him presents, and my friend asked them why they did so. They said they did it because he was a saint, and God took care of him. My friend asked them what the man did that God had to take so much care of him. They said: 'Every time he goes out he brings back something. He never returns to his house empty-handed. Sometimes it is a mule, sometimes a camel or a sheep; but it is always something. Now, that is a proof that God takes care of him.' This went on for many years, but one night the saint went out and never returned. Some time afterwards it was said that he had been shot and killed, God having forgotten to take care of him on that occasion. But the people believe that he will yet return, and bring something with him.

The custom of vendetta obtains among some tribes; in others the dia, or the price of blood. In the last case, if the aggressor and victim agree the law does not interfere. It rests with the murderer to offer to pay the family of the dead man the price of his blood, and if the family agree to this a document is drawn up, and neither law nor Sultan can interfere. The vendetta is handed on from father to son until vengeance has been carried out. The feeling is especially strong among the Riffs, who would consider it a disgrace to accept the price of blood. A murder thus becomes a legacy from generation to generation. As soon as the first murder is committed, the nearest relative knows that he must pursue the murderer and kill him. When that is done, the nearest of kin to the murdered man must pursue the man who killed his relative. Sometimes men take years in hunting for their victim. It even happens that the ill-feeling dies out, and the two families may be living amicably, when something unfortunate happens, and is attributed to the failure or negligence in carrying out the vendetta; then the man knows that he must take his knife or his gun and lie in wait and kill the unsuspecting victim, who for some years past has been living close to him in peace and friendship.

But vendetta is much worse where it involves a whole tribe. I believe this is the case with the Beni Hassan, a powerful tribe in the Marmora Forest. If a murder be committed by a man outside the tribe, then the whole of the tribe has vendetta against the whole of the murderer's tribe. There is a kind of running war between the two, for wherever the men of the two tribes meet it is their duty to kill each other.

Moors are capable of great fidelity. My Kaid El Hashmy, of a Sus tribe, was a remarkable instance; but he was not the only servant I had of proved fidelity. They will not trust a stranger, but their loyalty to people they know is striking.

The best and most faithful servants are the Riffs. They always carry arms, and I heard of households where as many as six Riffs were employed. They slept in the house, and the Europeans rested in security. The town Moor can never be depended upon, and even if he had arms given him would sooner open the door to a robber than risk his skin.

Every house of the least importance is granted a soldier, or even two soldiers, as guards, or a guarantee of protection from the Bashaw.

There was a Riff who was an oyster-catcher, whose acquaintance I made owing to the interest I took in fishing. He used to arrive at the Hôtel Cecil very early, and sometimes I had a chat with him after I had been out to feed my horse. One morning I was waiting for my breakfast, when the oyster-catcher came up the steps to the terrace, carrying his little basket, and made straight for my window. He had come upon some Roman coins when he was oyster-hunting, and from talking of these we went on to talk of the ruins of old Tangiers. This proceeded while I ate my breakfast, and we arranged to go together to visit the ruins. I had often been alone, and could go at any time, but the Riff suggested that he should take me. My breakfast was soon disposed of, and I shouted for my horse. By the time I was ready the rain was coming down. Nevertheless, having made up my mind to start, I handed out my blanket and saddle, and was soon mounted and off.

The oyster-catcher ran on in front—a tall, lean, active mountaineer, erect as a pine-tree. He went so fast that Conrad had to step out briskly to keep within a few yards of him. Along the sands we went, then inland over the sand-hills, down a lane to a ford; over the ford and under the shelter of the hill of Shaf; across the bridge and through the plain, which was a sea of mud in places up to my horse's knees; past little market-gardens fenced with aloes and prickly pear; down a lane flooded with water, where branches and blossoming thorns met overhead—and on to the shore again.

The rain left off and the sun came out, and the Riffian waved his arms towards the green hill and cried: 'Romanos! Todos Romanos! Una ciudad Romana!' It sounded like a lament, and the voice, as it died away over the green hill, harmonized with the wailing of the sea over the long-departed glory.

He ran on again till he crossed a little stream swollen by the rain, and here he carefully washed the mud from his bare legs and feet, and, pointing to the ground, said: ' Mucha aqua! Bueno por que se vé a los Romanos!'*

I did not quite understand him then, but I did so later, for it is these streams which, washing down the hillside over the site of the city, lay bare odds and ends, such as coins, for which his quick dark eyes were searching.

Again he ran before me, my horse following at a trot. We passed by a long low wall, black with time, or perhaps from fire. Waving his arms above his head, the Riffian cried, ' Puerta de la ciudad!' and ran before me through the gaping breach of what was once the port of a city.

The Riffian turned and faced me with an air of hospitable welcome ; my horse stopped, and I dismounted.

Green grass grew within the enclosure of the mighty massive walls ; palmata, asphodels and narcissus covered the hillside, growing between the stones of the ruins. Only a part of the walls remain intact fronting the sea, and about fifty yards running parallel to an inner harbour, which is now used for salt pans. The sea has receded since the days when the barges came to the quay, but its waves still lap to the foundations, and high tides roll through the yawning breach.† The city extended where at low tide there is

---

* The Moors call all foreigners Romans.

† The frontispiece represents the landing of Lord Sandwich as having taken place at the Anjera end of the bay ; from which it seems that the Tangiers of the English possession was originally a Portuguese town on the site of the ruins of Tingis. The inner harbour and the hill forts and surrounding country confirm this opinion ; and the proximity to the Anjera country and the low-lying site account for the continual attacks of the tribes. Probably it was for the greater safety of the town, and to protect the mole which they immediately began to build, that the English removed the town to the site of the Berber hill stronghold on the spur of the rock, where Tangiers, protected by the kasbah, now stands.

mud and sand, the wharf projected into deep water. The
river now reaches the sea a quarter of a mile nearer to
modern Tangiers.

I walked with the Riffian up the modern track, which
must once have been an important and busy street. As we
passed close to the spot where the argosies brought rich
cargoes from the outer world, he stooped, and with a cry of
delight pounced on a small bronze coin. He rubbed it
between his finger and thumb, and handed it to me, saying:
' Romanos ! Buenos Romanos !' I took it, and looked at
the head of Cæsar still crowned with laurel.

Other coins we found also—Spanish, Moorish, and Portuguese. The last were pathetically characteristic : on one
side a proud escutcheon, and on the reverse an ancient
castellated sailing-ship. They were clipped and battered
and worn, yet they linked our day with that of Prince Henry
the Navigator, whose austere life was devoted to his profession in order that a Christian Power might some day
wrest from the infidel the trade of the East. One English
farthing we found—the date of the English occupation,
when the ground where I was standing was British.

The heavy rains brought rivulets singing from the hill, as
though they carried messages from the asphodels, who
learnt them from the earth. They were the singers of the
deeds of olden times, telling of the exploits of heroes on
that spot ; of travellers and chroniclers who had landed
there and walked through its streets ; of the days of
pageantry — of great processions, of triumphs, of conquering Kings and retinues of slaves ; of men whom
time had borne away ; of those who had ruled and judged
and feasted ; of those who had suffered and sorrowed. Only
these battered coins were left, which once had passed in
exchange for all the city had to give. When evil days came,
people hid their money in the floors and walls of their
houses. In the scrimmage they were killed, or they went

over the sea and never returned. The walls crumbled—the
coins slipped away.

Another Riffian joined us who fell to praising the good
Romans. But soon—so he said—the herbs would grow up,
and then the Romans would be hidden, and he stooped as
he spoke to pick up another head of Augustus and slip it
into my hand. Only in winter-time, when there came
plenty of water from above, did the Romans come to light.

Thus spoke the descendants of the men who had broken
the power of Portugal and turned back the arms of victorious
Rome, even as my own people had done in the North of
Britain. Never to have been great is not unnatural, and
the path of that hope, which is 'the medicine of the
miserable,' lies before these tribesmen still.

I mounted my horse to ride back, and presently the
oyster-catcher's profession claimed him; and, bidding me
wait, he walked into the water, returning immediately with
two large stones encrusted with oysters, which, though
small, were more delicious in flavour than the English
oyster. Then he cut me a branch of yellow - flowering
genista, and with this in his hand he ran before me over the
mud and across the rivers on to the sand-hills again, and
back to Hôtel Cecil in brilliant sunshine.

Once I went out fishing, but as that relates to boating,
and has nothing to do with riding, I will leave my readers
to go to Tangiers and find out what it was like. Suffice it
to say that I enjoyed it supremely, especially the society of
the crew of Riff pirates, who wanted to sail to Gibraltar.
We caught a boatload of fish; and it was beautiful to watch
the solan - geese drop from the blue above to the blue
beneath. Before we returned we drew up alongside the
Sultan's man-o'-war and boarded it, being most kindly
received, in the absence of the captain, by the chief engineer
and another officer, probably a marine. They were both
Germans, and entered thoroughly into the humour of the

situation. The chief engineer had five Germans under him, and between them they kept the engines in an apparently high state of efficiency. But the crew, who were all Moors, changed every third day. They knew nothing at all about ships—nor would they learn. While we were on board we saw them occupied in their private and domestic affairs. Some had just come on board, and brought with them a quantity of clothes to wash; others were busy airing their bedding, others whiling away the time catching small fish over the side of the ship. The remainder did nothing but quarrel amongst themselves. The pay is excellent. They are three days on board and three days on shore, and they get their food on board and £3 a month. So good a berth is considered good enough pension for any friend or relation of the Sultan.

However much they may differ amongst themselves, on one point they are agreed—nothing will induce them to obey an order. If one be given, they dispute it immediately, and argue that it would be much better not to do it. Measures to enforce discipline are forbidden to be used. But the German officers can hale the crew before the Governor of the town. When this is resorted to, the Governor asks who the prisoner is. 'Oh! he's the uncle of the Sultan's wife,' or, 'The cousin of the Sultan's uncle.' 'Well, let the poor fellow go,' says the Bashaw; 'you shouldn't give him so much to do;' and there the matter ends.

On one occasion a little light occupation was found for one of the crew which it was thought he would not object to. He was to hold the office of lamp-trimmer to the ship. But he did it so badly—in fact, so seldom made any attempt at touching the lamps at all—that the officer remonstrated. 'Who are you to talk to me?' inquired the Moor. 'Don't you know that I am the Sultan's cousin?'—which disposed effectually of further lamp-trimming. 'It is your work to clean the deck, and therefore you must do it,' said the German when first he found it was not done. 'Why should I do it?' asked the Moor; 'you are a German, and you come here to work. Do it yourself. I do not come here to work. I am the cousin of the Grand Vizier.'

The situation was full of irony. We sat on a shockingly ill-kept deck, yet the ship was a smart modern Italian-built ship. The guns were of the best make and type. One Hotchkiss, which I asked to see without its cover, was so rusty that I wiped the rust off with my fingers. The crew could not handle them, and the Germans had more work than they could get through in the day. A grand state-room had been fitted up on board for the Sultan's use, and decorated in Moorish style; but he was never likely to see it, as he is forbidden to leave the shore.

Though I do not think Germans are capable of training natives (for even if they had permission to resort to disciplinary measures, they would never get in touch with them), still, the material provided—town Moors—was of the worst. 'In my country's service,' said the chief engineer, 'an officer says to his men, "Look here, this thing is white; but *I* say it is *black*. Therefore, in future you are all to remember *it is black*."' To a people who delight and excel in argument, what a delicious opportunity would be given by such an announcement! I found the country Moor not merely ready, but anxious to obey. But, then, they entertained an extraordinary opinion of the English; and if I put aside anything that they did, and said, 'That is the Moorish way, but now look at the English way,' they laughed and were delighted.

But on board the man-of-war kief and sleep made time pass for the Moors; laager-beer and cigars soothed the Germans; and they got on together about as well as most 'happy families' where incongruous natures are caged together—and live—without a vestige of liking or respect.

Returning to our boat, we made the crew put up the sail.
I wanted to see them do it, though they argued that it was
no use unless we were going to Gibraltar. There were
several kinds of gulls besides the ordinary herring-gull and
the tern, and I counted six solan-geese.

Trawling is practised in the deep-water part of the bay,
about half a mile from the town. It is that end of the bay
which will become the real seaport if Tangiers is ever thrown
open as a port in earnest. A river runs into the sea at that
end, which might be made navigable for small flat-bottomed
crafts for about two miles of its course, but not further.
Cattle or corn could come down from the rich valley beyond
the hill of Shaf. If irrigation works were started in that plain,
I should like to see a thousand acres put down in lucerne.

The sands in Tangiers Bay are always interesting. There
the life of the shepherd and fisherman meet.* There is a
continual traffic of asses, mules, and camels hurrying to the
market at Tangiers. Even at night, when the wide vault
above was lit with a thousand stars and the moon had
started on her journey across the sky, the sound of the
mule - bells reached my room, and I knew that belated
travellers from Tetuan, or from the old Portuguese fort on
the other side of the river, which serves as a caravanserai,
were drawing near to the city. Camels seldom came from
the Tetuan road, but strings of them from Ceuta forded the
river at daybreak, and passed with swinging strides, casting
long shadows in the early dawn. The ford was very attractive,
and I often rode there to watch people cross.

The European shore is always visible, and sometimes the
houses, and even the streets, can be seen in the Moorish
Spanish towns. The sea sparkles and dances in the sunshine,
and outside the bay there are the fishermen always at work
catching something, according to time and place.

---

* The fish netted and dragged ashore are very strange beasts, including
torpedo fish, snakes, mackerel-guard, etc.

'The herring loves the merry moonlight,
    The mackerel loves the wind ;
But the oyster loves the dredging sand,
    For they come of a humble kind.'

That distant shore was always alluring. Behind it lies all
that Africa has missed. But more—far more—than the
depths of the sea lie between them. Deeper than the
depths of ocean is the deceitfulness of human nature, with
its inexplicable affections, that no plummet has ever sounded.
More powerful for the good or evil of this world are the
strong currents, far out of sight, in human souls which bear
away for ever those who descend into them, though the
surface remains serene and smooth. No chart can tell the
contradictory winds which blow from zones of unrealized
pressure. We do not know where the storm has raged or
the ships have sunk. There is the wreckage on the shore.
And afterwards come days of halcyon calm, when the light
from heaven streams over sea and land, and it is easy to
sail the straightest course, while the waters hush themselves
to rest and we dream of the many whose lives have passed
to where tempests for ever cease, and of the challenge of the
daring adventurer on its surface, 'Bid me come to Thee
upon the water,' and of the monosyllabic benediction when
He said 'COME !'

CHAPTER III

ONE morning I started at 8.30 to visit the village of El
Minaar, the white koubah of whose saint's tomb is distinctly
visible from the terrace of the Cecil Hotel. I started early
in order to catch the tide for fording the river. I took my
Moor, Mohammed Jellally, on my mule Mooleeta, and we
went at a good pace, both of us being light-weights and the
animals young and fresh.

After we had left the second of the Portuguese forts behind
us, we climbed up a creek. This soon turned out to be the
wrong road. Mohammed had known for the last week that
I intended to go to El Minaar, and I had told him a dozen
times that he must inquire about the way, but, with true
Moorish procrastination, he put it off; and then, after my
horse was saddled, and I was ready to start, he suggested
that he should run to the soko and find out the road. Had
he done so, we should have lost the tide, so we started with
such directions as we could glean from a multitude of counsellors composed of all the Moors at Hôtel Cecil all talking
at once. Moors are always bad at a start. They are a
highly-strung people, and the least excitement makes them
lose the little head they have. They require great forbearance, and 'it weareth the Christian down.' Besides, as I
discovered afterwards, Mohammed was bent on going to
Cape Malabata.

2

In riding up the creek I saw that the river had been doing a little mining on its own account. There was plenty of iron ore laid bare, and stone which looked like black marble. The Moors believe that whatever is in the earth belongs to the genii, and that the spirits will slay those who come to rob them of their property. Even if dollars are buried in the ground for a certain time, the genii claim them, and it is dangerous for an ordinary man to try and dig them up. The spirits will come out of the ground and kill him, unless he be protected by a wizard.

Near Tangiers there is a marshy piece of ground where some natives of Sus buried their treasure. Years afterwards their children returned and camped on the spot, hoping to find the money, but the spirits came out of the ground and slew so many of them that the others fled in terror. What really happened was that malarial fever killed some of them, and the rest withdrew to the town. There appear to be two kinds of genii—the wicked ones, who are avowed enemies of the human race, and others who are harmless, and may even be helpful at times. The evil ones come up out of the sea when the tide is awkward. They also haunt rivers, and, being of an irascible disposition, they are apt to dispose by drowning of those human beings who do not treat them with tact. But of all the bad and dangerous genii, those who live in the earth and keep a tight hand upon mineral deposits are the worst.

It is well known that the Christians are very curious about mines, and if they are not closely watched and prevented they will dig up the property of the genii; and, unfortunately, the genii make no distinction between the Christian dog and the true believer, but as often as not go off in their anger and destroy the true believer. This gives a great deal of trouble to Moors.

But there are ways which Moors know of whereby the property of the genii can be obtained either with or without their consent. The Moors know how to do this, but the Christians do not, and they must not be allowed to interfere, for their ways are not good ways. If a Moor should want some antimony for enamelling tiles and pottery, or for painting the eyes of the women, he must first go to a holy man, taking with him a present. The holy man will come and say prayers on the spot, and the man must be careful to take with him something that will keep the spirits from laying hold of him, and this he can buy from the holy man before he starts. Then he may dig and obtain all that he wants in safety, but no unbeliever must be allowed to come near, or to see what he is doing, for if by chance one even happened to ride that way all the prayers of the holy man would cease to be of avail. The genii would be angry, and would kill the first person to hand, which would be almost certainly a Moor. This had happened many times, and Moors had learnt to be careful.

But Christians are powerful people nowadays; it seems that they are more powerful than Moors. Their Sultans are not boys; and they have many ships which come to Morocco and say, 'Bow!' Nowadays the Moors cannot help what unbelievers do. So it happens that sometimes they have interfered with the genii of the earth; but the Moors went to the Sultan, for they were frightened, and the Sultan put a stop to it. But yet, if they *can* find out where the genii keep their treasures, the Christians *will* dig. It is a bad thing for a Moor to travel with such a Christian. It is far better for a Moor to be servant of a senorita, who does not think of such things.

Besides the iron ore and the black marble, I saw clay shale, and further on some blue clay, but I did not see that the decomposed blue clay in the wash of the hillside had any mica in it. If there be a reef of iron ore in the small inner bay on the Tangiers side of Cape Malabata, where the water is deep, it would be easy to work it cheaply. A small pier

2—2

run out to the ships could discharge the ore in automatic
cars running straight from the quarry.   On the hills heather
grows, but laurestinus, olive, arbutus, and, I think, myrtle,
indicate that trees would grow if given a chance, but the
natives cut down everything for burning.

In a valley I found brick-kilns, and bricks seem made there
pretty extensively.   They were the flat bricks like those
found in old Roman buildings, and probably the Romans
taught the trade, and may even have made the bricks for old
Tangiers at this very spot.   Thence we made straight for
the saint's tomb, whose koubah shone, white and dazzling, in
its grove of olive and mimosa.   It was the prayer-house or
mosque of the village of El Minaar.

When we were a quarter of a mile from the tomb, I dismounted from my horse, for it would have been impossible
to ride through the trees owing to their thick growth overhead.   Climbing down into a narrow ravine, I began to
ascend on the further side, through dense growth, where I
could see nothing of any kind of track.

It was a lovely and solemn approach to the sacred spot.
I was climbing with every step, but the trees with bare stems
beneath met overhead and made a cool shade.   Flickering
patches of sunlight fell at intervals upon the ground, and I
saw that I was walking in an old graveyard on the mountain-
side.   The graves were ranged very close—some with head-
stones, others marked by a circle of stones, and all were old
and mossy.   The intense silence was broken by the singing
of a kind of thrush far above my head and out of sight.   He
might have been singing to the dead or telling of their lives.
Outside was the dazzling sunshine and the blue sky, but
where I stood was cool, quiet shade, and the graves all
round.

There had been a battle fought here between the Anjera
tribe and the Sultan, and these were the graves of those who
had fallen.   The peasants had planted the olive-tree, which

is a sacred tree, between the graves, and honoured the dead
by never cutting a branch. Nobody could remember anything
about Sidi Minaar, and his house and all his kindred were gone.
All that anyone knew was that he was called Sidi Minaar
and that he was a saint. He was just the titular divinity of
the village, a survival of the worship which makes men long
for a special god of their own, to care for their special needs
and be their particular friend. A high-class Moslem told me
disdainfully that peasants prayed for nonsense, such as that
they might not be ill and that their crops might be good.
True believers pray in an orthodox manner. He himself said
' Allah !' a hundred times a day, and Allah knew all about it.

I found the shrine locked. The rusty bolt made a noise.
I turned my head without moving, and saw, creeping stealthily
between the trees, a Moor who carried his slippers in his
hand. His eyes lit up disagreeably at first sight of me, but
I walked towards him and said ' Good-day.' Then I sat
down under the trees and watched him wash his toes in
mugfuls of water, which he took out of a large stone jar set
there for that purpose. Whether he was the muezzin, or
whether he had merely come to pray for good crops, I cannot
say. There was a dignity and solemnity in the scene which
affected me so powerfully that I felt much inclined to pray
for myself and for the peasants by the tomb of old Sidi
Minaar in the grove of olives and mimosa ; but I had mis-
givings as to what might be happening to Mohammed
Jellally, therefore I rose and returned.

The Moors at all times interested me as much as dumb
animals do. I enjoyed watching them. As I emerged from
the trees the group formed by Conrad, Mohammed and
Mooleeta was delightful. Mooleeta was only two years old,
and very precocious. It was her first outing with Conrad.
From the very first she had tried Mohammed, and now she
appeared to have imbued Conrad with her own taste for
mischief. Poor Mohammed stood between them looking

distracted, turning his head from one to the other till the tassel on his fez flew out straight. Conrad, who was usually kind, was doing his best to stamp on Mohammed's golden slippers ; while Mooleeta was manœuvring to jerk the bridle out of his hand and make off home.

Mohammed's face brightened at the sight of me, and it was with genuine relief that he handed me Conrad's bridle. It was 'all Mooleeta's fault,' he assured me. Ah, she *was* a Mooleeta! It was lucky the senorita had come ; or Mooleeta might not have been there.

Then we set out to find the village of El Minaar. It was once the scene of mining operations undertaken for coal. But upon coal being discovered and proved to be good, the Sultan ordered the mine to be closed. I could not even find the spot.

I wanted to buy some forage from the villagers for the animals, but they would not sell me any. The streets are narrow, only allowing one mule or horse abreast, winding between the houses ; and each house is enclosed in a fence of prickly pear. They usually consist of two houses inside the fence, built very low, with the thatch coming forward in front and making a little stoep or veranda. Each dwelling has a cooking shelter and a store attached to it, and a rough stable for the calves. At night the sheep and goats are driven into the yard.

I looked over the prickly pear, and saw rather a nice old lady. I asked her in Spanish for something for my horse to eat. She paused, and, without answering me, asked Mohammed Jellally where I came from and who I was. Mohammed said I came from Tangiers, and that I was English and very distinguished. Then she said she would fetch some straw for my horse. As she was doing this, a man appeared, and I took out 50 cents to give him ; but he declined it, and invited me to come into his house and bring the animals inside the hedge.

I jumped down and led the way with Conrad. The peasant was an elderly man, with a good countenance. He brought a rope and tied Conrad at one end of the yard, and Mooleeta at the other. Then he ushered me into his house, the entrance of which was very low, and I sat on a carpet which he spread for me. It was the sleeping and eating room of himself, his wife, and one daughter of about fourteen. In the other dwelling opposite lived a married daughter and two children.

Though poor, everything was clean, and nothing was ragged. The man's jellaber was a good one, though only the ordinary striped jellaber of the Anjera peasant. His wife brought me fresh milk, butter, and eggs. Mohammed Jellally produced my luncheon-basket, and I got out my spirit-lamp and made some coffee. They watched the operations with interest, and the peasant told me that he was for some years in the service of Colonel Mathews. Both he and his wife evidently entertained the warmest recollection of Colonel Mathews, and they added that seeing me reminded them of those good days when they worked for Colonel Mathews and saw him and his family every day. They drank some coffee with me, and Mohammed fried me some eggs in a small earthen vessel on the top of my spirit-lamp. I had some oranges, which I gave the children, and so we had quite a feast.

I was much struck with the loyalty of these people to the memory of their old master, who had evidently been a kind friend to them. I was shown a paper—the certificate of protection, or mohallet, for Mammed Ben Mohammed, which, of course, accounted for the comfort and the well-to-do air of the little home.

The subject of conversation turned upon different nationalities. The Spaniards were the nation they despised most, and they are the people they would like to fight. The French they feared most. To the Germans they appeared indifferent;

the English and Americans were much the same. The next
time they fought it would be with France; 'but,' said
Mammed, 'I hope the English and Americans, who are
friends of the Moors, will do something to keep the French
away.

In this part of Morocco a certain class of Europeans are
very greedy to obtain landed property, and will resort to
very mean tricks by the aid of the Legations, and by taking
advantage of the corruption of Moorish officials. I was told
of some peasants who discovered a good spring of water on
their property, and upon this becoming known a Spaniard
asked the Sultan for a concession of the land. The Sultan
agreed to give them the property (that is to say, for a consideration, which he or his Bashaw would pocket). The
peasants were in great distress, and said, 'Sooner than let
the Spaniards have it, we will give it to the English'; and
this I believe they did, by getting English subjects to take
them into partnership, in which case the English Legation
would protect them; but if the story be true, it must have
happened some time ago.

As the sun was beginning to soften, I bade farewell to my
kind hosts, and Mammed himself accompanied me to the
outskirts of the village to put me on the right track. The
country was mountainous, and the scenery was very romantic,
but it was a very hard fighting country; for either cavalry or
guns there was not much chance. These villages are very
quiet during the day, only the old men and old women
remaining at home, and the children being at school, kept
by a foki, apparently, all day.

The village fokis are graduates of Fez. After they have
finished their studies, they start on a tour, walking from
village to village. On arriving at a village, where they are
always sure of hospitable entertainment—such is the Moor's
respect for learning—they begin a dispute, a wrestling match
in words, with the village fokis. The subject is generally

some argument drawn from Aristotle, and the contest generally lasts for several days. If the village foki own himself vanquished, the new man takes his place; otherwise, after a few days' rest, the traveller goes on his way again.

There was one old woman who lived in a village I frequently visited who made pottery inside the little enclosure surrounding her house. She brought the clay up from the river, and made the pots sitting on the ground and turning a small wheel with one hand, while with the other she moulded the clay. Then she collected firewood, heated an oven, and baked the pottery. And when she had got enough pots she hired a donkey from a fellow-villager and took her wares into the soko. There was generally a child or two belonging to a headman, and sometimes, in return for medicine obtained from herbs she knew how to select, the child brought her an egg, a little milk, or a mealie cob, and so she lived a gentle, blameless, and industrious life—a poor widow, grinding her own corn in her own little hand-mill, and praying to her special saint by his tomb on the hill.

CHAPTER IV

THE ride to Tetuan is the expedition usually prescribed for the more adventurous tourist, who lands at Tangiers and places himself in the hands of an hotel guide, or Cook's agent. More than one 'Mrs. Brown' went to Tetuan on a mule to make a first acquaintance with the East while I was in Tangiers; and, as many of my readers may do the same, it may interest them to learn my experience. The man I had with me was ambitious of becoming an hotel guide; but at the time I employed him he had not so far ruined himself, and I found him an excellent servant, though very soon afterwards I had to give him up, and leave him to the enjoyment of preying upon the tourists which the weekly steamers land in Tangiers.

A feeling of insecurity on the back of a donkey, and the unsympathetic nature of the hired mule, had decided me upon buying a Riff pony, about thirteen hands high, a silver gray with black points. He was very much out of condition, having been owned by a Frenchman; but he was only two years old, and I believed that good treatment and care would improve him. We got to understand each other and became the very best of friends, for he had plenty of life, and was sometimes in the wildest spirits; but there was not a scrap of vice in his whole nature, and he was so sensible that, even in the middle of a gallop, I could stop and get down to recover my stick or pick a flower, and he would stand like a rock for me to mount again. I stabled him at the hotel, paying for my own groom and feeding him myself. It is one of the good features of Tangiers as a winter resort that horses can be bought cheaply and kept economically.

But I rode to Tetuan on the regulation hired mule like any other ' Mrs. Brown,' being determined to see what that kind of travelling amounted to. It was of the kind which hurries by the way in order to reach a fondak for the night. We scrambled through in the day, first crossing a plain where the Portuguese built cities in old times, placing watch-towers on the hills; then through a gorge in the mountain to a fondak, where I camped for luncheon, and down the other side to Tetuan. There were villages perched on rising ground, sheltered and protected in most cases by crags, and sur-rounded with thick hedges of prickly pear. The little houses or huts were neatly built of mud, generally whitewashed, and thatched with the coarse rush of the swamps.

Before sunrise the peasants were on their way to the soko in Tangiers, with their donkeys' panniers full of produce. The women carried loads on their backs, bending double under them, with seven long weary miles to tramp. A woman's transport capacity is equal to half a donkey-load, and when it comes to fording a river the donkeys insist that the women cross first. The courage and hardihood of these poor creatures is marvellous; but is it surprising that their infants die, far more often than they live ?*

To English eyes these peasants present a very poverty-stricken appearance; but they are well off compared with those in the South. I never heard a satisfactory reason given for the difference, but the following are worth quoting : First, the North resolutely refused to pay the tax for the indemnity claimed by Spain after the war, and therefore the

* I often asked them for their children, and tears welled up into their eyes as they answered, ' Dead ! Dead !' One woman told me, counting on her fingers, that she had seven who were dead.

South had to pay the whole.* The second reason given me was that, there being richer products and more wealth in the South, there was greater temptation for the Kaids to plunder, especially as they were further removed from Europe and the eyes of the Legations. Thirdly, the old kingdom of Fez is largely under the mosque, whose dealings are more regular than those of the Sultan, though the mosque is bad enough.

Each peasant cultivates a plot of ground pretty much where he pleases without fencing it. It is only round the house and fig-garden, where a few vegetables are grown, that there is a fence of aloe or prickly pear. The goats, sheep, and cattle are turned loose to graze on the mountain, herded by lads, whose limbs are partly covered with tattered goat-skins, often recalling the 'St. John Baptist' of Murillo. This kind of herding offers plenty of opportunity for quarrels and disputes. As a rule, the headman of the village, who is elected by a kind of popular vote every year, settles these disputes; but sometimes the peasants drag each other before the Bashaw, who seizes the opportunity of squeezing money out of either or both parties. I was told that the peasants in the North suffer from the usurious practices of the Jews. This is possible, because they are better off than in the South, where the Abda and other tribes have been robbed till they are practically dying out.

The maladministration in the Bashaw's courts has resulted in the peasants doing justice among themselves, and many fearful cruelties ensue. The commonest crime amongst them is theft—they steal each other's implements or cattle. When a man is suspected of theft, he is tried roughly by the villagers, and if found guilty he is punished on the spot by the loss of a hand, or an eye, or both eyes. A sickle is heated in the fire and the eyes are hooked out; then the wretched victim wanders into the town, and sits by the gate

* This allegation, however, is not true. See page 33.

holding a little wooden dish and reciting verses from the
Koran to move the hearts of the charitable to contribute
to his maintenance.   Certain sums are disbursed by the
mosques on holidays and every Friday, and the beggars live
on the alms of the faithful.   I used to notice that the poor
gave more often to them than the rich, but not in coin.   A
lump of charcoal, or a little piece of kindling wood drawn
from the bundle before they take it to market, would be
laid gently down by the blind man's side, and the example
would be followed by others, till he had enough for one small
fire; then another would place an egg beside the charcoal, or
an onion ; and perhaps one would rise to half or even a whole
loaf of bread.

The sole bond of unity amongst the tribes is the Mohammedan religion, which consists not so much of the practice
of the law of the Prophet, as a feud—a bitter heirloom—
of centuries of warfare against the Christian.   Admirable
disputants do not make good logicians, as those who travel
in Morocco soon discover.   Someone has said that the desire
to know 'why' is a specially human gift.   In these people
religion has obliterated any such want.   Ages of endurance
have taught them not to go to the root cause of anything
respecting the principles of government.   They accept the
cruelty of their Kaids as a matter of course; and it is only
when stung to some sudden madness by the most wicked
oppression that they fight to get rid of an individual, not
with any intention of changing the government.   When
they have been taxed beyond their ability to pay, would it
console them to know that they fought on an established
principle?   They would add the information to other
aphorisms, and perhaps recite it with their prayers.

Neither religion nor government nor tribal custom has
nurtured in these people the love of either God or man or
Nature.   Of civilized philanthropy and the Christian religion
they would understand only enough to squeeze and lick these

entities, as a pariah dog which has by good luck found something that is neither corrupt nor unclean.

For centuries the Kaids have robbed the people, and
robbed the Sultan as much as they dared. The mosque has
clutched at all it could get, and men steal from one another,
so that no man trusts his own brother, and all men go
armed. The very villages are fenced, and each house has a
barricade of thorn-bushes, with a narrow gateway, closed at
night. But so long as a people can and will fight its man-
hood is not wholly extinct, and there are tribes in Morocco,
which contrive to keep at bay the worst atrocities of the
Sultan's rule. They have never been completely subdued,
and in the fastnesses of their rocks and the density of their
forests they preserve their distinctions of race and customs,
and form concrete existences. To people possessing so much
of the elements of nationality it would be possible for a
civilized Power to offer terms, terms upon which modifica-
tions might be grafted which should soften the ferocity, and
lighten the horizon by showing them that it is in their own
power to improve their condition.

And as I rode on my way to Tetuan and watched the
peasants in their scanty rags, ploughing with primitive
wooden ploughs drawn by small oxen, and knew that even
from the time of ploughing the fruit of the coming harvest
might be wrested from them—if, indeed, it was not already
forestalled—I thought of the pæan of the liberated slave, who
on his release from captivity could, while denying himself,
find hope for his labour, and I longed to do something to set
these people free and give them assurance and a future.
'He that now goeth on his way weeping, and beareth good
seed, shall doubtless come again with joy, and bring his
sheaves with him.' But the peasant bent over the poor
wooden plough of homely pattern such as they make themselves from branches of the cork-tree. He lifted it bodily
over the boulders or patches of palmata-scrub, and the little

oxen lowered their heads under the yoke and responded to the goad. The toiler was so single-handed on the small patch in the wide plain; and the white cranes walked behind him over the clods, looking smart and well-dressed gentlemen of leisure with nothing in life to wish for.

I saw rabbits running in the scrub and among the rocks. The herds ran after them with sticks, and killed them after fairly running them down. The peasants hunt rabbits on horseback. They use the mares for this purpose, and ride them with only a single-rope rein. The mares hunt by sight. I think the remarkable eyesight I noticed in my pony was due to his breed having hunted in this manner.

The glory of the bird life was the white crane. Whether singly or in flocks, they had a beautiful appearance. Sometimes they darted through the air with the swiftness of pigeons, making a long, slow swoop round as they descended. They followed the plough and perched on the back of cattle with the independent air of officials or persons of very exalted rank.

The route was marked by wells, where the cattle collected while the herds drew water by letting down skins on ropes, and pouring the contents into roughly-hollowed stones.

There were no trees except a few old olives. I saw what looked like cypress-trees growing on the very tops of the mountains, probably the remains of a forest. Oleanders grew vigorously along the banks of the streams; but everything, except the olives, which attained any size was cut down and burned for charcoal. There was plenty of the spirit which cuts down, but none of that which plants. Destruction was rife everywhere, but no one thought of repairs or restoration.

The moment a native shows the least enterprise, such as making a well, the Kaid calls upon him for extra taxes. If he fences a piece of ground and stocks it with fruit-trees, the first time there is a crop he is sure to be squeezed upon some pretext or other. Natives dress poorly, lest they should attract the notice of the Kaid. If they have a dollar to spare, they hide it in the ground; for were they known to spend it the Kaid's suspicions would be aroused, and they would be imprisoned and flogged to make them disclose what money they had. What wonder was it that they were reckless and that their spirit 'ran cunning'? The reckless-ness which says, 'Let us eat and drink, for to-morrow we die,' was stamped on the face of the land.

The Shereefian Court has always been the theatre for every variety of intrigue, and it is extremely difficult to get at the truth of anything in Morocco, so much is it the custom to veneer and drape facts. We are accustomed to a code which we call 'Western standards,' but in Morocco things occur in which Westerns are interested wherein the consular voice may ask, 'What is truth?' and things have been done which are as little likely to be obliterated as the sin of Pilate by any amount of 'washing.' Highly-agreeable social amenities clothe lives which even a poor Moorish peasant might criticise, and those who sit 'in the seats of the mighty' may tremble with Felix. Only after-generations will see in them men who missed great opportunities—men whose conduct indicated the decadence of national character.

One morning in the soko of Tangiers I saw a nice little ox and a good little sheep being sold by auction. Owing to the number of Government officials and to the crowd round them, I made inquiries as to the sale. They were the pro-perty of a peasant, who had cultivated a nice little farm and stocked it carefully. A case had been trumped up against him by the Kaid, and he was imprisoned, while his property was gradually being sold off. His wife and children were turned out to beg or starve; they had gone to a Jew, who, it seemed, was trying to help them. But when the man came out of prison, if he ever did, he would be ruined, and in the Jew's debt for the remainder of his life.

In some gaols the prisoners are given a limited amount of bread. In others they have to buy everything, even the water they drink, and pay for their irons and for the smith who rivets them. They are nearly always ironed; but to the peasant from his mountain home the confinement and want of air and exercise is a deadly punishment, which it is scarcely worth while to hasten with the lash.

If the Kaids grind the people unmercifully, they are in turn themselves ground by the Court. The quickest way to fortune in Morocco is this farming of the revenue; but it is a dangerous game, and few play it out to the end, and even those who die wealthy and prosperous are liable to have their estates seized after their death, and their sons beggared or imprisoned.

A curious incident in the revenue record was the raising of the Spanish war indemnity of 1860. Spain claimed £4,000,000. It was paid out of the Customs revenue. Spanish administrators sat in the several customs offices checking the duties with the Moorish officials. The arrangement was that half the revenue should go to the Sultan and half to the Spanish Government. So far as I am aware, no statement of accounts was ever published by the Moorish Government; but the debt was declared to be paid about twelve years ago, and all the Spanish officials left the country rich men. It offers a singular comment on the official life that a foreigner should be permitted to occupy such a position.

CHAPTER V

THE road down from the kasbah was very bad, and progress was slow. At length the city of Tetuan came in sight. It lay like a white chalk-mark placed purposely in the centre of a picture in which the sea and sky formed the background and rocks and boulders lay piled up in the foreground. It was still about ten miles distant, and the Hadj began an argument with the Kaid as to the hour at which the city gates would close. The mountains intercept the light and deprive the town of about an hour of day. When we at length reached the plain and could make better progress, a strong wind sprang up and blew right in our teeth. I shall never forget the bitter cold of that ride. The Hadj had tried to persuade the Kaid to ride on and stop the guards from closing the city gates. And to this suggestion the Kaid returned a curt refusal. It transpired subsequently that he had done this when he was escorting a party of Jews, and after he had left them they were set upon and robbed of their mules and their merchandise.

Then the sun jumped down behind the mountains, and immediately the evening gun boomed over the plain.

It was a lovely scene, and the moon, like a great brazen disc, rose slowly above the citadel, casting a pale yellow light on the squares and oblongs of Moorish architecture.

But the stink of the city came out to meet us before we got near the walls, at the bottom of which the filth gushed out from open conduits and flowed wherever it pleased.

Feeling that we were now safe, the Kaid rode on ahead, and to my satisfaction I found the port open, and could see the pale blue of the evening sky through the Moorish arch of the gateway. I asked the Hadj what he would have done if he had found the gate closed. 'Oh!' he answered, 'Kaid Rahool knows how to talk to those people He would have got it open for you.' 'No doubt,' I replied, 'he would. But what explanation would he have made?' 'He would have said, "Here is a lady from the British Legation in Tangiers who has ridden on this mule to see the city of Tetuan; therefore the gates must be opened." Then the guards go to the Bashaw—perhaps he sleep, anyhow he don't know—and they get the keys, and the gate is open.'

The Hadj showed the delicacy not to refer to the little incident of 'bakshish' which would have been the motive power in the transaction.

I was glad to be spared waiting in the wind, and most thankful for the shelter inside the walls. But it was rapidly getting dark, and I could only distinguish that the city had a large garden within it, where orange-trees and bananas grew vigorously. Then we passed under low archways and into very narrow streets. Suddenly my mule's bridle was seized, and I was brought to a standstill in front of a low, dark door. I could see turbaned heads all round me, and understood by gestures that I was to dismount.

It was an old Moorish house in which a family of Spanish Jews lived, and here I was to pass the night. The atmosphere was overpoweringly close, and strongly flavoured with a smell of ill-kept drains. But they gave me a fairly large-sized room upstairs over an archway, and served me a little dinner far better cooked than I expected. An omelette, half a grilled fowl, and some oranges made an excellent meal, but I rejected the coffee, being suspicious of the water, and sent the Hadj to get me a bottle of wine. He returned with some canary sherry, which had not much flavour, but was a refreshing, and certainly inexpensive, beverage.

The room was frightfully chilly, but the bed was clean, and I soon got into it, having heaped upon it all my wraps; and very shortly fell into a sound sleep.

I was awakened by an unearthly noise. There was a melancholy horn being blown which conveyed an idea of menace. Blast after blast, with short intervals between, during which the wailing cry of the muezzins from the fifty mosques of the city seemed to fill my room. Then, louder than all, came the raucous Arab voice accompanying a barbarous ejaculation with a terrific banging on the doors of the houses in my street—my own included.

It was the midnight call to the faithful to rise and pray —to cook food and eat it in preparation for the fast, which would commence with the firing of the gun at sunrise.

The whole neighbourhood was immediately in a commotion. The Moors came out of their houses and crowded the streets on the way to pray in the mosques, while their households busied themselves to cook a meal. I lay awake with my candle lighted, rather enjoying the novelty of the situation, for I had never slept in the heart of a Moorish town before, and it was more than unusual to have my door banged and be called to pray and cook at midnight.

Very early the following morning a Moorish family next door were greatly upset by the conduct of a young slave-boy of about fifteen. I watched the scene from my room, which, being built across the street and having a small grilled window on either side, enabled me to get two good views of all that happened, except when they got actually underneath my room. From all I could glean, the slave had slipped out at midnight when his master went to pray, and did not return till after his master had come back, and part of the inconvenience caused by his absence without leave was that the master was kept waiting outside the door of the house.

On his return, the slave gave a gentle tap at the knocker, doubtless hoping to be admitted by some fellow-slave, and to slip in without being noticed. But when the door was opened he was face to face with an elderly lady closely veiled, behind whom appeared another slave considerably older and stronger than himself. He uttered a cry of horror and made a gesture of despair.

Acting upon a sign given him by the old lady, the slave seized the delinquent and gave him a severe shaking. Meantime the lady, in a high-pitched voice, harangued with vehemence, accompanied by occasional gestures and signs which resulted in renewed shakings. The boy cried and even shrieked, and the voices went on vibrating as it were against each other. The elder slave also joined in, and a perfect Wagner opera was the result. At last all three drew under the archway, and, from the sounds which followed, I believe the boy was beaten, yelling savagely at each stroke. This went on for some minutes. Then the old lady went back into her house, the boy followed her, and the rear was brought up by the elder slave, who throughout had behaved in a prompt and business-like manner. The door closed after them and perfect silence reigned.

After my ears had recovered from the noise, I could distinguish the soft patter-patter of slippered feet, or the almost rhythmical pitter-pat of the eternal donkey, or the hurrying step of the bare-footed slave, which interested and roused me so effectually that there was no more sleeping. A good deal of business is done in what may be called slave-dealing in Tetuan. There is no open market, but the wealthy Moors can afford to give good prices, and Tangiers competes to a certain extent, so that the dealers throughout the country remember Tetuan when a well-trained black for a servant, a good-looking girl for a concubine, or a likely boy-child to

make into a eunuch comes in their way. In some of the
houses that I visited in Tetuan, I saw some very handsome
blacks, both men and women. They appeared to be kindly
treated and to be perfectly happy. But of course there is a
great difference between the pampered favourite of a Shereef
or official and the defenceless drudge in the house of a small
tradesman ; and these slaves are rarely blacks, they are more
often Moors who have sunk to the very lowest degradation
through one cause or another, or have been stolen as children,
as they frequently are in Sus. It was to this class that the
boy belonged who was beaten under my room in Tetuan.

Before I had finished the breakfast, which was laid for me
on a small table in my room, and consisted of hard-boiled
eggs, rather good fresh butter, brown bread and honey, the
Hadj arrived, and announced that he had found a better inn.

I was fairly satisfied, except that I should have liked more
air, but, on the other hand, the change might bring fresh
experience, so I rolled up my effects, paid a very moderate
bill, and departed with the Hadj, who led the way to the
outskirts of the town. Here, although it was within the
walls, new houses were being built on the site of those which
had fallen at the time the Spaniards bombarded the town in
the war of 1860. It was a new house built in the Spanish
style with European windows. Both bedroom and sitting-
room were built on the outside city wall, and commanded a
magnificent view of the valley, which followed the course of
the river, and was studded with white villas surrounded by
well-planted gardens, the summer-resorts and hunting-boxes
of the rich Moors of Tetuan. A delightful and refreshing
breeze blew in from the open country, and I felt that the
change would be advantageous in more respects than one.

The country which I saw from the windows is inhabited
by the Anjera tribe, a spirited and warlike race ; but the
name of Tetuan is supposed to be Riffian, and the Riffs form
quite as marked a feature in the town as the country people

or Anjeras. Most Moorish towns have a legend attaching
to their names. Of Tetuan it is said that the name is derived
from a Riffian word thêtáwîn, meaning 'eyes' or 'springs.'
Mr. Meakin favours this latter idea on account of the number
of fountains or springs, which he says 'add such grateful cool-
ness to the better-class houses,' but he admits a Moorish
tradition that the name originated in the cry of warning
while the walls of the city were being built, which meant,
'Open your eyes!'—*i.e.*, to see the enemy approach. He
also refers to Leo Africanus, who says that the city was
called Tettáwan, 'an eye,' because under the Goths it was
once governed by a woman who had but one organ of vision.

Which of these stories might be true mattered but little to
me, who enjoyed them all. I also found it a great treat to
walk out and explore a city which was not a wooden township undergoing its first 'boom.' It was refreshing to me to
have no wide streets to waste my time in crossing, and I
could not forbear crowing with delight when I found that by
stretching out my arms and standing somewhere about the
middle of the street, I could with ease touch the walls on
one side with my stick, on the other with my hand.

The city is on the borders of the forbidden land; and the
valley on which I was looking out would lead me, if I
followed it, to the wildest and most anti-European part of
the Empire—the country of the Riffs.

But the Riffs come down into the town to 'shop.' They
are fine men, dressed in a short brown jellaba (a smock with
a hood to it). They do not wear a fez, but they shave their
heads, except for one lock, which is sometimes plaited and
sometimes hangs like a tassel. This hair is left for the
Prophet to lay hold of when he desires to add them to the
faithful in heaven. The Riffs come into the town for
pleasure; but the Anjeras come to work, and there seems
plenty to be done in Tetuan. New houses are being built
as residences. From the roofs of these there resounded a

melancholy howl accompanied by dismal thumping. I went to find out the meaning of these wretched sounds, and found a cheerful party of labourers, mostly women, in very large hats and swaddled in yards of drapery, who were stamping with wooden stamps on the cement roof of a new house. They seemed amused at me, and smiled at the questions which I addressed to the Hadj.

Tetuan is as much a manufacturing town as any city in Morocco can be. I even saw one small engine, though the power which worked it was a human being. This machine was for gun-cutting. It consisted of a big wheel and a small one, and by its means the barrel of a gun could be rifled very deeply. Great numbers of these guns are made in Tetuan. I found it rather difficult to see much of the gun-cutting. The Hadj was most unwilling to take me. In one shop the stocks are made; in another they are inlaid with mother-of-pearl, etc., while the smith's work takes place where the whole is actually fitted together. These guns discharge bullets, and the bullets are also made on the spot, but the gunpowder is generally imported. I did not see it being made anywhere during my travels. There are two kinds of guns made in Tetuan. One is on the old Portuguese pattern, as used by them in their invasion. Probably they taught the people, after they had beaten them, how to make and repair guns in the cities which they built. There the thing is, with a barrel about 5 feet long, clasped with silver (sic), a thin and elegant stock, stained to look like ebony and inlaid with ivory (sic) and mother-of-pearl. It is fired by a flint, and I am told that the natives make excellent practice with it, using shot for small birds; which seemed strange in a rifled barrel. There is another gun, also made in Tetuan, of a more modern pattern. The barrel is not so long, and the stock is modern in general outline. It is a muzzle-loader, and fired with a percussion-cap instead of a flint. In this gun the Moors seem for the time to have laid aside their habitual overlay of ornament. They told me that these guns shoot very well, but they recommended me, if I wanted to buy a gun, to get one of the former kind. They carry the ornamental antique weapon in a long red flannel bag, which looks very smart on horse-back in contrast with their white cloaks; but the effect is spoilt when they put the shorter-barrelled plain gun into the case of the long gun, for the extra length of red bag droops gracefully over the top of the muzzle, and looks very foolish or 'wanting,' like an empty stocking.

On one occasion, as I was walking through the market, I saw a young fellow from the country carrying what appeared to be an army regulation rifle of rather an old pattern. He would not show it me. But the Hadj induced him to hand over the gun, and himself showed off the movement of a breech-loader which was quite old-fashioned. There was no magazine, and I feel certain that the gun was an old, but very good, Spanish army regulation rifle. It appeared to be very well kept.

What troubled me was the fuss the Moors made. They came out of their shops and from all directions, and made a great noise, gesticulating and looking very cross. Their good manners deserted them, and they were almost as rude as Germans. In fact, had I been trying to photograph a fortress on the Rhine, Kaiser Wilhelm himself could not have been more surprising.

I told the Hadj to return the man his gun. This much I saw—that the rifling in the barrel was deep and close. What the length of range might be I could not even guess, as I had not time to look at the sights. Of the gunpowder used by the natives I never had a chance of forming an idea. Several times I was told that it was made in the country. Of course, the value of a gun depends largely on the powder it will take, as a popular song ascribed to a modern General says:

'What is the gun that makes them run?
You bet your boots it's the gun that shoots
The high-velocity shell.'

Further down the coast I found the natives had Win-
chesters of the old pattern, which had been smuggled into
the country in considerable numbers; but what I never
could learn was how they got the cartridges. Someone told
me that they kept the old cases, and were very clever at
refilling them. I heard everywhere—and it was never con-
tradicted—that the Moors in general are very good shots.

Tetuan is a great place for the making of shoes, or, rather,
slippers. Oh, those slippers! Picture a whole country
going about in slippers!—slippers which are invariably
yellow (only the women wear red ones), flat in the sole, and
down at the heel. I feel sure that the people who wear
boots outside Tangiers, which is practically European,
number but a hundred. I adhered to wearing boots till I
reached Marakish; and there I went about in a pair of canary
slippers like the rest of the world. But one does not get an
unmixed satisfaction out of them. It is almost impossible
to pull up the heels, and they are always trying to come off.
If the Moors have a fight, their slippers are sure to fly; and
whenever I was in a hurry I left my slippers behind, and
the Kaid picked them up. Thus I learnt to walk bare-
footed before I left Morocco—a practice which I believe to
be not unwholesome, and in so hot a climate is a very
refreshing one.

These slippers are made in thousands in Tetuan, and form
an item in the shipments from Tangiers. A great number
go to Egypt. The Jews collect them, and take them overland on mules to Tangiers. They trade them all over the
country, selling them in Fez and in the country soks, and
keeping the price for a pair of slippers about even all over
Morocco. Tetuan could never consume a third of its manufactures, but what it might do in trade if it were ever im-

proved as a seaport it is impossible to say. The industries are there; the cleverest and best-trained workmen imaginable, and abundance of the very best raw material.

At the time the town was founded it was a sea-port, but that was very long ago, and the sea has retreated, and possibly the river, which is not navigable, although it is still tidal, was then wider and more important. What surprised me in Morocco with regard to rivers was the extent of their tidal water and the strength of the current. I believe that the bed of the river is often considerably below the level of the sea, and when once the sea has got over the bar it rushes up the river with tremendous force. The port which Tetuan uses is approached along seven miles of good road, which was made by the Spaniards when they landed in 1860. I suppose it would never be a safe port, owing to strong winds, one of which was blowing fiercely when I was there; but Nelson came here for supplies, and the Spaniards effected a landing. Ships call occasionally, but there is nothing approaching a regular service of any kind, and even the export of shoes for Egypt goes overland to Tangiers. Besides shoemaking, there is a great deal of weaving. The striped black-and-white jellabas and the wrappers of stripes and checks worn by the native women throughout Morocco are made here in great quantities. The whole system is medieval, for every manufacture goes through its entire course. The skins for the shoes are brought from the slaughter-ground to the tan-pits, and the manufacture of a shoe can be seen from the time the leather leaves the animal's back. The fleeces are also shorn and washed on the spot; the carding, spinning, dyeing, and weaving all follow, till the complete article is offered for sale to the public in one of the shops or by public auction. It would be quite possible to choose the animal whose hide was to make one's shoes, and watch the whole process till they were on one's feet. I bought a very fine striped blanket, as I intended sleeping at the kasbah on my return, and most fortunate was it that I did so.

There is silk which, I believe, is produced in the neighbourhood. Later I saw plenty of cocoons offered for sale in the streets of Marakish, and as the mulberry-tree flourishes in Tetuan (one of the gates is called Bab Tût—'the mulberry gate'), I think it is probably true that silkworms are also cultivated in the city. I saw hanks of golden silk hanging in the dyers' sheds, side by side with yarns. But the Moors say the worms will not spin if a Nazarene sees them, so they keep the matter dark. The Riffian women bring into the market a kind of green moss, very similar to that which I have seen growing on the mountains of Scotland; this they sell to the dyers, with other herbs which were not familiar to me. Beautiful, warm, unbleached and undyed blankets are woven at Tetuan; but mine came from Rabat. Its stripes were irresistible. There are also hat-makers, who weave the large hats worn by the Anjera women, and finish them by sewing on ornaments of wool in the shape of little pom-poms in rich colours, to tempt the purses of the well-to-do.

After all, the chief interest and great pride of Tetuan is its tile and pottery manufactory. Outside the city, in a cave, the workshop is one of Nature's making, into which man has fitted himself and his art. The little wheel, the spot itself —the whole process is probably as it was in the days of the Romans, or earlier still. It recalled the old astronomer poet of Persia who knew, with a skill truly Oriental, how to use the most ordinary incident of life as a device for graceful imagery, and I found myself repeating his verses:

'For I remember stopping by the way
 To watch a potter thumping his wet clay,
And with its all obliterated tongue
  It murmured, " Gently, brother, gently pray."

'I think the vessel, that with fugitive
   Articulation, once did live
And drink ; and, ah ! the passive lip I kiss'd,
   How many kisses might it take—and give !'

When I arrived, the potter was thumping his wet clay on a ledge of rock, kneading it as though it were dough, and dusting over it a dry dust of clay out of a basket, till he got it to the right consistency. Then he jumped down into a low pit, and turned a small wheel with one foot, and, lo ! there grew up under his touch a most graceful water-jar, and in almost the same instant another of a different pattern but quite as good. This clay is so valuable that it is an export from Tetuan by sea.

The glazing of the tiles is done with antimony, dug out of a mine in the neighbourhood, but I could not learn where the colouring was obtained. The tiles vary from those of Fez, being cut into various shapes : octagons, crosses, stars —in fact, every shape except a curve. The Fez tiles are always and invariably square, and I only saw them in two colours, blue and white. The secret of the blue colouring of the Fez pottery has been so well kept that no one outside Fez has learnt it—yet for how many centuries has it been handed down !

Painting upon wood is one of the industries of Tetuan. The door, bracket, or mirror-frame is first made by the carpenter, and the painter overlays it with colour. The foundation is a bright red ; then, without any aid from drawn lines, he proceeds, apparently without thought, to cover it with an arabesque pattern in dark blue, white, green, and yellow. When the whole is toned by almost a hundred years of Moorish atmosphere, the effect is very soft and rich, and does not give the impression of painted wood. The iron hinges, clasps, etc., are gilt with a beautiful old gold. These decorative arts are used in beautifying the houses of the rich Moors. The town is divided into a Belgravia, an East

End, inhabited by low-class Spaniards and poor Moors, and a Mellâh, inside which the Jews are locked at night.

Though the modern Moors spoil their houses by intro-ducing modern trash, using cheap druggets instead of their own beautiful carpets, and Manchester cottons instead of native drapery, still, they are grand habitations, with a rich-ness of colour and a dignity of form due to spacious patios and the horseshoe arch, to marble columns, and gardens which are bowers of greenery, where bright water gurgles deliciously into tanks full of gold-fish, and the air is heavy with the scent of orange-flowers, jessamine, roses, and heliotrope.

One lady received me very graciously, and I was taken expressly to see her wardrobe by her old nurse—a hideous old black slave-woman, but with a not unkindly face. Certainly the clothes were numerous and magnificent. There were three suits in particular—of jacket, waistcoat, and knickerbockers — of a pale blue cloth heavily em-broidered with gold, of a maize-yellow cloth embroidered with silver, and a rich rose crimson embroidered with dark navy-blue silk. These, with brilliant sashes, must have looked very fine. The linen, too, was extremely delicate, and beautifully washed. In the middle of the room, upon the floor, was a mattress, and in front of it a cheap little looking-glass, such as one might find in a poor cottage at home. A double string of real pearls, but of indifferent quality, hung on the mirror. Some white pigment for the face and other similar arrangements lay about. The lady was really very handsome, and she had a dignified but pleasant manner. She was the one wife of the Moor, and had a son of about ten years old and a daughter a good deal younger. She seemed struck with wonder, mixed with a disapproval which she appeared to try and overcome, at my attire and appearance ; and evidently wishing to be civil, she politely indicated her admiration of the stud which fastened

my collar. I thought she would have liked it, but my offering to give it her was a great mistake, and for a moment she seemed vexed.

As I walked down the steps to regain the Hadj and the Kaid, I thought of the immense difficulty of getting the East to understand the West. This woman was all that was kind and courteous, but I felt that she was simply diametrically the opposite of myself. And yet I thought how many Western women put their faith in fine clothes, and perhaps it would be easier to approach these Orientals in something more elaborate than a travelling suit. The words of an old Scottish song recurred to my mind, and I fear the Scots are as a rule neglectful of appearances, and apt to be satirical on the subject :

> 'He put on a ring, and a sword and cock'd hat,
> And wha could refuse the Laird wi' a' that ?'

The East is far from the West, and the distance is as great in domestic as in political matters. This house was, I feel sure, a bright example of domesticity. Everyone, even the black slaves who were preparing the dinner, was clean, well dressed, and smiling. The children were both good specimens. There was, so far as I could ascertain, no other wife and no harem; yet one felt confronted by a steadily maintained difference of opinion which nothing would change, and a different standard of happiness.

CHAPTER VI

THE kasbah at Tetuan is old and historically rich. It was destroyed by the bombardment in the Spanish War, and only a part of it is used as an arsenal, which I could not get permission to enter. But from the kasbah hill I could overlook the city. In old times these narrow, winding streets and low archways were a defence, especially in the days when bows and arrows took the place now occupied by magazine rifles or revolvers. The arrow that flieth by day would have to fly round many odd corners if it meant to travel far in Tetuan. These streets probably account for the favourite weapon being a nasty dagger-like knife ; for it would be far easier to hook an enemy out of a dark corner than shoot at him, especially with one of those long-barrelled guns.

The Moors are possessed with an inveterate hatred of the Spaniards. The feeling is so fierce that I wonder how any Spaniards can live in the country. Its origin dates back to the time when the Moors were driven out of Spain. They left with the determination to return, and brought with them the keys of their houses in Granada. It is said that many of these keys and other relics were in Tetuan in the houses of the aristocratic old families who came from Andalusia, till the Spaniards took them away when they occupied the town in the war of 1860.

The beating which they gave the Moors in that war is

still deeply resented, and when the time came that I understood a little Arabic I often heard it alluded to. They
watched the Spanish-American War with a keenness they
have never felt in foreign affairs before; and laughed at the
Spaniards whenever a fresh disaster befell their arms. When
some of them were in sore anxiety and distress at the
claims put forward by France for the murder of Monsieur
Pouzet on the Riff coast, they comforted themselves by
reflecting upon the American-Spanish War. 'Truly,' they
said, 'Allah does things in His own way. And it may yet
befall France as it happened with Spain. Allah permitted
the Spaniards to beat the Moors; but He prepared for them
the humiliation of being beaten, not by Moors, nor by the
English, who are a great people, but by the Americans, of
whom no one has heard much.' Someone suggested that
the Americans were some kind of a tribe of English people.
'That may well be,' observed the Moor, nodding his head,
'and probably it accounts for their being able to beat the
Spaniards, which the Moors could not do because Allah did
not will that they should.'

As I was walking in Tetuan a woman seized the Hadj by
the arm and appealed to him for fair judgment. She was a
Riffian, and the two men who were with her were Riffians,
and they looked very great scoundrels. She was in deep
distress. Her face quivered, her cheeks were wet with tears,
and tears hung on the long dark lashes of her fine eyes.
She pleaded her cause in a voice which vibrated with indignation, and I never saw anyone so desperately in earnest.
Every gesture told, every movement was an added emphasis.
A rabbit was the bone in the dispute. The sum claimed
was half a real. The man had offered to buy the rabbit
from her before she got to the market, and she agreed with
him for three reals. He took the rabbit from her, and paid
her only two reals and a half. There was a little scene.
The rabbit's corpse was flung from one to the other back-

4

wards and forwards, till the Hadj, with perfect gravity, grasped its legs and held it while he gave judgment. Some coins also which were flung on the ground were carefully gathered and retained by him. Then he said that either the rabbit was to be paid for to the value of three reals, or it should be returned to the woman, and the man receive back his two and a half reals. In the end the man took back his reals and the woman regained her rabbit. But before we moved on the scoundrel turned on the woman with an evil look in his face and roared at her some deep-toned abuse. 'What was that about, Hadj?' I inquired. 'Him great scoundrel,' said Hadj sententiously, 'she poor woman. Him say, "If I get you outside I kill you."' 'Why did she appeal to us?' 'She see me with you. She think European protect me. I no fear to say what I like.'

The Mohammedan feeling is strong in Tetuan. Even the Riffians, when they come into the town, go to some special mosque, and send their children to a foki. I watched a party of them arrive—two men, a lad, two women, and a little boy and girl. The men busied themselves with the animals, and the women prepared to sell produce, but the little boy and girl ran to the fountain. She was sent for water, and carried a little water-pot. He was older than she was; I dare say he might have been eight years old. He began washing himself, and she assisted him by pouring water over his feet and hands. All his gestures were an exact imitation of those of a grown-up Moslem. 'Who can have taught that child to wash like that?' I asked. 'He go to pray, and his teacher have taught him wash hisself so,' answered the Hadj. I was glad to think that something was taught; but when I asked why the freed slaves in the soko in Tangiers who were Moslems were not taught to wash— for a dirtier, more disreputable and miserable set it is impossible to imagine—the answer was not satisfactory: 'They have no money to pay a teacher.'

There is a greater sense of wealth and grandeur about the
Moorish houses in Tetuan than elsewhere. The rich Moors
are out of reach of the intrigues which, sooner or later, level
everyone within reach of the Court. Most of them made
their money originally by getting some appointment which
enabled them to farm the revenue. They then invested
their money in commerce, and very often in real estate in
Tetuan, which they have managed to rack-rent; and now
protection secures not a few of them against the depredations
of their own Government.

On my return journey, I decided to take the mules half-
way and sleep in a peasant's hut the other side of the kasbah,
proceeding next day to Tangiers. Meantime the wind had
changed, as it frequently does in the morning after it has
blown hard for a couple of days from one quarter. At ten
minutes past eleven we rode out of the city gates, and I
drew deep breaths of pure air as I went on my way, but we
were not out of sight of Tetuan before the first drops of rain
fell. Some Jews with horses laden with goatskins hurried
past while we were taking the best precautions we could
against the threatened drenching. Some Spaniards were
flogging heavy-laden and exhausted mules towards the same
destination. We passed a dead horse lying on the road,
whose back was a mass of galls and sores, which had eaten
down to its very bones. Even in death it bore an expression of excruciating fatigue. Its last load had been released,
its journey was over; it would lie there till the dogs
ate it.

As we got nearer to the mountains, the rain became
heavier and the air colder. It was a case of butting one's
head against a cutting wind, feeling sheets of water like ice
descend upon one with such force that they seemed to intend
nailing one to the saddle. I was caught unprepared. The
'aqua scutum' coat I wore was soon like blotting-paper. I
had no gaiters, and the water ran down my stockings into

my cowhide boots and stayed there. A bad stumble on the
part of my mule on the road down to Tetuan had slightly
ricked my back, and now its rough paces hurt me, especially
when the ground became slippery and she slid about in all
directions except the one expected.

Africa will never be civilized or behave like other conti-
nents. She must always be burning one alive, or else
drowning one in a flood, wearing one out in a whirlwind, or
choking one in a dust-storm. She is always untidy, always
unfinished. She makes her people barbarous, and though
Egypt did wonderful things, there is not in all history a more
marvellous page than that which barely outlines the suc-
cumbing of Egyptian civilization to witchcraft and idolatry.
Of all their science and invention, we have left to us only
dead bodies and tombs, while the most that remains of its
history is the life of a freed slave. Here in Morocco, the
learning and science which once illuminated Europe has been
ineffectual against the elements introduced by the black
blood, which even the strength of Islam could not withstand.

As we climbed higher up the gorge, the rain became mist,
and I decided to get down for a moment and empty the
water out of my boots. So I slid down to the ground, and,
to my amazement, found myself stuck fast. I could not
move a foot. I had kept the reins, and the mule went round
me. Seizing the stirrup, I tried to get leverage to raise one
foot, but utterly failed to do so. Morocco is indeed a 'gum-
boot' country. The Hadj came to my assistance, and, seizing one ankle, hauled the foot up, and set it down on a
boulder, with several pounds of clay attached to it. It
struck me at the moment as most meritorious to convert
this clay into bricks, and I praised the export business out
loud. The Hadj unlaced my boot, poured the water out of
it, and replaced it. He did the same with the other foot,
and then I jumped from the boulder into the saddle again.

We had now only four or five miles to make to reach the

kasbah, but the rain came down again, this time mixed with
sleet, and I decided not to go on to the peasant's hut, though
I was sorry to give up the experiment. At half-past four,
as it was getting dark, we entered the kasbah. Leaving the
mules in the yard, which was already full of other pack-
animals belonging to Jews and Spaniards, who had hurried
on to take shelter, I followed the Hadj up a narrow staircase
to a fair-sized room, bare of any kind of furniture, and
lighted by a narrow shot-hole in a deep embrasure, protected
by a grill. The wind whistled through this aperture, but I
managed to close the ill-fitting wooden shutters, and finding
my matches dry in a metal box, I lighted a piece of candle
and glued it by one end to the floor.

My hold-all was wet through, and all the contents were
damp; fortunately, the blanket I had bought at Tetuan
was fairly dry. But having on several layers of clothes, and
being as wet as if I had been dipped in a pond, was not the
worst of it. The worst was that none of my baggage was
waterproof, and that I had no mackintosh sheet to spread on
the floor.

I left home with all my camp sleeping equipment complete,
packed in a Wolseley valise; but it was stolen from the hotel
at which I stopped for one night in London, and I had to go
on board ship without a rug or warm wrap in the middle of
winter. The journey to Tetuan taught me the impossibility
of travelling in Morocco in winter time without proper
mackintosh equipment.

A charcoal brazier soon warmed the room, and the next
thing was to find something dry to put on. The Hadj had
brought me his sleeping carpet, which was thick and warm,
and finding an ulster with a thick lining, which was less
damp than the rest, I put it on and rolled myself in a blanket.

The pleasant glow from the charcoal brazier and the
warmth engendered by soup and whisky made me feel that
my retreat was princely—all the more so that the rain and

sleet had recommenced, and the wind howled round the
tower in which I was lying like an evil spirit. I felt that a
determined attack was being made upon my stronghold. I
could have drawn in charcoal on the wall the evil spirit of
the weather, as the rain came thrashing down on the roof
and the wind rattled at the shutter and made the candle
gutter. There I lay like a fugitive cavalier; and I wondered
whether the good deeds of my forefathers in their own time
were being returned to me in the third or fourth generation.

The Hadj had brought home from Tetuan a cooked fowl,
some bread, oranges, and half a bottle of wine; and after
a time I rose and made a good meal, heaped some more
charcoal on the brazier, which, as it stood on the window-
sill near the badly-fitting shutter, had sufficient ventilation,
and then went to sleep. But at midnight the Moors woke to
cook and eat, and the noise roused me. Soon after daybreak
I woke again, and after a hasty breakfast of coffee and eggs
started for Tangiers, dressed in such garments as were only
damp.

The rain had ceased, and there was a thick mist like a
November fog, which made the air very chilly. But I decided
to start at once, lest the rain should recommence, and I was
determined to get the better of the weather devils. The
track was desperately slippery, and my mule was very heavy
on my hands. She did not actually fall, though whether she
kept up owing to luck or good management I cannot say. I
know there was an indecision somewhere as to whether she
should sit down on her hocks behind or flatten her face in
the mud. I saw the Kaid's mule slide further than it stepped.
What happened to the Hadj I never inquired, but whenever
I turned my head I saw the mule lying down and the Hadj
on his back with his legs in the air, looking like a dining-
room table upside down.

He expended immense energy in cursing the mules in
Arabic. He concluded a perfect tirade of abuse with a word

which sounded like 'Abimelech.' I had never considered
that cognomen in connection with mules, but in the mouth
of the Hadj, and spat out crisp and hard as the last of many
strong adjectives, it had a decidedly good effect. At last I
asked him what Abimelech meant, but he only tittered and
held his peace. Afterwards he rarely used it, and when he
did so dropped his voice suddenly to a very subdued tone.
He assured me that mules knew the difference between Moors
and British; and added significantly that they did not fear
the latter.

As we rode through the mist, black carrion crows flew
from one side of the gorge to the other, making a hollow,
dismal croaking. This bird is supposed to call the rain.
The cranes were also flying about restlessly. These birds
have very short tails, and make good the deficiency by
stretching their little black legs so that their toes add to
their tail when flying. I suppose birds use their tails to
steer with, but a long tail would manifestly be out of place
in a bird which frequents marshes. The water-birds of the
duck kind have most characteristic tails. I never can help
thinking that their hearty 'quack' is a laugh. The humour
comes out again in the tail, which always turns up, and in
the drake positively curls. There is no other bird, neither
the peacock nor the wagtail nor the widow bird of the Transvaal, which can put half so much meaning into its tail; and
what pleasant companions they are on the sea or lake! I
know no more melodious sound when one lies awake at night
than that of the water-fowl feeding by moonlight.

The road is interesting, being marked by old Portuguese
ruins and battlefields, where they fought the natives with the
new invention of gunpowder, and overcame their slings and
bows and arrows. Besides the ruins, the way was rendered
interesting by a very decorative thistle. It had shed its
down. It was dry and withered, but it stood there glistening
white like frosted silver, and spiritualized beyond the beauty

of a mere flower. It was rendered all the more striking by the
ascetic setting of dry stubble. Some spring flowers there
were, notably the white pheasant's eye narcissus, but nothing
was so striking or so beautiful as this dry silvery thistle.

We passed a little cemetery, where the peasants buried
their dead, each grave simply encircled by a ring of stones.
They were not enclosed, and the goats browsed over them
and the cattle trampled round; and close by stretched the
open fields that in life their hands had ploughed and reaped;
and I myself was journeying by the same winding road to the
city they had trudged so often, till the day came when they
went by ' the ancient path ' that all our fathers have trod to
the great Silent Land, where they laid their burden down
before the Lord of Death. I thought of the passions which
were for ever laid to rest, of the struggles and tears, of the
hopes and fears, of generations which stretched into the
world's dim ages as the mountain ranges swept on to the far
horizon; while over all extended the far blue sky, symbolizing
the Eternal Patience who watches over all men and races
and creeds, and who 'knoweth all things.'

CHAPTER VII

A RIDE DOWN THE COAST—THE CAVE OF HERCULES—THE
FIRST NIGHT IN CAMP—CROSSING A RIVER—THE CITY
OF AZÎLA

I DECIDED that if I saw the coast towns and the country
which maintained the ports, and visited Marakish, I should
gather a fair idea of the *status quo*—the value of Morocco—
and the aims and wants of the merchants.

It did not take long to procure an outfit. Fortunately, I
was able to persuade my kind friend, Mrs. Greathed, to
accompany me for the first part of my journey; and her
intelligence and sympathy with things Moorish added very
much to the pleasure of the ride.

At half-past four in the afternoon of Thursday, April 4,
we rode out of Tangiers on the Cape Spartel road. I was
mounted on Conrad, and Mrs. Greathed rode Mooleeta.
We were preceded by Kaid El Hashmy, and our baggage
had gone on with Shereef Moulai Hammed and Mehemmet,
as muleteer and tent-man, and my old groom Mohammed
Jellally to act as general servant, and to be at times a
general nuisance, for the poor old fellow was getting very
blind. I had ridden to Cape Spartel in broad daylight, but
I thought the scenery infinitely more interesting as the
twilight fell. The road lies over high land commanding
Tangiers and the Straits, with plenty of places where land-
ings could be effected in fine weather, and rising ground
where guns could be mounted which would sweep the

country right and left and from shore to shore. A hopeless
country for cavalry manœuvres, but affording plenty of cover
for infantry; in a word, it was Africa once more.

One glimpse of the sea, where some gray crags cut the
sky, showed us far down below a steamer quietly and evenly
pursuing her way. She was going down the coast, and
bound for Casa Blanca. The rock cistus was in blossom,
and its large white flowers showed ghostly in the gathering
darkness; then, as we descended a steep hill by a road
winding down almost to the sea-level, the great lighthouse
rose before us with its light burning very brightly. Very
stately and protecting it looked, gazing out to sea—the sea
of so many hard fights—for Trafalgar Bay is almost immediately opposite. The scene, too, of many cruel wrecks, for
it is a dangerous coast; and, in addition to Nature's moods
and the storms from the Atlantic, many wrecks were con-
trived of set purpose by the coast Moors and pirates.

The tents were pitched close to the lighthouse. The first
evening was one of some confusion. The tent was new, and
there was not much room to stretch the ropes. A high wind
blew till it became a gale, and this and the difficulty of finding our things on that first night made it late before we got
any dinner. However, by perseverance and by hunting for
one thing and finding another, we managed to get a good
bowl of soup, which, with a dish of bacon and fried eggs and
some coffee, made a decent meal. The horses and mules
were tethered outside, and they all objected to the weather.
Several times in the night I had to go out to Conrad. The
moon was shining brightly, and it was cold. I had strapped
his saddle-blanket round him, but he was wretched, and
would not lie down, imploring me to let him come into my
tent.

The next morning, having sorted our things a little, we
started at about eight o'clock, descending over a stony track
to the shore, and across a mile or more of sandy beach

covered with small shells. Then we began to climb over rocks, and at the head of a narrow pass close to the sea Mehemmet made a sign to me. I slipped off my horse. Mohammed Jellally took the reins, and Shereef Moulai Hammed helped Mrs. Greathed to dismount, and I went on, following Mehemmet through a path which grew narrower at every step, and descended over steep rocks and among bushes, till I called to mind as I watched the turban bobbing along in front of me the words of the old tale: 'After the robber had made his way among some bushes and shrubs that grew there, he very distinctly pronounced these words, "Open, sesame. . . ." The captain of the band had no sooner spoken them than a door immediately opened, and having made all his men to pass before him and go through the door, he entered also, and the door closed.' I was still following Mehemmet, but stooping very low, until we came suddenly into a large vaulted hall in the heart of the rock, dimly lit from above by rays of warm golden light. It was like the interior of a magnificent cathedral or ancient palace. The drip of water from hidden springs sounded clear and musical, as though fairies were playing upon silver bells; and strange lights—some pale silver and others red gold—fell upon masses of rock and converted them into heaps of hidden wealth. I almost fancied I could hear the ring of dollars, and saw strange forms bending over them engaged in loading the panniers of their asses from the pirates' horde. Then a rumbling sound which broke into a hoarse roar burst on my ears, as if our approach had waked the guard from sleep. But, advancing nearer, I saw at the far end a pointed arch which opened straight upon the sea, and admitted the waves with a rushing, furious sound, as though the dragon of the deep hurled itself into the cavern, jealous that one of its secrets should be known. There was just a touch of recent human presence which lent additional romance, for human hands had carved millstones out of the rock. For ages and ages, from the days of mythical heroes, men had come here for millstones. One dreamt of magic wine in golden cups, and fairy laughter, and age-long feasts. It was one of those spots in the world where to be alone is best ; and I stayed for a time by myself in the cave, dreaming that I had forgotten the upper world and my home and country and kindred.

From the Cave of Hercules, as it is called, we went on in a wind which blew the sand into ridges and made travelling very hard for the pack-mules. We came to ironstone rocks running down to the water's edge, and passed the wreck of a steamer which had been driven on her beam upon the sands.

By two o'clock we reached a stony beach between a river and the sea. This river we were to cross by boat, but in spite of shouting on the part of our men in chorus, led by the Kaid, the people would not bring the boat across. They were busy washing their clothes; and then they went out fishing. Meantime the tide began to rise. It came with sudden rushes of great force, and three times we had to seize our rugs and fly before it. For three mortal hours we waited, lying on our rugs in the eye of the sun. The wind was so fierce that there was no chance of making a fire for a cup of coffee. At length I got tired of the game and mounted my horse. I told the Kaid that I would wait no longer, and should ford the river on horseback. This threat altogether exceeded my expectations. The Kaid fired his shot-gun, shouted something across the river, which caused a sudden alacrity among the peasants, and immediately the ferry-boat was brought across.

The tide had gone down to the level it had reached when we first came to the river, and getting across was not difficult when once we were in the boat. They brought a light boat for us and some of our baggage and Mohammed Jellally. The horses, mules, and the Kaid, with the other men, followed in a heavy boat. A Moor who had ridden on a

baggage-mule and gained the river an hour before we did
had been kept waiting, and crossed with us. This fellow
was in a great hurry to reach Azîla before nightfall, and
persuaded my Kaid that he must do so, as he wanted the
escort of my soldier in the dark. I had no intention of
accommodating him, and told the Kaid that we must put up
at the next village. The Moor had preceded us in order that
I might pay the transport of himself and mule across the
ferry. When we rode on he joined the Kaid, and began to
assert himself, riding up to me with a frown on his face, and
telling me in Spanish that I must hurry, because 'it was
necessary to get to Azîla before night.' I called the Kaid
to me without answering the fellow, and asked him to whom
the Moor belonged. The first name given me was that of
one of the Legations, but on my saying I did not believe it,
the name was changed to that of a missionary, who I knew
was not travelling anywhere in the North of Morocco. I
therefore ordered the Moor to leave the camp, and told the
Kaid I would not allow him either to ride with us or to
camp near us. I rode my horse forward, and made the
Moor turn his mule out of the line and go to the rear. I
rode last myself, and took care that this impudent native
did not come within a quarter of a mile of me or my people.

The sun had set, but the first part of our road lay on land
which was lower than the seaboard, and we could watch the
waves raise themselves on the sand bar while the light shone
through them before they broke upon the shore. It was a
mingling of gray-green water and golden and brown sunlight,
like a liquid opal, a living gem. Then there were wide, still
pools like burnished gold, wherein frogs innumerable sang in
chorus as we passed; while silhouetted in strong relief were
bands of storks standing in the water in solemn consultation,
listening to the chant of the frogs, who pleaded their right
to exist in an epic descriptive of their amours, and their
deeds of daring in two elements, and of their high rank as

one of the plagues of Egypt. Then we left the shore, and climbed a track through cultivated land cropped with peas and beans, till the barking of dogs announced that we had reached the village we were bound for that night.

The stars were shining brightly when we reached the highest point of the hill overlooking the sea on two sides, and while our tents were being pitched the headmen of the village came to dispute with the Kaid our right to camp there.

About a score of voices joined in, all talking at once in all manner of keys, and I heard the Bashaw and Sidi Mohammed Torres, and even the Sultan, mentioned. I fetched the letter of Sidi Mohammed Torres, which gave me permission to camp anywhere at any time. This, being held before the villagers in the light of a lantern, had a soothing effect, and they became very friendly, selling us straw and charcoal, and anything else that we wanted.

I could have wished that Sidi Torres' letter would have influenced the village dogs. They made a noise at intervals all night, and, though we were tired, they effectually roused us more than once. These horrid brutes startled the storks, which we wanted to photograph on the roofs of the houses before going on the next morning.

It was barely two hours' ride from this village to Azíla, and we went slowly. We passed the ruins of an old Roman city, called Tahaddart, at the mouth of a tidal river, which we forded. The ruins of the old town were covered by the tide. Whoever built it—and I have heard it suggested that they were Phœnicians—chose for the site the deepest part of the bay, where fishing-boats can still find a little shelter. The foundations of the houses and walls were formed by uniting the low flat rocks with concrete. The tide was out when we passed, and it was easy to picture in the squares still filled with water that here was a Roman bath, there a pavement or terrace, or there a judgment-hall.

It must have been this abandoned city whose ruins we passed which was possessed by the Goths, till in 713 the Arabs took it. It is one of the few places in Morocco with an English tradition, for it is said to have been seized and destroyed by the English in 933. But that we should have penetrated so far afield is hardly stranger than that there should have been a Moor among the followers of the Conqueror William.*

Then the town lay in ruins till a Cordovan Kalîpha rebuilt it a mile further off, on the rocks where Azîla now stands. Its history thenceforward reads like most of these Moorish coast towns. How it was depopulated by the plague; how a Moorish Governor of Ceuta, finding it a stronghold of the Spaniards, destroyed its fortifications; how it became the prison of a Portuguese Prince, brought there as a hostage for Ceuta, which Prince was allowed his own Christian church; how it was the scene of martyrdom for a Franciscan friar—all these things are part of the history of those white walls which stand in ruins to-day. Perhaps strangest of all is that it was once the scene of a vigorous sea-fight in 1471, when it was attacked and captured by the Portuguese King Alphonso V. in person, who brought 300 vessels and an army of 30,000 men, with which he besieged the town for ten days. After its fall, the chief mosque was converted into a church, and dedicated to Our Lady of the Assumption.

The religious spirit which animated the Portuguese, and was responsible for most of their prowess, has left with Azîla one remarkable tradition. When the Jews were expelled from Spain by Ferdinando and Isabella the Catholic, they landed at Azîla on their way to Fez, a line of retreat which seems to have been frequently pursued by Moors, and which brought Leo Africanus from Granada to Barbary. The Moors attacked the fugitive Jews,† and drove them back

* Meakin, 'The Land of the Moors,' p. 223. † *Ibid*, p. 224.

to Azîla, where 'they were forced to purchase shelter by sub-
mitting to a sprinkling from the friars' mops at work above
the gateway, as with broken hearts they passed in.'

Though the Moors finally gained possession of Azîla, the
Portuguese have left their mark upon the place, for the whole
of it is of Portuguese foundations, scarcely touched by the
Spaniards, and merely adjusted by the Moors.

We were most fortunate in our approach to Azîla, for there
was a heat haze, which partially obscured the town. The
long rows of white breakers rushed in upon the beach, and
ran on to the shore, past the walls, which rose straight from
the water itself on a foundation of dark-brown crags. The
outlines we were looking upon were practically the same
that all travellers had seen for some 300 years. We
could not see the slowly crumbling condition of the walls.
To us it was a perfect medieval city, with grand and simple
outlines of graceful watch-towers and strong defences.
Through the haze which concealed the ruins shone the
gleam of a white-domed mosque, and the fringes of stately
palms rose here and there, adding to the dignity, the
antiquity, and the grace of the city, which was a prison for
a Prince, the scene of a martyrdom, and the object of a hard
sea-fight.

As we drew nearer, the sense of disaster and of dread
came out, as it were, to meet us. On the towers there were
no watchmen, but the storks guarding their nests. In the
little chapelry on the wall there was no bell. No guns
looked out from walls or bastions; no royal standard was
flying in the breeze. There were no sentries at the city gates,
no crowd passing to and fro, no hum of city life. It was as
though a great plague or fire or famine had laid its hand
upon the place and left it an empty shell. We seemed to
be entering in from the outer world, as the vanguard of a
victorious army into a city that had surrendered; and there
was the feeling of compassion and of regret for greatness

which we found in ruins, and respect for a brave defence which had availed nothing.

But our approach had been watched and noted, and people come out to meet us and ask who we were and where we came from, and as we rode in through the gate we were followed by some half-dozen curious Jews. Then began the disillusion, which was almost comic. We were bound for the house of Mr. Bensheeten, whose roof supported the flag-staffs for the colonies of four European nations. Azîla is forbidden to import or export anything, and in the squalid streets, where heaps of filth accumulate and are never moved, cattle are herded at night, while in the old houses peasants find shelter.

Mr. Bensheeten received us most kindly, and placed his servant at our disposal during our stay in Azîla, with in-structions to find us camping-ground to our mind, run our errands, and show us all that was of interest in Azîla. I have visited wooden townships, pegged out with a view to a magnificent future, but never have I dreamt of stone cities with nothing but a past.

CHAPTER VIII

THE population of Azîla consists of about 400 Moorish families and 100 Jews, who are not confined to any special street or quarter. Of Europeans, besides a few Spaniards, there are none. But the system of protection obliges the countries to have a Consul on the spot, and Mr. Bensheeten transacts the affairs of the Italian, the Austrian, the English, and the Spanish nations. The only business which is done in the place is in selling to Spanish fishing-boats which put into Azîla for water and fresh provisions; but, as no imports are allowed to be landed or exports to be shipped, there is little enough done in the way of trade. Of course, it is open to suspicion that the Spanish fishing-boats do contribute something besides fish as payment, and the laxity of Moorish customs would render a slight infringement of regulations a very tempting little business; but the people are very poor, and at the markets, which are held once a week in Azîla and on different days in the villages round, it is the Jew who collects eggs, poultry, butter, and a little fruit, for the lowest possible prices, and runs them on mules into Tangiers or Laraiche. The former, being largely European, and having some half-dozen hotels, absorbs a good deal of fresh produce, besides shipping quantities of poultry for Spain, which can be done more regularly than from Laraiche.

We pitched our tents on a green hillside outside the city,

preferring to do so rather than remain in the heat and smells of the town. After we had refreshed ourselves, and bitten as long as we could at a very tough grilled fowl, we set off to walk to the town, taking with us the Kaid, Mr. Bensheeten's servant, and Mehemmet. On the way we visited some orange-gardens, the property of an Italian protégé, a friend of Mr. Bensheeten's Moor, who picked us oranges hot with the sunshine, and sprays of blossom. Some of the trees were white with blossom, as though weighed down with snow. There was more blossom than leaf. The fruit was perfectly delicious. Nowhere on our travels did we meet with such beautiful oranges.

We walked round as much as possible of the city walls, but they would not admit us inside the crumbling batteries, though they were empty. The walls were overgrown with a large-leafed thistle in the vigour of its spring growth, and it was interesting to see our bare-legged Moors negotiating these thistles. They marvelled greatly, and were evidently perplexed as to our interest in these walls, but resigned themselves to our being slightly demented as part of our English nature. In Tangiers the English are called 'the mad Christians' to distinguish them from the others. But madness is not altogether a thing to be despised, for among the Moors it is regarded with a reverence that is partly superstitious. The Kaid could not face the thistles, but he made an address to the other two men, exhorting them to take every care of us, and on no account to take us out of his sight. Then he sat down with a groan on a piece of crumbling stonework, and kept his eye on us. A great wish possessed me to insist on climbing somewhere out of reach and out of sight; but I believe had I done so the Kaid would have fired his old shot-gun, and made such a noise that the whole city would have been roused.

We came to a little chapel on the walls, which the Moors had dismantled and used as a praying koubah for the guards.

Now it was the nesting-place of innumerable pigeons. Here and there were half-defaced inscriptions in Spanish and Portuguese; but the most interesting part of the ruins was near the seaport. The inner construction of a vaulted chamber had a very ancient appearance, and might have been Roman; but the Portuguese had changed the shape of the windows and made them semi-Gothic. I came upon the opening of a passage in the thickness of the wall, which might have been used for heating purposes for baths. If the vaulted chamber was a temple, it was not unlikely that baths were connected with it. There was another passage which ran along under the wall, and which might have been an aqueduct, except that I could not see where the water came from to fill it.

I noticed as I walked through the streets that almost every woman was tattooed on her chin, and one had a cross very beautifully tattooed in the centre of her forehead. These women were peasants, and dressed as Riffian peasants. Mr. Bensheeten, on whom we called again, told us that the town was inhabited by these tribesmen and Anjeras, who had been deported from the other side of Tangiers by the order of the Sultan as a punishment for rebellion. A more unsuitable class for an urban population it would be impossible to imagine. In the evening they drove all their herds down the hill into the town, where they slept, in such shelters as they rigged up for themselves anywhere they pleased, or in the ruins of the citadel or the old walls. After we returned to our camp, as we sat drinking tea, it was delightful to watch these peasants crowding down the hill in an irregular procession, driving their herds before them towards the city gates. They were ragged and half clad—a wild horde of semi-barbarians, but light-hearted and contented enough. Our tents interested them, and they came near to gaze wonderingly at us. One reason why they preferred to sleep in the town was that it secured their immunity from malaria, but safety for their flocks against the raids of cattle-thieves was another potent argument.

Besides the four guards who were allotted to us, and who duly came up for payment in the morning, there was one old gentleman who was quite irresistible. He was clad in the loose flowing raiment of unbleached wool common to the peasants there, and had a long gray beard and a mild, venerable expression of countenance. He carried in his hand four enormous ancient keys, the keys of the city of Azîla, which I should dearly have loved to carry away with me. This old grandee—for he had magnificent manners—made himself very useful, holding our horses, and acted in a benign and patronizing manner, as though his visit were purely complimentary and the half-peseta I slipped into his hand as we left was a mere detail.

People say that the country round Azîla is flat; but we found it very much the contrary. On leaving we rode straight up the hill on to a plateau, and then higher again and into a region of steep gorges and rich valleys, a land which was a veritable garden for fertility. On the side of one valley we came to a grove of ancient olives, on whose tops the storks had built their nests, and beneath whose shade a mixed flock of sheep and goats rested from the noonday sun beside a clear stream, herded by a lad in a ragged sheepskin, who was plaiting palmetto leaves.

The scenery does not lend itself to photography. Photography deals with facts. It stereotypes, it records. It never idealizes. It is like Mohammedanism. The landscape could only be painted in detail. A group of Moors and cattle, a mass of rocks and marvellous vegetation, or even a piece of the winding track itself, with a solitary hawk the only feature against the perfect blue of the sky. Each contained form, line, colour, and breathed a poetry all its own.

We must have climbed to a considerable height, for when we next saw the sea we looked down upon it with the clouds

beneath us. They were low-lying vapours gradually rolling
back to the sea from which they had come. At length it
was our sad fate to descend to the shore, and find ourselves
enveloped in a cold Scottish mist. The tide was coming in
very fast, and on our left the rocks rose precipitously. We
fairly raced the tide to get past a bluff, and very threatening
the bold bad rocks looked; for even if we could have climbed
on them out of reach of the waves, they would have baffled
the baggage-mules. The Kaid became anxious, and the
baggage-mules had to be hustled, while he set spurs to his
old white horse and galloped past us with a great show of
dash, and took up his stand at the bluff facing the ocean,
while we hurried past him in single file. Then we all
breathed freely and the mules had a little rest. The sands
widened out, the mist disappeared, and the sun came out
fiercely. The way after this was monotonous, and the continuous boom of the sea was wearisome. At last we reached
an oasis, a grove of oleanders with a patch of brilliant green
turf, where the animals could graze while we sat down to our
luncheon in the deep shade of the grove by a murmuring
stream. After a good rest we started again, turning inland,
passing through evergreen bush where charcoal-burners were
at work, and then over a wide grass country like parts of the
county of Dorset.

The scenery was very beautiful, for an immense valley and
plain stretched before us, reaching to the distant hills round
El Kasar, and a magnificent river, the Wád Lekkûs, which
it seemed strange should not be navigated, made a grand
curve before it passed away into the distance. Then, as we
passed over the top of a sand-hill, where many sea-birds were
at work, we saw sailing-ships in the harbour of Laraiche
flying Spanish and Portuguese flags, and behind them the
old fortified white city itself, with its domes and kasbah, and
gay with the flags of innumerable Consuls, for it was a feast-
day.

Once again it was a case of fording a river by boat, and
we had to wait about half an hour for the boat while a cargo
was being laden at the port and deposited on board a Spanish
ship near to our landing.

There are at Laraiche very fair facilities for the landing
of cargo for such ships as can get into the river. The large
steamers have to lie out in the roadstead and discharge into
lighters, but if the weather is bad the lighters cannot go out.
So far, however, as the quay is concerned, it is a very marked
improvement on Tangiers; and yet Tangiers is not a bar
port, and has everything in its favour except that bar to all
improvement, the presence of the Legations, whose business
it is to maintain the *status quo*.

On landing at Laraiche we divided. Mrs. Greathed went
to select a camping-ground with Mohammed Jellally and
the muleteers, and I rode to the British Consul's house to
ask for our letters.

Mr. Lewis Forde was expecting us, but, as it was getting
late, I did not remain long at the Consulate, but, taking the
letters, went on almost immediately to the camp.

The tents were pitched on some grass outside the city
walls. It was the usual camping-ground for travellers, and
two caravans of growling camels were arranging themselves
for the night at about 50 yards from us. Mehemmet went
into the town and bought some fresh meat, new bread, and
other provisions, which were very acceptable. We did not
hurry to go to bed. The old city walls were right in front
of us, and immediately beneath us the dry moat, where some
enterprising European had cultivated a vegetable-garden,
turning on a small sewer by way of irrigation at one end.
Old houses had been built into the wall, and looked out with
one scanty window here and there. There were rows and
rows of storks' nests, and storks on guard along the walls.
Now and again one sounded an alarm by clapping his beak,
and instantly the signal was repeated right down the wall

like a *feu de joie*. The sky was soft above like velvet, and
the stars shone brightly, while at our feet the charcoal-fire
glowed and was pleasantly warm, for the nights were still
chilly.

We decided to remain a day at Laraiche, and find out,
amongst other things, if the road were open to El Kasar. I
brought a letter for the Italian Consul, who could talk
English very well and had a very nice Italian wife.

The trade of Laraiche is hampered by a bar port on the
sea side, and by bad roads on the land side. The business is
mainly a forwarding one, the goods going through to Fez on
camels, where they are handled by merchants, who distribute
them throughout the North of Morocco, and to Tafilet beyond
the Atlas. A good many of the caravans go direct to Sefroo,
six hours beyond Fez, and there diverge.

Laraiche is well served by steamers. The Forwood line
calls once, and French and German boats sometimes twice,
once on the way up the coast and again in returning. It
seems strange that, though Italian trade is increasing, there
is no regular line of Italian steamers calling at Moroccan
ports.

By combined action the Consuls had induced the Moorish
authorities to provide the port with a serviceable tug for
towing lighters over the bar, and considerable improvements
have taken place in the lighter service. When I remembered the scene of confusion at the port of Tangiers, I was
astonished to find at Laraiche good order and good management, sufficient, well-kept warehouses, and things proceeding
with clock-like regularity.

The Moors are not really a seafaring or water-loving race.
If a Canadian had to deal with such a river in so rich a
valley, he would invent a craft which would navigate the
river to a certain distance, negotiate the bar, and keep
the channel clear. I believe the superior management at
the port was due to the Consuls being business men, whose

main object in life was to sink differences, and find a *modus vivendi* with each other and with the Moors by which trade should be facilitated.

Laraiche is the nearest port for Fez ; and for long it was the favourite port for the Fez trade, and a much more important place than it is at present. Were the harbour accommodation improved, it would advance immediately to take a front place among Moorish ports. There has been some talk of straightening the river to get a rush of water sufficiently strong to clear away the deposit of alluvial soil which blocks the mouth. But the enterprise would be costly, and, in common with many similar undertakings, could not be safely entertained under the present rotten government.

It is not difficult to imagine Laraiche a delightful residential spot, situated in a beautiful and romantic country, and with a lovely river for boating ; but up to the present time only the Italian Consul has ventured to build a house outside the town.

CHAPTER IX

THE CITY OF LARAICHE—A BLIND SAINT—START FOR EL KASAR—FLOWERS—PHŒNICIAN RUINS—A RIVER IN FLOOD

WE spent a very pleasant day in Laraiche, winding up with a tea-party at our camp, which greatly excited our Moors, who were most anxious to join the company, and had every now and again to be despatched to a respectful distance.

There is a fine gateway leading from the country into the great sok, or market - square; but the imposing market-place, with its colonnade, recalling the Rue de Rivoli in Paris, is scarcely in keeping with the narrow, irregular streets which lead from it. At the far end of the market-place there is an open space, clean and well kept; and close by is the kasbah, or residence of the Bashaw, and two prisons, which are generally full. One was empty when we were there, as it was undergoing repairs. I went inside, as nobody seemed to object. It was very bare, but there was a good water-supply; the courtyard was open to the sky; and though the sleeping accommodation was only a bare, dark recess, probably very damp, and the sanitary arrangements practically nil, I did not see any evidence of close confinement or dark dungeons. To an Englishman such conditions would be torture; but taking into consideration the state of most Moorish houses, I did not think the prison was bad. We went to see the other, which was full, and took some bread with us; but the prisoners were not at all eager for it. They looked well fed, but most of them wore leg-irons.

As we had some bread left, the Kaid and Mehemmet
asked us to give it to a saint they knew who was blind.
They guided us to a street corner and sent a messenger to
fetch the saint. But first there appeared a sick woman,
who walked leaning on a friend; then an old blind man.
And when they had each had a loaf, for which they appeared
far more grateful than the prisoners, the saint came, a man
about five-and-thirty, with fair hair. His eyeballs were
perfectly white and prominent. I wondered what had made
him blind. He was dressed in a very thin, old jellaba. The
face was pale and emaciated, and there was no question of
his poverty. Mrs. Greathed by means of Mehemmet, who
could speak Spanish, told the saint that the English wished
to give him the bread. He answered nothing, but the face
with the blind, staring eyes lightened with the nearest
approach to a smile that I should think it ever wore, and he
stood for a moment or two holding the loaf in both hands.
I wondered what might be passing in his mind, and what he
thought of the Christian dogs. I wondered most of all why
Mehemmet and the Kaid, who were strict Mohammedans,
should have proposed that we should give bread to one of
their saints; but the fact is that Moors' minds are so con-
structed that they are prone at all times to a kind of hero-
worship. I soon found that they felt a pride in belonging to
us, and wherever we went they impressed the people with
the illusion of our immense worth and distinction. I believe
the feeling dated from the time that I ordered the impudent
Moor with his luggage-mule out of my camp; for they are as
a people, like all dark skins, most appreciative of a firm hand.
Giving alms to a saint they look upon as a transaction. On
one hand, the saint needs the alms, but the giver benefits by
the prayers of the saint. I believe they thought it a good
thing for the saint to get bread, and they believed they were
doing us a great kindness in securing for us as Nazarenes
the exceptional and rare benefits of saintly prayers.

Laraiche was a very strong place in the time of the Barbary pirates. They ran their vessels into the river, and until the Portuguese, by establishing themselves at Azîla, could keep them in check, they made use of Laraiche for every purpose, including the building and repairs of their ships. The name of Laraiche is supposed to be a corruption of the Arab word *Arasi*, signifying 'pleasure-gardens,' referring to the orange-groves, which produce the finest and best-flavoured fruit in Morocco. The Spaniards, who built the grand walls outside which we were camped, pronounce the name 'Laratchi.' But its old-time grandeur and prosperity were due more to piracy than pleasure.

There is very little business done in Laraiche itself, for there are not many European residents, and very few well-to-do Moors. It has been the point from which many expeditions have turned inland to Fez, which is only four or five days' easy ride. Dr. Leared has graphically described one of these missions to Fez, proceeding with all the pomp and display of semi-barbarous state in which Moors delight. He mentions also the band of European instruments which the late Sultan introduced; and the musicians who had been taught to play English popular airs, and whose selection was sometimes calculated to cause surprise, if not consternation, to Europeans, playing the Portuguese Minister into Laraiche to the tune of 'The Rogue's March.'

The country lying outside Laraiche is very fertile. The cork forest, known as the Mamora Forest, begins here, and stretches beyond Casa Blanca. At one time there were fine oaks, which the pirates used for their ship-building. The valley of the Wád Lekkûs is very rich, and even with the primitive agriculture in vogue at the present time, it produces a great quantity of beans and peas for shipment, besides grain, which is not allowed to be exported. Oranges have been tried as an export, but the uncertainty of being able to ship them, owing to the state of the weather frequently preventing communication on the day that the ship calls, has proved disastrous to fruit export.

But it is also a fine sheep and cattle country, and ranching might be carried on on much the same principles as those obtaining in South Africa. The finest wool produced in Morocco is grown in this neighbourhood, and shipped direct to Dunkirk by French steamers. The hill tribes buy the best quality for their own clothing, and give a higher price for it than Europeans. There seems to be an idea that they do this purposely upon principle, to prevent it from leaving the country. There may be something in this, for when a famine broke out after the late Sultan gave permission for the export of wheat, all the fokis and immams agreed in declaring that the famine was due to the vengeance of God, because the faithful had allowed wheat to go out of the country to feed the infidel. Poultry is consigned overland from here to Tangiers, and comes down this way when the roads are bad between El Kasar and Tangiers. Eggs are shipped direct from this port to Cadiz.

The following morning we started for El Kasar, travelling by the upper road to avoid the swamps occasioned by the late heavy rains.

Riding across a high sandy plain, I saw many grasses which I had met with in Bechuanaland, and which constituted the 'sweet veldt.' There was also one grass called in the South 'sticky grass,' which sheep and goats eat freely, but which is injurious to the fleeces, making them matted and difficult to clean. It was evidently a dry country in the dry season, but in the early spring it afforded excellent pasture. At intervals there were bushy little scrubs such as sheep and goats delight to vary their diet by browsing upon. It struck me that this veldt had been rather spoilt by overfeeding with sheep, for many of the best grasses only grew where the little bushes protected their roots and prevented them being nibbled out. In one place, about

three-quarters of the way to El Kasar, I passed a stretch of
what was called 'sour veldt' in Bechuanaland. The ground
was a plateau, with low-lying swamps on either side. The
change of pasture was doubtless beneficial, for I saw that it
had all been grazed.

After we had proceeded about four miles out of Laraiche,
we entered the cork forest. Some of the trees were very old
and delightful in their quaint outlines; others were quite
young, mere saplings, and were growing much too close.
It was like a scene in an English park.

The beauty of the flowers by the way was a sight never to
be forgotten. I do not know what half their names were,
but it was like riding through a very beautiful garden.
Little African marigolds and flowers like coreopsis, with
scabious and gladioli, formed the bulk of the first array.

To our left we saw the old stones of the ruins of the
Phœnician city of Shammîsh. A mystery hangs about these
ruins which hitherto the old stones have not divulged.

It is said that the name implies that its founders were
sun-worshippers and came from Egypt. Others, again,
ascribe the city to one of the four Berber tribes which
inhabited Morocco prior to the Arab invasion, but if so a
city with such stones argues a high rate of civilization.
Anyhow, the great stones were very attractive-looking, suggesting the genius of an inventive or scientific people, and
had it been possible I would have visited the spot and
camped there. Whoever founded the city chose a spot
inland—up the reaches of a beautiful river, in a fruitful land
with a noble forest—which proved that they had more than
a coastal interest in the country. But by what curious freak
of destiny a city so founded should be utterly swept away,
leaving nothing but these gaunt forlorn stones, surpassed all
my understanding. But as with people and cities so it is with
individuals. Those who seem to possess everything have a
hollowness within them, and they pass away. A Power

whose wisdom is inscrutable 'hath put down the mighty
from their seats, and hath exalted the humble and meek.'

Meantime our flowers changed to a rock cistus, which
grew close to the ground in tufts between bunches of a rich
dark violet sage. Then we came to a green country where
the grass was short and close, as it is on English downs,
and there were waves of swelling green hills, with yellow
genista growing as gorse grows in England, and smelling
quite as sweet. We had luncheon by a stream where the
animals had a bite of grass, and then we went on into
lower country to the cistus again, and I saw a small and
marvellously coloured iris of a dark coffee colour with
delicate gray shading. It was a mysterious-looking flower,
and seemed as though it were intended for an emblem,
or to convey a warning—hardly a flower to love, and not
one to put in a bouquet. I noticed that it always grew
alone in solitary state, and it appeared to be rare even in
its own land.

At length we came to a grove of very ancient olive-trees,
whose foliage half concealed the white tomb of a saint. On
the tops of the olives storks were nesting. I drew rein, and
as I was looking at the scene, which seemed so strangely
set in the wilds so far from human habitation, I heard the
cuckoo for the first time that spring. Nightingales were
also singing, and, in the absence of all other sounds, these
songs about the tomb and the cool, pleasant shade of the
delicate olive foliage formed a harmonious whole, in keeping
with the dignified retirement of an honoured death.

The Moors have a festival which appears to be similar to
our All Saints' Day. On this occasion they pay more than
usual attention to the graves of their friends, spending hours
in praying beside them. I remember seeing one old man
who could not expect to live very many more years. He
was spending the festival sitting alone on his father's grave,
chanting in a quavering voice what might have been a

lamentation, but which was probably an invocation. They
are deeply impressed with the sanctity of tombs, and it is
sacrilege for a Christian to set foot in one of their cemeteries,
for they are holy places. Not that I was very often tempted
to do so, for the graves are very shallow, and if the jackals
do not clear the contents the scent is very strong.

Seeing how they reverence the resting-place of the corpse
—which, by the way, is not always there—it is strange that
they should have so great a horror of death. I have heard
from those who have witnessed the deaths of Moors that
most painful and frightful scenes occur at the last owing to
the frenzy of terror which overwhelms them at the approach
of death. This does not appear to have much to do
with good or bad consciences, for the late Grand Vizier,
Ba Ahmed, who was one of the most wicked even of Moors,
died with singular calm, although he realized fully that he
was dying. The Moors are capable of exercising great
powers of self-control. I have often marvelled at them.
But if they lose their self-restraint for an instant, a torrent
of the most violent passion rushes away with them, and they
behave suddenly as though possessed. They scream like
fish-wives, and I have even seen middle-aged men cry like
naughty, passionate children.

Something of the kind must happen to them when they
have to face death. They have no object in further restraint,
and simply let their feelings go free in frantic expressions.
Like some children, they will 'be good' exactly as long as
they feel sure something is to be gained by it. This is the
childish side of their character, and the one which is most
appealing. They are a hospitable and not a mean people,
and capable of feeling kindly, and, I believe, of acting justly,
where it is not obviously to their personal gain to do
otherwise. I know they can be extraordinarily devoted as
servants, and where a Moor trusts a European he trusts
him implicitly. There is a term now amongst them which,

I am told, they look upon as more sacred than any oath ; it is ' English word.' That, to the Moor, implies perfect good faith ; and if, after making a promise, he puts his finger to his lips and says ' English word,' he may be relied upon as having every intention of acting honourably. I asked one of them once why it was they used this term. And he explained to me that the English were a very strong people and were not afraid of anything. When an Englishman said a thing the Moor found it came true ; and he added : ' It is good for Moors to have to do with English people '— a circuitous way of arriving at a conclusion that it was worth their while to treat English people decently.

From the tomb we descended a hillside into a plain, more or less bogged up to our horses' hocks. Then we came to a river which was still swollen with the floods. It was sufficiently deep for my horse, and I rode him over and sent him back for Mrs. Greathed.

We were destined to cross the same river again lower down. There were about fifty natives, some partially clothed, others without a stitch of raiment about their persons, employed in helping travellers across the river, which was coming down very fast between steep banks. It was about a hundred yards wide, but in crossing it a detour had to be made to avoid the holes and whirlpools. Some natives who aspired to be thought modest wore little shirts twisted round their necks above the water line, and one of these untwisted his shirt and let it drop to his waist before he came forward to offer to lead my horse. I appreciated his good feeling, and said he might walk in front to show me the way. Conrad is especially good at crossing water and negotiating a stream, even when it takes him off his feet ; but he always objected to being led. However there is no accounting for what these horses will do, and in the present instance my pony selected the middle of the stream to cut capers, which he would not have done in

6

ordinary circumstances. I sent him back for Mrs. Greathed, relying not in vain on his chivalry, and then we had to wait some time for the baggage-mules, as they had to be relieved of their packs, and our belongings were carried over on the heads of natives.

With much shouting and wrangling we started afresh. The animals had much enjoyed the cool water after being eight hours on the road, but coming back to the dusty track again soon sobered them.

CHAPTER X

A VERY beautiful legend accounts for the origin of El Kasar.
The Sultan El Mansûr (the Victorious), a contemporary of
Richard Cœur de Lion, was out hunting, and missed his way
in the marsh. His suite were out of sight, and on looking
round he spied a poor fisher 'getting of eels,' and asked him
to show him the way back to his palace. The fisherman was
a philosopher, and the dialogue which followed, as narrated
by Leo, between the Sultan in distress and the eel-catcher,
who did not realize the stranger's rank, is quite delightful.
It ended in the fisherman offering the hospitality of his hut
to the Sultan and setting before him roasted eels, while he
dried his clothes at the fire. Early the next morning the
courtiers came whooping and holloaing through the fens to
find the Sultan, and were greatly rejoiced to discover him
safe in the fisherman's hut. 'El Mansûr,' says the chronicle,
'turning him to the fisher, told him what he was, promising
that his liberalitie should not be unrewarded. Neare unto the
place were certain faire castles and palaces, which the King at
his departure gave unto the fisher in token of his thankful-
ness.' The philosophical eel-catcher became an excellent
Governor, and a town grew up called El Kasar el Kebir,

6—2

which means 'the great palace.' 'And because the soil near
unto it is so fertile the King used to make his aboad there-
about all summer-time, which was a great benefit to the
towne.' The extraordinary fertility of the soil in the neighbourhood, and a market to which the Arabs resorted, made
the wealth of the people, who built 'many temples, one
college of students, and a stately hospital.'

Nevertheless it is situated so low down as to be subjected
to annual floods. But what it would be without the cleans-
ing of the floods it is difficult to imagine. In all probability
the stench from the accumulations of filth would cause a
plague such as would sweep away the whole population. A
flood had taken place before we arrived, and I marvelled,
as I noted the high-water mark on the walls, how such
crumbling buildings could stand such severe treatment—but
the East falls slowly.

This old city has a record of comparative peace, though
'the Portugals' from Azîla harried the country, and one of
the greatest battles in Moorish history took place in the
plains, and was called the Battle of El Kasar. There
Portuguese ambitions of conquest received their final
overthrow.

El Kasar is situated on the Fez road, and there is a large
through trade, some goods coming by Tangiers, when the
roads permit, and others from Laraiche. The caravans
carrying up Manchester cottons, green tea, candles, and
crockery stay the night in El Kasar. They return loaded
with grain, hives, wax and honey. Towards Fez are the
plains which grow the finest wheat in Morocco. There is
also a great deal done in the cattle trade for export from
Tangiers to Gibraltar.

The great Mohammedan University, the royal city of the
ancient kingdom of Fez, is only four days' ride from
El Kasar; and the Fez Moors, who are the most influential
and aristocratic in the country, are under the influence of

the mosque, which is more powerful than the Sultan, and they make themselves felt all through this northern part of Morocco. Fez is strongly anti-European, and practically Moslem. The Moors are well-to-do, some of them even wealthy merchants, and they are so keenly alive to the benefits of trade that they do more to secure it by keeping their word than any other Moors in the country

Whilst in this neighbourhood I heard a good deal about the French. Just before we reached El Kasar the French Ambassador had been there travelling incognito, but he was recognised before he left. He occupied himself in making very careful notes. I constantly came upon Frenchmen travelling for no very clear reason. One man told me that he was studying the religions of the tribes ; but as all the tribes are Mohammedan, the reason assigned is obviously a strange one. He could not give me any definite idea as to the discoveries he had made, and he seemed most unwilling to acknowledge in which direction his investigations had taken him. The French would probably rely on these tribes to provide a kind of standing army, officered by Frenchmen, and would allow them to retain their own government. France is always anxious to provide fresh material for an army, and has recourse to means which no other civilized nation employs. Another I met with was more occupied with endeavouring to dissuade me from travelling than to give me any information which could assist me. He drew terrible pictures of the hardships and obstacles I should find in my way. In some places the French were civil and well spoken, but further south they assumed another tone, and in Mogador they were inclined to be outrageously rude, with the Jacobin manner which is purely French, and never to be met with in any other people.

The Fez Moors were very anxious at the encroachments of French arms, and they were dissatisfied with the Sultan for not doing something to keep the French at bay. There was

no doubt in my mind that any attempt on the part of France
to bring force to bear would mean the arming of the
tribes.

I heard a good deal about the methods of French warfare
on the borders, and if there is any truth in the stories which
filtered through, the conditions in that secluded and savage
land produced by French interference may well cause dismay
among the Moors. As they were reported only on native
authority I do not care to repeat them. But shortly before
I arrived at El Kasar, three fugitives, deserters from the
2nd Regiment of the Legion Étrangère, which had its depot
at Sidi Bel Abbas, in Algeria, arrived in El Kasar. This
regiment is not the Lost Legion, but it is composed of
foreigners who have for one reason or another left their own
country, and desire to pass into oblivion. The accounts
which these men gave of the brutal treatment in the French
service made the deepest impression on all who heard them;
but I incline to think that their veracity was borne witness
to by the hardships which they had faced in deserting.

Terrible as existence in the service evidently was to them,
to desert and walk through the Atlas, with no money and no
means of support, was a desperate enterprise. The Moors,
seeing their miserable plight, helped them on more than
one occasion, and practically kept them from starving. One
story which they told I feel may be safely repeated. They
had spent the night where there was to be a market the
next day, in the hope of picking up a little food. But in
this they failed, and they were making up their minds to
walk on, when they stood looking hungrily at some bread
which the women had for sale. A Moor saw them. 'Are
you English?' he asked. None of them happened to be
English, but they said 'Yes.' He gave them a dollar, and
said, 'Go and eat.' This relief kept them alive, and enabled
them to reach El Kasar, which they did in an almost
dying condition. Yet through all this suffering they never

regretted the step they took when they deserted from the French service.

The site which Mrs. Greathed had selected for our camp was outside the city of El Kasar, near to some beautiful orange gardens, fenced with bamboos, and watered by narrow conduits of clear water, which made a pleasant gurgling sound. From our tents we could see the lofty minarets and towers of the mosques for which El Kasar is renowned.

The Vice-Consul, Mr. Carleton, walked back to the camp with me. He took his soldier with him, and while he remained chatting with us he repeatedly sent his servant to fetch for us anything which it struck him we might require. Shortly after he left us the last thing to arrive that evening was a large dish of kouskous, served in Moorish style and sent out to us under the straw conical hat-shaped covering always used by the Moors.

The following morning, before we had finished breakfast, Mr. Carleton arrived to walk with us into El Kasar, and show us as much of the city as we could see before the heat of the day began.

Not only are the streets in El Kasar never cleaned (the mounds of filth were in some places piled so high against the houses as to be on a level with the top of the front-door), but rotting in the sun at the entrance to the town were the carcases of dead mules and horses, and the stench from these was truly appalling.

The Jews form a large addition to the population of the town, which is supposed to number about 10,000. There is no Mellâh, but some Jews we visited were inhabiting a fondak. Several brothers and their families lived together. Most of the transport business is in Jewish hands. They trade goods from the coast through El Kasar to the country markets, or sokos, in the vast region between the Mamora Forest and the Riff country, where there are no towns. The subject of the flood still exercised people's minds, and the

Jews told me that no one knew how many people had been
drowned. They seemed highly amused at Mr. Carleton's
going out to rescue his horse and swimming back into the
town to his house. These Jews regaled us with the wine of
the country, which is a thick, dark liquid, made by boiling
one-half of the juice and adding it to the other half, and
with a sweetmeat made of preserved orange-flowers. The
Jews make wine every year, but they have great difficulty in
getting sufficient grapes. The Moors object to wine being
made, and will not sell them grapes for the purpose. As
they are not allowed to own land they cannot grow them for
themselves. Morocco is a country where the inhabitants
are all on edge with one another.

The ruinous state of the mosques was even more striking
than their grandeur. Entrance being forbidden, we could not
go inside them. As the flood had swept through some of
them, they were probably in a bad state inside. The
peculiarity of El Kasar is its want of central interest. The
Jews live scattered through the town, and the markets and
streets are crowded with tribesmen from the hills and from
the plains. There are merchants from Fez and traders from
the coast ports. El Kasar is looked upon as a camping-
place, or, at best, as a distributing centre, and nobody cares
to make it smart or attractive. As somebody said of railway-
stations, they were places which nobody wanted to stay at,
so that decoration was wasted upon them. Only one saint's
tomb and praying-house seemed kept in any kind of repair.
By the grill in the window, set in old Fez tiles, it was customary for Moors to seal their oaths by kissing the outside
of the window. The white dome of the koubah, and the
green fig-tree in the courtyard, and the general grace of the
outline, made this old tomb especially picturesque. But
there were many corners in El Kasar delightful for an
artist, which photography would fail to convey any impression of. The grand old houses, which had been built in

Photo by Miss Loyde

SLAVES

days when a very wealthy class of Moors lived there, who drew their resources from the agricultural backing in the plains, were all more or less ruinous. A large building, now inhabited by numbers of poor Moors, was pointed out to me as a flourishing hospital before the Portuguese took possession of the town in the seventeeth century.

' In the multitude of councillors there is safety,' says the proverb ; but El Kasar has a multitude of governors. The Bashaw of the town is responsible to the Bashaw who appoints him. The adjacent country is governed by a Kaid, appointed by the Sultan to rule a very numerous tribe called Klôt. But all the tribes who come into the town are responsible to their own governors, and not to the authorities of the town. Europeans are governed by their Consuls.

The walls of the town suffered great damage at the hands of Mulai Ismail, and now, though the gates are closed at night, it is not difficult for the tribesmen to get in and do much as they please. I was shown a house near the gates where a Jew lived who had given umbrage to a hill tribe, and consequently they came down one night, and finding the gates shut, made a hole in the city wall close by, through which they crept. They broke open the Jew's front-door with axes, and smashed all his furniture and crockery. They took nothing away, but they broke all they could find ; and they would have killed the Jew if he had not escaped by the roof. There was a rude sense of justice at the bottom of the escapade, but these people have their own way of doing things.

About a month previously they had stolen some women out of a house in El Kasar, and had taken them away to the hills. They stole them because they could dance well, and these tribesmen will not allow their own women to dance. The captives improved in their dancing so much that their fame reached another tribe, who bought them for a high price. It was said that they would probably be sold again, and so handed on from tribe to tribe.

The theft remained unpunished. There was a collusion
between the hill men and the plain men. The hill men
found the money, but the plain men arranged the affair—
it was said that a town Moor in El Kasar helped them.
These tribes have a government of their own, and though
they owe the Sultan allegiance and pay him tribute, he has
very little to do with governing them. His position is
similar to that which history has left us as the King of
Scotland's towards the Highland clans. But instead of
hereditary chieftainship, every year a headman is appointed
by popular vote, and he appoints two or three headmen to
help him in council, or in the investigation of cases. He
acts as administrator, and when there is anything exceptional
to be done he summons the whole tribe and gives them his
opinion in a speech, and if they agree with him it is done.
The hill tribes are Berbers, fair, tall men with blue eyes of a
Scandinavian type, and, as a rule, they speak their own
language, and seldom can even make themselves understood
in Arabic. A great many of them were in El Kasar, having
come in to the market. They strode through the town with
a lordly air, indicating supreme disdain for the town Moors
and plain men. They have vendetta against the plain
men individually, but in their own tribe the price of blood
is accepted. The customs of different hill tribes vary; but
I am giving here the particulars which were given me of
the hill men I saw in El Kasar. They were a tribe, so far
as I could learn, with no divisions, and this tends to make
them more powerful. The Beni Hassan has as many as
ten divisions, and if any one division has a blood feud
against any individual in any other tribe, all the divisions
must join. The vendetta will be a difficult problem in
governing the country, more especially as it is justified by
the Koran, which says that it is more honourable to take
the life of your enemy than to accept a ransom.

Even the plain men take the law into their own hands

under certain circumstances. I asked a Moor once about this, and he told me that if a man is known to steal, perhaps his neighbours will hale him before the Governor, or Kaid, and if for any reason the Kaid fails to satisfy their sense of justice, they go back to their village; but after a time something happens to the man. Perhaps he falls sick and dies. Perhaps he goes blind; and if anything is said about it— Allah is great, and it is the will of Allah. As I thought of the blind beggars sitting outside the city gates raising their mournful chant my blood grew hot, and I told the Moor that where my country governed it was the will of Allah that such things did not happen But he looked incredulous, and said English people were different to Moors.

The hill tribes are adepts at cattle stealing, and this causes many a fight. Four days before we arrived at El Kasar, a hill tribe came down and stole the town cows to the number of thirty-two. They took the herdsman away with them, and he was found afterwards with his throat cut. This was done to prevent his revealing who they were that had taken the cattle. Then another hill tribe offered to return them to the town at six dollars a head, declaring that they had bought them at that price, not knowing them to have been stolen.

At El Kasar the coinage in circulation is entirely Moorish, and very poor it is. Eight copper coins of the roughest description go to the half-real. There was at one time a good copper farthing made of native copper. One of these farthings was worth four Moorish flous. The Spaniards collected these farthings and took them to Spain, where they were melted down for Spanish currency.

From the Jews' house we went to visit the ladies of the Bashaw's harem. They were enjoying a picnic, having been brought in from his country-house to one in the immediate neighbourhood of the town where there was a nice garden. Here they sat on mattresses on the floor, singing a weird chant and drinking unlimited green tea.

The Bashaw had quite recently divorced a wife and married another.   Mohammedan divorce is very easy to obtain under the law of the Prophet, and its practice in Morocco is a grievous iniquity.   A man can divorce his wife at any time by going to the fokis and stating that he wishes to do so. He pays a small sum of money, and they give him a paper, which he hands to the woman.   She takes it and goes away. There is no provision made for her; thus, from affluence it is but one step to destitution.   If she can, she may work for her living as a servant; but the probability is that, untrained and unaccustomed to the slightest physical exertion, she breaks down under it, and takes to vicious courses for her support—and the viciousness of some of these women is simply inconceivable.

The harems are little better than lunatic asylums, with this difference—that whereas in a lunatic asylum the patients are encouraged to employ themselves rationally, and to strengthen such minds as they have, and to practise self-control, the régime in the harem is the very reverse.   The poor countrywoman who toils along the road bending under her load is less to be pitied than the pampered wife of a Bashaw; for these grandees are not permitted to do anything. The stigma of slavery attaches to work, especially household work; therefore they spend their time in painting their faces and dressing themselves, tattooing their hands with lace patterns as though they wore mittens, and finding some fresh spot on their cheeks where another mark can be added.   They are bedizened with savage jewellery, in which huge emeralds play a large part in Morocco; though I could not judge whether they were real.

The favourite wife in the harem of the Bashaw of El Kasar assumed a languid air, as though it were almost too much trouble for her to look at us; but the other three made a place for Mrs. Greathed to sit beside them, and began at once to show her their jewels and to examine her rings.

Meantime the concubines had started singing, clapping their hands to mark time. They were of all ages and all shades of colour. Two were very pretty girls, apparently peasants, and wearing the simple dress of a peasant, which was far more becoming than the atrocious make-up of crude coloured silks, dyed eyes, false hair, and rouged cheeks of those four wives. One concubine was so young that she was hardly more than a child; she might have been seventeen, and she was the prettiest there. The singing was led by an old woman, who, I believe, composed the ditty on the spot. They sang one verse over and over again till it flagged, then she started another, clapping her hands and calling attention. Could I have understood the words, I feel sure they would have conveyed an atrocious meaning, for the expression of the old hag's countenance, which reflected itself on some of the other women's faces, and her gestures, were vicious in the extreme. What tried me exceedingly in the Bashaw's harem was the presence there of a little boy about seven years old; and the child's eyes and ears had no other occupation than to drink in the lasciviousness and wickedness of this hell.

It was by no means the first harem that I had visited, and it compared favourably with others. There were in all about twenty women, and as they were on a picnic, they were in a more friendly and sociable mood with one another than was usually the case. I have been in some harems where there have been sulks and ill-humour, and some of the women were looking positively murderous.

The harem is one of those perversions of the natural order of things—a crooked thing which nothing can straighten. It is better to be a concubine than a lawful wife, for a concubine cannot be divorced, and has some provision and status, though no better than a slave; just as it is better to be a slave for whom a price is paid, than a free peasant under the tyranny of a rapacious Kaid. This is the way the East has gone on reforming itself backwards.

The view which the Moor takes of womenkind is that they
are naturally impure and worthless. It is a misfortune
common to all men that their wives will betray them if they
are given the least chance. It is the inevitable destiny of
all husbands who cannot imprison their wives with sufficient
security. To repine, or to allow chagrin to disturb their
repose on the score of feminine conduct were folly. The
wretches must be punished, and what punishments are
inflicted inside those high walls, God only knows, and their
fellow-men praise them for gratifying their resentment. They
never regard their misfortune as singular; besides, God is
good, and affords them the consolation of seeing the wretches
suffer. It is a weakness for a man to allow his happiness to
rest on a woman's fidelity; for all women are wantons. The
Moors take for granted that a truly virtuous woman does not
exist, and that nothing can equal their malice; yet by an
odd contradiction they put a premium upon chastity.

This was the ancient view of womenkind in the East. We
have only to read the early books of the Bible to see what
were the popular ideas of women in the dawn of history.
But Mohammed understood the nature of his followers in
allowing them four wives. It is to a certain extent a safeguard against the inconceivably greater evils of concubinage.
The Oriental, except in most rare cases, which do not form
a class, must be a polygamist; that is his nature, and it is
the chief obstacle to his becoming a Christian. We do not
think so in England; but then our views and our ways of
doing things are different.

After we had drunk tea, and the ladies had satisfied themselves that their apparel and their jewels were far better than
ours, we took our leave. They were puzzled up to the last
as to our motive for travelling as we were not missionaries.
Mrs. Greathed's acquaintance with Indian natives made it
easier for her to talk to them, which she did in Spanish.
I felt their civility, and I believe that even the detestable

singing was partly intended for our pleasure. They gave me
the only chair to sit upon, and Mrs. Greathed was provided
with a nice cushion in the seat of honour between the wives.
But I could not express the least appreciation of the singing,
which had a monotonous entreaty, with a hungry sound at
the bottom of it, and no kind of melody; and I was thankful
when they ceased beating a wooden jar with parchment
stretched over it and clapping their hands all round me.
The tea was not otherwise than refreshing, being made in
Moorish fashion—about a tablespoonful of green tea to a
quarter of a pound of lump sugar and a bunch of seven or
eight sprigs of green mint, all put in the pot together. We
drank it out of little handleless cups of imitation Crown
Derby, probably made in Germany. The wives pretended
to be annoyed at our departure, but they shook hands with
us and asked us to come again.

From the harem we went to see the Bashaw. He was
administering justice in an alcove under an arch, or portico.

The first thing that struck me as we drew near was the
sight of two fat mules tethered in the archway, with smart
red cloth saddles. A large brass tea-kettle was spouting
out steam on the top of a brass tripod containing charcoal.

The Bashaw was a fat, dark-looking man, with a 'tigerish'
expression, which came into his face at intervals, and
temporarily extinguished the good humanity which was
there at times. I was told that 'he is fond of flogging,' but
that 'he does not torture.' He had just returned from visiting the Sultan—a pleasure, or rather obligation, which had
cost him 40,000 dollars; and, of course, he had to get this
money by some means or other. The Shereef who sat
beside him to give him assistance was Hammed Bekeli, the
descendant of a calipha. He had a fine, manly countenance,
with a very intelligent and fearless expression. He had the
reputation of being a just and wise man. His manners and

bearing were most distinguished. I was told that no other
Shereef had so large a number of followers.

Both the Bashaw and the Shereef were evidently taken
aback at our appearance. It seemed, to use a common
expression, 'to knock the breath out of their bodies.'
They each seized a cushion ; the Bashaw slapped the one
which he caught hold of, and invited Mrs. Greathed
to sit on it by his side. The Shereef hurled his at me,
indicating by a nod that I was to sit down on it there and
then. I did so exactly opposite the Shereef and the Bashaw,
who, having secured Mrs. Greathed by his side, was studying
her countenance intently.

Mr. Carleton had followed us and sat down in the
entrance, on a bundle of green food which was deposited
there for the two mules.

As soon as the Bashaw could speak, he asked Mr. Carleton
who we were and what we wanted. The Vice-Consul
explained that we were two Englishwomen who were
travelling for the pleasure of seeing the beautiful land of
Morocco, and making the acquaintance of the Moors.
They were visibly astonished, but pleased. They wished to
know whether we were Christian missionaries. Mr. Carleton replied that we were Christians, but not missionaries.
This was perplexing but satisfactory. The Shereef wished
to put the question as to our business more clearly. He
said we were probably ' doctrinas,' and it was well known
that the business of ' doctrinas ' is to travel in order to find
people to doctor. His view seemed to be that ' doctrinas '
were a breed of Christians kept for certain purposes, as, for
instance, fox-terriers are kept to kill rats.

Mr. Carleton said, ' No ; these women are not " doctrinas."
They merely travel. That is the way with my country-
women. There are some who *must* travel, just as there are
some who *must* doctor. These women mean well to the
Moors, and one has a son who is a judge to the Moors who

are in India.' This gave complete satisfaction, and I really
thought the Bashaw would order in a case to give Mrs.
Greathed the chance of trying it with him. But instead he
called for the tea-kettle, and the two scribes, who sat
together, but a little apart from the Shereef and the Bashaw,
were told to make tea.

The Shereef observed that he had never met women like
us, and the Bashaw emphasized the remark by adding that
he had never *heard* of any like us. He took for granted that
it was our custom to assist in presiding in courts of justice;
and I gathered from something that passed that he believed
Mrs. Greathed to be of great use to her son in the discharge
of his duties in India.

The Shereef, who had been looking at me attentively,
asked who my father was, and Mr. Carleton described him
as a kind of Shereef, to whom people came for advice, and
that his business was to tell people publicly how they ought
to behave: that he did this every week, and that it was the
duty of the people to go and hear him.

They then asked what we thought of the Moors. We said
that Moors had been kind and helpful to us in travelling. I
added that I was particularly interested in the hill tribes,
and that in my own country I belonged to a tribe.

They then began to talk about India. They said the
Sultana, who was just dead, had been very good to the
Moors in India, and allowed them to practise their own
religion without interfering in any way. They assured us,
with gracious bows, that the Moors and the English were
like brothers. The Shereef remarked that the English were
sad because their Sultana was dead; and the Bashaw,
wishing to say something specially pleasant and consolatory,
leant forward and told me that now I had a Sultan, which
was, he thought, very advantageous. This was almost more
than I could endure. The thought of his horrible harem
rose before me—but I could make no excuse for him, and I

7

longed to punch his head.   I said that the Sultana had been
very good to her Indian subjects, and kept some always near
her.   Both the Shereef and the Bashaw said that that was
quite natural and to be expected.

Tea was now ready—very strong of mint and very sweet
of sugar.   We all partook of it, sucking it up with great
gusto.   Then I wrote down the name of the Bashaw, and
the name of the Shereef.   Whereupon the latter, who looked
with great interest to see if I could really write, and listened
to Mr. Carleton's repeating his name and to my attempts at
pronouncing it, determined to follow suit.   He snatched up
the reed-pen which lay in front of the nearest scribe, and
called for a piece of paper.   But the whole court did not
contain such a thing, and I was about to supply his want by
tearing a leaf out of my note-book, when I bethought me of
my card, which I handed him.   He examined it carefully,
as I might a curio from the Sandwich Islands.   Then he
gravely turned it over, and proceeded to write my name and
address in Arabic characters, pronouncing each word in
English as Mr. Carleton said it.   Having completed the task,
he shook a little black sand over the writing, and then put it
briefly and without comment into the folds of his garment.

Meantime the business of the court was delayed.   The
witnesses had crowded into the archway behind us, and
were standing as near as they dared, and looking over each
other's shoulders, raising themselves on tiptoe to see what
was happening.

The scribes having been ordered to make tea, never ceased
from doing so, and were proceeding to hand us a third
edition when the Shereef interposed.   He said that he had
made up his mind that we should drink the next cup at his
house.   He spoke with an air of royal command, and rising
with great dignity, made a sign to us to follow him, which
we did after shaking hands with the Bashaw.

The way lay down a few narrow, tortuous streets, with

rubbish heaps lying across them. The Shereef strode in front, turning round every few yards to beam benevolently upon us and make sure that we were following, or to address a few words to Mr. Carleton.

It was very hot, and the cool shade of the courtyard or patio of his house was a delightful change from the streets. While we were kept waiting a moment for the women to be given time to retire, I noticed a whip with several cords hanging in the entrance, and a gun against the wall of modern pattern. Then we were escorted to an apartment opening to the courtyard, which was the old gentleman's bed and sitting-room combined. He sat down on a cushion in the entrance, and we sat on a mattress within the room. There were two four-post beds at either end of the room, while on the floor, midway between them, was a narrow mattress with a large leather pillow, at the back of which stood a cheap eight-day clock. It was the noisiest thing in the place, and I made up my mind that the Shereef must have nerves of brass to sleep with it ticking so close to his head. Beside the bed stood a beautiful old brass candlestick with three branches to it, and on the wall above his head hung his dagger and a gun in an old red cloth case. A looking-glass and a comb were on the floor close by.

The Shereef called a slave—a black girl gorgeously attired in coloured muslin drapery, who immediately brought the inevitable tea paraphernalia and the sprigs of green mint. After the Shereef had delicately bruised the mint with his own hands by folding it in a fine handkerchief, and beating it against his palm, he crammed it into the teapot after the tea, and put in an extra lump of sugar to keep it down. The slave poured the boiling water from the kettle into the pot, and then the Shereef set down the pot for the tea to " draw."

While these preparations were being made I was able to take stock of our host. He belonged to a hill tribe, and his

round well-shaped head and expression of strong common-
sense, with a certain balance about him, was more like an
English gentleman than a Moor.   He had strong but refined
hands, and I believe there was not a trace of black blood in
his veins.   He possessed the Bedouin hospitality, and I
think this cup of tea he was offering us under his own roof was
intended as a civility to us as English, and to show us that
he accepted and understood the difference between English
women and Moorish.   It was the difference in kind—as
between horses and mules, or bees and ants, a curious or
scientific fact—for they are as God created them.   Still, to
receive us as he did, he must have been setting aside some
prejudices, and I admired him for it.   Every now and then
he asked Mr. Carleton some question about us, and our
interests and views.   Then he gently remarked that it was
strange that we took an interest in many things that Moorish
women never troubled about.   When we left he shook hands
with us very cordially, and we both felt that it was one of
our pleasantest experiences to have met this fine old Shereef.

We lunched with Mr. and Miss Carleton, and in the afternoon the two Mr. Carletons and their sister, and a gentleman
who was on his way to Wazan, and had just arrived and
pitched his tent about a hundred yards from ours, came to
tea at our camp.

CHAPTER XI

THE GAOL OF EL KASAR—AN OLD BATTLEFIELD—HORSE-
BREEDING—A SOKO ON THE PLAINS

I was sorry when the time came to leave El Kasar, and felt I could have spent some days longer there and in the neighbourhood. The last place we went to visit after saying good-bye to Miss Carleton was the gaol, which, like everything else in El Kasar, is in the last stages of disrepair. It was quite as dirty and smelt as bad as the prison at Tangiers, but it was better lighted. We went on the roof and looked down on the prisoners through a wooden trellis. I was told that a few months before a man had come to the gaol, bringing with him eight other men and a carpenter. They overpowered the guards, and took two men out of the gaol and went away with them. It was a curious incident. The escapade was ascribed to a Moor who was protected by an American citizen. There was probably ground for the charge, for the Sultan complained to the American Government. But the Moor who was under suspicion went to some adools, and, with their assistance, was able to put in an alibi. It became, consequently, one of those cases on which people form opinions as they please.

It must add enormously to the difficulties of ruling a country when each consul governs the stranger within the gate according to the law of the country to which he belongs. Yet this is the case in Morocco. It is wheel within wheel—jurisdiction within jurisdiction. There is nothing to lay hold of to form a national life except the Mohammedan religion, and that does not include either Jews or Spaniards. There is practically no hope of doing away with old prejudices by one common form of education which might evolve a national aim. There is no strong personality on which the people can fix their eyes, for even the personality of Mohammed has passed away, and left a crowd of small saints, whose intercession is prayed for with loud-voiced persistency.

Missionaries have come in to raise another ideal, but the country is not in a condition to be worried by any additional religious question. The whole population of Moslems, Jews, and Roman Catholics are sensitive, if not slightly mad, on religion. If a man has a recognised mania, the wise would establish friendly intercourse on a ground of common interest. Great discrepancies and differences necessitate the subordinating of that private sentiment which, be it remembered, is not always in accordance with public good. The reformer who enters with exalted schemes for the mote in his brother's eye is sure to become the prey of rogues and impostors, with the result that the little good he might achieve concerning the mote misses the goal, for the level-headed body of the people reject him and his companions.

The faddists who clamour for ' sympathy and imagination ' in the government of native races mistake the nature of the case. The overwrought, war-distracted people need peace. It is peace which this distressful country sighs for—the peace of a strong hand, the even balance of cold, dispassionate justice, the calm of a common ground. And often when night came and I lay down on my camp-bed with the day's events passing before my mind, I remembered these lines from a poet who followed hard on the wild scenes of the French Revolution :

> ' O Life ! Without thy chequered scene
> Of right and wrong, of weal and woe,

Success and failure, could a ground
Of magnanimity be found
For faith mid ruin'd hopes serene,
Or whence could virtue flow ?
Pain entered through a ghastly breach,
Nor while life lasts must effort cease ;
Heaven upon earth's an idle boast.
But for the bowers of Eden lost,
Mercy hath placed within our reach
A portion of God's peace.'

From El Kasar we were bound for a village where there would be a soko the next morning. It lay out of the road, but I was anxious to see one of the markets which supplied the backing to support such a city as El Kasar must have been in days gone by. It was only a short ride, but our people chose to take us to a village where they had friends. Fortunately I discovered the trick before the tents were put up, and rode on. They had taken us so far out of our road that it was nearly dark when we reached the village.

Nevertheless, the ride was one of the most enjoyable in my travels. At first we crossed the plain, which was very marshy in places, but settled with a few huts and some grain-crops here and there.* After luncheon we began to climb from the plain, and came on to a wide plateau, where there were more fenced villages and a great many horses and

---

* It was in this plain that the battle of El Kasar took place between the invading Portuguese and the Moors. It is thus referred to in Dr Brown's introduction to 'Leo Africanus': 'In 1500 the Portuguese had possession of all the best parts of Morocco, and were gradually extending their outposts into the interior, with the intention of seizing Marakesh. This design, as well as the capture of Fez, they would unquestionably have accomplished, had not Dom Sebastian's death and defeat on the plains of El Kasar el Kebir (1578) discouraged any further aggression.' There is a footnote to the passage quoted, which says · 'The actual locality of this famous fight—the "Battle of the Three Kings"—was near the Wad M'Kamsen,' and this river, I believe, we forded near the site of the battle. We stopped for our luncheon in an old half-ruined garden of pomegranates, oranges and figs, which a little primitive irrigation from this river rendered fertile.

cattle grazing, but I saw very few sheep. The horses
interested me especially. The mares were good. Where
they got the breed from, I cannot tell, but I am confident
there was English blood in some of them. They were light
horses, such as would make good hunters or smart carriage
horses. At home we should say they were three parts
thoroughbred. One thing which struck me particularly was
that they were a very good whole colour. The Moors have
no mad fancies such as the Red Indian indulges for hideous
markings. I never saw a piebald the whole time I was in
the country. Roan is very rare; but they have a great many
grays—some nearly black; others a silver gray, with mane,
tail, and legs almost black. The next favourite colour is
black, and white stockings are rather rare. They have good
dark browns. I only saw two very good chestnuts, and that
was in the south. Bays were common.

In shape, these horses have very good short heads and
long necks, which I believe they stretch by continual grazing.
Their fore-legs are admirable, the hind quarters not so
satisfactory. I believe this defect is principally due to using
them as pack-horses when they are still foals. I have
positively seen a yearling following its mother to the market
with a small load on its back. The mare only carried a
woman and a baby. They do not load or work the mares,
and their hocks are usually sound. The feet are remarkably
good, and about these horses in the north there is not the
puffy chest which is so ugly a defect in the spoilt cart-
horses down in the south. Their shoulders are good, and
should render them serviceable for light harness work. Not
the least remarkable feature is their eyesight; but they are
apt to shy if something that is strange and incomprehensible
be in sight and they are not given time to satisfy their
curiosity. They are very curious. I also believe that when
they are cutting their four-year-old tooth they shy, whether
from nervousness or not I cannot say. My pony would buck

a little, but not seriously or viciously. Sometimes they will rear, but I cannot say I ever met with a horse in Morocco which had any faults or ill-temper to be compared with other horses. As to paces, it would seem that these are much a matter of training. For centuries these horses have been trained to be good walkers, and they will walk all day without food. They have also been trained to be chargers, and they will charge short distances of about three hundred yards at a headlong rate, and then stop dead, to the damaging of their hind-legs. But they can be very easily cured of this absurd trick. I have been told that they cannot trot, but this is very difficult to be certain about, for there is not much trotting road. People do not trot their horses. I made mine trot, and he would trot for short distances evenly and well. It was distinctly a pleasant pace. As to constitution, I should think they were the hardest horses in the world. They will eat anything except prickly pear and aloes. It is said that the breed down south has been spoilt by the introduction of English cart-horses, which some evil genius tempted George III. to send as a present to the Sultan, and which these deplorable Moors admired. The result is that though they select their mares well, the stallions are not the best, and I much fear that the breed is getting more and more mixed and spoilt. The Abda breed, which was once pure, and of the pronounced Arab stamp, is very seldom met with. I saw one, which was a very pretty animal, but not a horse according to English ideas. It would have made a charming pet, and whoever rode it in the Park would have been well stared at and remarked upon.

It was nearly dark when we rode into the village, which lay on the side of a slope in the middle of a prairie on a plateau. The huts were square, and there was the tomb of a female saint near to a mosque built with two aisles and a little tower, exactly like a village church. When we arrived,

the women were crowding into the tomb of their saint, and
the muezzin's plaintive entreaty sounded from the minaret.
The men went into the mosque, but the women are not
allowed there except on rare and stated occasions.   Human
nature vents itself in prayers, and the women to whom Allah
is denied, draw near to the dead saints as their friends and
intercessors with little theology but much faith.   It was the
month in which the Shereefs collect their dues, and one was
established for this purpose in a tent in the centre of the
village.   It was very chilly, and we were glad of all the
wraps we had, and some hot soup was most acceptable.

The market commenced with the shooting up of streets of
flimsy tents soon after daybreak.   Any old rug or mat does
for a tent, but a tent gives standing to a tradesman.   No
one would place the same value on a cobbler's work if he sat
out in the open as they would if he had a mat on two sticks
and made believe it was a tent.   By the time we got there
there were streets of shoemakers, of sellers of Manchester
cottons, of blacksmiths, who even set up a small anvil, a
charcoal fire, and a boy to work the blast.   An old woman
sold small wooden bowls carved out of solid cork-wood.
There were beautiful rush mats for five reals, that is, less
than a shilling English.   Ploughs were exhibited, and this
part of the market was like an agricultural show, only there
were, of course, no new designs.   These ploughs were very
light.   They were made of cork-wood, which is very tough,
with a coarse grain.   There was not a single nail used in
them.   The iron share, like one long tooth or an exaggerated
narrow hoe, was fixed in a socket and wedged.   They worked
with a long pole and a crossbar, which passed under the
bellies of the oxen.   A moderate amount of native pottery
was offered.   There was some wool and grain.   Charcoal was
in abundance, and there was a slaughter-yard in operation.
The principal business appeared to be the sale of sheep,
cattle, and goats, and their slaughter then and there; and

everyone who comes to the market secures, if he has the wherewithal, a little piece of meat or offal. The feature of chief interest in the market to me was the beauty of the mares, but they were not for sale. They had come in carrying their masters. There were streets of chemists, or, rather, herbalists, where spices, rose-leaves, sulphate of copper, zinc, leather charms, talc and sulpher were offered in very small quantities. Some very poor-looking old men brought upon very poor-looking old donkeys great blocks of rocksalt. They said they came from the mountains, and the whole thing looked weird and wizened. They would not tell me where they came from. A preacher or foki of some kind sat under a bamboo-stick. A piece of white paper was inserted in a slit to indicate that it was a place of prayer. He sat there reading to himself, and was dressed in a ragged creamy-white jellaba, and the worn copy of the Koran or saint's life was bound in real red Morocco leather. The people gave him coppers, but he sat under his bamboo absolutely unconcerned, and apparently disdainful of worldly things in general.

Unfortunately, the Jews were absent, owing to the Passover. It struck me that their methods of collecting goods at these markets and disposing of them again was the business of the Moors themselves in former days. That it has passed into the hands of the Jews indicates that the whole trade of the country is tending in that direction. I heard it said that no one but Jews know how to deal with Moors. And unquestionably there must be a very valuable training to be acquired in these sokos. I was struck with the absence of any commercial traveller.

Independent trade, that is to say trade in the villages themselves, is impossible. The system of the country is to confine trade to markets. However much the condition of the natives may improve under protection, there is no opening for a trader who in South Africa would fill his cart with

goods suitable for native trade and trek from village to village.
Of such a trader the Moors would be suspicious. Neither
would it be desirable for a trader to stay too long amongst
them. The idea of travelling in Morocco is to go on a
distinct business errand, to tell them plainly what it is, and
having completed it, to return. To linger in a village offering
goods for sale, not being the custom of the country, would
arouse all manner of conjectures, and probably lead to difficulties. Any attempt at village trade would be not only
contrary to the customs and feelings of the country, but very
hard to manage, for the Jews carry the cash into the sokos.
I believe there is very little in the villages. All transactions
in the sokos are in cash, and practically all the cash goes
back again to the Jews. It is much as follows : A woman
brings three or four fowls for sale. A Jew buys them for five
reals. She buys some olive-oil from one native, and her
husband has the mule shod by another. The man she buys
the oil from buys a new jellaba from a Jew (or Moor who is
a Jew's agent) with the proceeds of his day's sale. The man
who shod the mule buys some candles from a Jew trader.
Thus the cash passes from hand to hand very much like
counters in a game.

It had rained heavily during the market, and we rode away
under a very threatening sky across a marsh and over some
round green hills, where the soil was sandy and full of large
stones, probably limestone. The road was interesting on
account of the horse-breeding, and broken at intervals by
crumbling old tombs of saints. At length we came to a
Moor who was a friend of Mr. Carleton, and who was most
anxious that we should camp near his house. This we were
afraid to do, for the weather seemed very broken, and we
were most anxious to get down to the coast, believing Rabat
to be much nearer than it was. The Moor's neighbours and
friends came out to join their entreaties to his, and finding
that we would not agree to his request, he became sulky, and

sat down on some rubbish in a pet. I felt that this would
never do, so I sat down by his side, and looked at him. We
soon straightened things out by the aid of Spanish, and when
we at last rode on, he walked by my side, sometimes laying
his hand on my horse's bridle in a friendly manner, and
pointing to his crops of maize, which were really excellent;
and when we reached the end of his land he wished us a good
journey, and begged us to return and visit him soon.

That night we stopped at a village called Ain Filfil, where
we struck the plains of Tlemsan, the lagoon country, which
stretches down to the Sebou River.

CHAPTER XII

THE peasants here received us with presents of eggs and
fresh milk. The headman himself came to see us, and sat
at the door of our tent to receive our thanks for a grand dish
of pastry, cut into strips, and baked with plenty of butter.
His name was Si Mohammed al Heil, and he belonged to
the order of Hamdouchi. The dish was borne to our tent
by Mr. Carleton's soldier, who had been kindly lent to
Mrs. Greathed to look after her mule. It was then that we
asked Si Mohammed al Heil to come and see us, which he
did, though he was rather nervous. He was a fine-looking
young man, with an open, fearless countenance and perfect
manners. He sat down on his heels, and told us how he
had made the tart for us himself, because he was sure we
were good people, and he promised to send us a guard for
the night. We might sleep in peace, for he would take care
of us. Then he rose to his feet, and salaamaed with great
dignity and withdrew. Nothing could have been more
charming than this simple peasant, with the air and bearing
of a prince.

We were cold and very glad to wrap up in our blankets.
But the night did not get colder, and the rain held off.

Before I had finished dressing the next morning Si

Mohammed came again, and Mrs. Greathed received him. He inquired how we had slept, and on Mrs. Greathed's assurance that we had slept beautifully, he sighed, and said that he had not slept, for he had been watching over us. This, together with the assertion that he had cooked the tart, was merely figurative. His appointed guards had done the watching, and his ' house' had made the tart.

Then he and his headmen sat in a row at a little distance from us, watching us prepare and eat our breakfast with breathless interest, questioning our people about us, and trying hard to understand our extraordinary ways, and amazed at the numbers of strange things we used.

We were the first English who had stopped at their village, and they were glad to see us.

Presently the headwoman of the village came slowly up the hill, pausing from time to time with an air of great importance. There was no nervousness about her. She was very old, being the headman's mother. She leaned on a staff, and was dressed in all her finest clothes. Her cheeks were painted. In addition· to the tattoo - mark between the eyes and on the point of the nose, she had a star on either cheek, and a hieroglyph on the chin. Her hair was braided, and seemed to be dyed a very dark brown, but as there was not enough to make two long thick plaits, dark blue yarn had been introduced to thicken the braids and lengthen them. The lines in her forehead which time had ploughed she had completely stopped with a clay like fuller's-earth. Her hands were so elaborately tattooed all over the backs and up the arms and round the wrists that she had the appearance of wearing long lace gloves. The insides of the hands were dyed with henna, as were also the finger-nails. Her drapery was spotlessly white, of a light cambric material, but she wore a bright-coloured sash above her pantaloons, and a coloured handkerchief, or veil, which flowed from her head down her back. Two large ear-rings, a massive chain, and brooches and rings of silver, all very old, completed her attire.

She extended her hand to us where we stood by our little breakfast-table with a gracious but languid air of great condescension, and kissed the tips of her fingers after she had shaken hands with us.

We brought out our camp-stool, and begged her to sit on it; but she declined, and subsided gradually and with marvellous dignity on to her heels. She expressed the liveliest curiosity as to what we were eating, and I offered her some of the stew, which consisted of rice-beans and bacon, but the headman called to her in a voice of stern authority and forbade her to eat it. We offered her tea, and to this he did not object. So she had a cup of English tea, sweetened to a syrup, and some of the fresh milk the peasants had sent.

This refreshment caused her to smile and to chatter while she drew in the nectar with long gurgles expressive of satisfaction. She was dumfounded that the señorita was not married, but politely endeavoured to conceal whatever shock the discovery gave her. She said the English were good people, and that we were especially good people. She wished us to know that she was called the M'ra de Mallam Mohammed bin Ain Filfil, and that she was the mother of the headman.

By this time the lower-class villagers had drawn near, and they ate up the remains of the stew with gusto. It was a scene like a village-school treat. The old men played with the children. One little child, who was an especial darling with them all, was just of the age to play the autocrat. He was chased by the other children, and ran to the men, who caught him up in their arms and kissed him, and put him on their shoulders and on their heads.

Meantime our people had struck the tents, and we were soon mounted and riding away over the crest of the hill, the headman accompanying us a short distance to put us on the right road.

Thenceforward, until we reached Mehîdya, at the mouth of the Sebou River, our way lay alongside the lagoons, or, rather, winding between them, for the water was deep after the winter rains, and the track disappeared into them continually, obliging us to go a long way round over the high ground.

The conical huts of the plainsmen were now the rule, mixed with tents—the dark-brown tent of the Bedouin or Arab. These huts were merely plaited bamboos, and so light that they could be carried. I met four men carrying a hut between them, and they did it quite easily. The scenery was like the Norfolk Broads or the Fen country. The lagoons were dotted with green knolls, which stood up out of the water like islands, and on nearly all of them there was the ever-recurring saint's tomb—zawiya, or sanctuary.

On some of the rising grounds there were fig-gardens which were never submerged. The villages and the gardens, both fenced with prickly pear, had every appearance of continual habitation, and they had one long square-roofed hall or barn in the middle of them for some common purpose. There was always a saint's tomb in the garden ready for prayers.

The most beautiful of these island sanctuaries was that of Sidi Mohammed Minsoo. A large mosque was beside the tomb and some conical huts, and as it stood, with its stately white tower reflected in the water, I thought of Ely and the story of King Canute. I could not learn much about Sidi Mohammed Minsoo, but there seemed a belief that he was a great general. That is not uncommon to the saints, who were more often powerful and warlike—at best of the Robin Hood type, but capable of a good outward show of religion, by which they sucked plenty of profit in this world. That idea is very rooted in the Moor's mind. It was in Morocco,

8

from one who, though not a Moor, had lived a lifetime
amongst the Moors, and understood them thoroughly, that
I heard the remark made that Kruger's two millions 'meant
a deal of Bible work.' And as time went on, and I grew to
understand scraps of Arabic and the trend of conversation,
I found how entirely the conversation relating to trade or
war is interlarded with religious expressions or pious refer-
ences.

But most repugnant to one's Western ideas was the adula-
tion shown to Shereefs, especially if they were rich. The
poor rushed forward to kiss their hands and feet or the hem
of their garment. The polite salutation among the men is
a kiss. 'He said, Hail, Master! and kissed him,' was the
tableau continually presented to one's sight.

The rushes had not grown above the water's edge, but the
ducks were already collecting for breeding, and I saw one
or two beautiful divers. There were flights of white cranes.
Sometimes we were within sound of the sea, but we never
saw it. It lay the other side of the green hills of sandy soil
growing fine crops of barley. The barley was good, but
there was not much wheat, and what there was was the
bearded kind. We passed some locusts preparing to lay
their eggs. We had met a flight near the cork forest on the
road to El Kasar, but they were far more numerous further
south. In one place the natives were busy driving them off
their crops. They are keenly alive to the mischief these
abominable creatures inflict; and are glad to collect the eggs
and get the Government payment.

As evening came on we drew away from the track half-
way up a hill, just above a few huts, which looked very poor
and squalid.

The peasants came out, and objected to our camping.
They were a ragged, desperate, half-starved set of fellows;
but I believe they were thoroughly afraid of us. They boldly
declared that they were thieves, and said that if we camped

there they would steal our cattle, to which our genial Kaid responded by at once handing them the bridle of Mrs. Greathed's mule, and ordering the others to go to work, pitch our tent, fetch water, and find barley for us. They obeyed, but they were very cross, and I gathered that they were saying bad things of the Christians. But they did not speak loudly, and appeared to be thoroughly uneasy and perplexed.

When the tents were pitched, and the animals hobbled and turned loose to graze, the Kaid sat down on the ground and gathered the villagers round him. He talked to them like a father, with a firm air of authority, but very kindly, and then offered to buy from them fowls, forage, milk, or eggs.

A child was sent to bring us a fowl, which we bought, but it was nothing but bones and feathers. Another came with some milk which was sour.

The manner of the villagers was still suspicious. Guards! No, we should have no guards. They would not be responsible for us or our animals. Bit by bit, however, they softened, and at last they became quite reconciled to our presence.

The dogs at this village were particularly savage. Mooleeta, who had got loose from her hobbles, took it into her head to gallop down to the lagoon to drink, and I thought I would go after her, leading Conrad. It was getting dusk, and it was not safe for Mooleeta to go out of sight. About halfway I was set upon by the village dogs, who rushed out to attack me in a body. How the thing might have ended I do not know. I had stood my ground, and was meditating having recourse to strong measures.

When Mr. Carleton's soldier came down to my rescue, sent by Mrs. Greathed, he and another Moor, Mehemmet, had the greatest difficulty to drive back the dogs. But I went on to the water, where Conrad had his evening drink,

8—2

and the independent Mooleeta galloped back in front of us,
kicking her heels and throwing herself down to roll at
intervals.   On our way we had the same trouble with these
dogs, and I think it would have served the villagers right
if one of the brutes had been shot.   But I suspected that
these people had recently been harassed, and I felt sure that
they had only too much reason to be suspicious and on the
defensive.   They gained confidence the more they saw that
we had no intention of hurting them.   But our people
decided to mount guard themselves.

However, after we were in bed and almost asleep, the
guard came up, played by the village band.   It was
exceedingly funny to hear them coming.   The band consisted of a tin horn which had only one note, a tom-tom,
a banjo of negro description, and some cymbals.   As this
noise grew louder and louder, I lighted the lantern and went
out to see what was happening.   On reaching the camp
they sang, and the guards, who had no instruments, clapped
their hands.   They drew up the other side of the animals,
who were tethered in a row in front of our tents.   The Kaid
came out and attempted to address them, but he could not
make his voice heard.   They were bent on a frolic, and only
made the more noise.   They then began to dance, and,
thinking that Mrs. Greathed would like to see this curious
sight, I took hold of the man with the banjo, who was jumping up and down and yelling louder than the others.   He
stopped, and I told the Kaid to tell them that I wished them
to come nearer to my tent.

It was a clear night, the moon was shining 'as bright as
day,' and, with the help of the lantern, which the Kaid held
up, we could see this mad circle, their loose drapery flying
as they capered backwards and forwards and whirled themselves round, singing and performing on their instruments
at the same time.   Some had their jellabas pulled over their
heads, and looked like monks of some white order, while

other heads were simply covered by their natural black hair
closely cropped.   They were at times convulsed with
laughter, and their white teeth shone in the light of the
lantern.

I asked what they were singing about, and was told that
they sang that the señoritas were very good people, that
the Moors were very good people, that all the people in the
world were very good people.   Thus they had arrived at a
highly optimist frame of mind.   The Kaid watched them
with a fatherly air, but not without anxiety.   The other men
were intensely amused.   Mrs. Greathed was speechless with
laughter.   Little Shereef Mulai Hammed, who was a very
prim, decorous little Moor of natty habits and almost dainty
ways, was so upset by the scene that on turning round I
found him sitting on the provision chest, and quite unconscious that the remains of the bony fowl were between
his person and the chest.

But the dancers became wilder and more excited, and
as I have seen dances which resulted in fits or seizures, I
thought this one had better terminate.   It was called haidus,
and was intended to do us honour.   Probably they regretted
having refused the guards and missed the chance of payment, and this dance was to make up for it and to convince
us that they meant to post them.

They were made to stop by each of our men catching hold
of one of them and holding him tight.   They then announced
that they were going to commence a feast in our honour,
but I stipulated that it should be held the other side of the
horse-line, and that there was not to be enough noise to
keep us awake, to which they agreed, though they begged
to be allowed to play the horn to keep the guards awake;
and, not liking to be too exacting, I agreed to the horn.

At this village of the dancers I saw great heaps of mussel-
shells.   I was puzzled by these people.   They were the
lowest type of any I met with on my travels.   One woman

who came to sell us eggs had teeth like a wolf, short, small, and square in front, and with two long eye-teeth like fangs. The jaw was long and narrow, and when she opened her mouth her lips went back into her cheeks. She was dark, but by no means black. This country suffered frightfully in all the wars of the kingdom of Fez; and is populated now by a very mixed race. In the lagoons I saw nets set with corks and baskets which looked like eel-traps, and I wondered if the tortoises crawled into them by mistake. There were great quantities of sheep and cattle in places; but I wondered how far they were really owned by the people themselves, who, generally speaking, looked poverty-stricken.

At one place a herd—a lad of sixteen—came jumping down over the rocks, carrying with marvellous balance a wooden bowl full of milk, which he offered to us. I constrained myself to drink a mouthful; but I am not fond of drinking out of native vessels. He was a wild young hawk. His type, like that of most of these people, was Arab, and I believe there was very little black blood.

CHAPTER XIII

I COULD not help contrasting the state of these lagoons in
Morocco with their condition had they been in America.
There, instead of people lifting their houses out of the way
of the water, the water would have been dyked and dammed
and made to serve a thousand purposes. There would have
been reservoirs to store the catchment of the hills for irrigation, and I could picture myself on board a smart little light
draught steamer, with my animals in a barge or scow, completing the journey in a third of the time. I could see trees
planted as a wind-break protecting prosperous fruit-gardens
running the whole length of the waterway, and the drained
land supporting a population thousands strong. Further-
more, I could hear that booming sea, and imagine how comparatively cheaply a way could be pierced through the
sand-hills to allow at least smart cutters to run in and out
for fruit, eggs, wool, and poultry. At all events, I saw
enough to convince me that the lagoon country is worth
studying and surveying by itself. But, to make it as successful and as prosperous as it might be, it should be placed
under one control, and not treated in sections.

We stopped for luncheon at the farm of a man who told
us that he was protected by Mr. Nathan, the missionary at
Tangiers; and that evening we arrived at a village on the
crest of a little hill not far from a saint's tomb—Sidi

Mohammed Balkeir. It was about six o'clock, and the headman was in council with his tribe, and I never saw men in so anxious a frame of mind. They met me effusively, and came with gifts. The front of my tent was choked with an accumulation of fowls, eggs, bread, milk, and barley. I sorted out these provisions and paid for them. Then a beautiful little lamb was brought to my tent to be killed—a painful incident which I begged should take place further off, so it was carried to the tent of the men. I knew that to try and save it would be hopeless. It is the custom of this country, when the people have a favour to ask, that they first bring an animal and kill it in front of the house of the person whose favour they solicit. I have seen a procession of the very poorest peasants leading their best ox to the Bashaw's house in Tangiers, to slay it there before asking him some remission of taxes or some right to keep a well. Sometimes the meat is distributed to the poor; sometimes they make a feast, which is also an honour to the Governor, cooking and eating the carcase there and then. I was expected to eat this lamb myself, and presently its skinned and cleaned body was brought to me for me to choose how much I would have, in order that my Moors might eat the rest.

Hardly was this settled, and I was debating how I could ascertain what it was they hoped to get out of me, when I was begged to accept a cow. I asked its price. They said they did not want money, only that I should lay my hand on it and call it mine. I consented to do this, on the understanding that it was not to be killed. We were drinking coffee at the time, and I gave some to the headmen, hoping to find out what they wanted.

I walked out, accompanied by the Kaid, who carried a lantern, and at about fifty paces from my tent there stood a lad leading a very pretty little cow, which I patted and admired very much, feeling thankful that its life was not demanded of it.

On my return to the tent, I found Mehemmet busy cooking dinner, in which the lamb figured largely. Then the headmen wanted to speak to me, but I decided that we must dine first. It was very cold, and we were glad to sit inside the tent and to have the brazier brought in.

The Kaid came and talked to us with Mehemmet. It seemed that the headman was afraid his Kaid would put him in prison and squeeze him for extra taxes. He assured me that they had paid all that they ought to pay. But what they dreaded was to have everything taken from them. They seemed to have collected round them very good cattle. Their sheep were beautiful, and their crops this year were unusually good. In order to save their property, and especially to save themselves from imprisonment, Abd el Kader wanted to have some cattle belonging to me upon his farm; in fact, he wanted protection. I do not think that I have ever seen grown-up men in such an agony of suspense. Their distress, borne with a stony air of rigid control, was positively painful. They wanted me to give them a letter saying that the cattle on the farm were mine.

I did not think that such a letter would be of the least use. The Kaid would come down on them to hand over the money I had paid for the cattle, failing which they would be put in prison, and in the consular court I should have no receipt to show that the money had been paid.

However, I thought it possible that the possession of such a document might cause delay, and meantime something better could be done. So I wrote a paper certifying that the herds and cattle on the farm of Abd el Kader were mine, and signed it, adding my address and registration number as a British subject. Then I told Abd el Kader that he must accompany me next day to the British Vice-Consul.

The following morning I found all the village in good spirits. We were asked to go and see the women in Abd el Kader's house. It was a square house, though many of

the huts were conical. We went in and sat on a rush mat,
and all the women crowded in to see us, dressed in their
silver chains and brooches.   Some of them were exceedingly
pretty girls, and their manners were very gentle and affectionate.   The thing that struck them most was that, when
I took off my hat, lo ! my hair was white.   They indicated
that now they belonged to me as well as the cattle, and that
I must come again and stay among them.   There were
abundant evidences of comfort and prosperity, and I was
particularly struck with the absence of any sickness or
suffering.   Well off they certainly were.   Still, I must own
that my breath was fairly taken away when Abd el Kader
came to accompany us on a magnificent bay charger, sitting
in a richly-embroidered saddle.   He looked grand, with his
coal-black hair and beard, fine dark eyes, and round, well-
shaped head.   His drapery was creamy white, and through
it shone a brilliant scarlet robe.

But I began to feel seriously uneasy.   I had nothing to
put on this farm except my horse and mule, and though I
was anxious to leave them in the country with somebody
trustworthy, I had no business account to show to justify me
in giving protection.   Even if I bought Abd el Kader's stock,
which I might have done, and treated him as my servant, I
could not have prevented his being imprisoned on some
charge trumped up against him.   However, I hoped something could be done, for it was an intolerable thought to
think of these thrifty peasants reduced to ruin or lingering
in a gaol.

As we rode down the hill, we saw the tent of the old
Shereef of Wazan, which he had pitched while he collected
his dues.   The father of this man once asked for British
protection.   This was refused him, and he turned to France,
where he obtained all he required.   He married an English
wife, by whom he had two sons, who at present live in
Tangiers as Shereefs of Wazan.   They were educated in

Algiers. One of them served in the French army, and such influence as they possess will be French, and in French intrigue these half-breeds will be made the most of.

The Shereef of Wazan is a true descendant of the Prophet, and I found that he had many followers, who paid him tribute in money or kind. This business had taken him on his travels, and he had several pack-mules waiting to be loaded with gifts, which he would sell on his return to Wazan.

The position of the Shereefs of Wazan is worth defining, not merely as a chronicle of some interest, but on account of the use France will undoubtedly try to make of them when she is prepared to add Morocco to her other possessions, which, in the opinion of the *Temps*, it is a ' vital necessity ' for her ' not to cease thinking of.'

In the course of ages the title of Shereef has been greatly abused, and it is now bestowed on any rogue who has the wit to give himself occasional airs of inspiration; but only those can really claim to be Shereefs who are descendants of the Prophet, and a very few whose pedigrees date back to Bashalates exercised by their forefathers in the time of Mohammed, and to his first Kaliphas, who held the most delicate offices in the Grand Sanctuary of Mecca. In addition to the Shereefs of the first class, there are a few who are descended from some saint who during his lifetime was adopted patron of a kabyla or douar. The descendants of the Prophet are first in rank, but even those who are accepted in the third estate enjoy considerable influence and many privileges.

If a Shereef be sufficiently rich, he establishes a settlement on unoccupied land which is azáib. In each azáib they plant by degrees isolated khoimas, which in course of time increase and become large douars. The people who are thus collected are considered as belonging to the Shereef, and in virtue of his saintship they have a right to certain immunities. If they are haled before the authorities they can appeal to their Shereef, who is sure not to slander them, and any case arising between two of them can be settled finally by their own Shereef.

The azáib, generally speaking, contains the tomb of a saint, and is therefore a sanctuary of special safety. The living saint, or Shereef, would object to a refugee being dragged from his azáib, but Moslem fanaticism would rise at the violation of the tomb of a saint.

The Shereef possesses the power of settling with the administrators of the Sultan respecting the payment of agricultural taxes. He pays what he wishes, and that is never much, and would doubtless be nothing at all were it not for the religious veneration paid to the Sultan as Head of the Faithful. But occasionally it does happen that he pays nothing at all, his ancestors having been exempted by pious or fanatical Sultans. As the population in the azáib increases, the inhabitants cultivate lands outside, and refuse to pay taxes for them, declaring that they have already paid them to the Shereef.

It is easy for anyone to realize the devotion paid by the poor to the powerful Shereefs. Their azáibs, saints' houses, farm lands, and sanctuaries, are scattered all over the empire, and are even found in the Sahara. From all parts the pious send them alms and presents of slaves, cattle, first-fruits, gold, carpets, and even in some cases the most handsome daughters of their families. They also leave legacies to the saints, or Shereefs, according to their means.

The destruction of Basara (979 to 984) was followed by the dispersion of the Edrisite Shereefs, some of whom went to Sus and the Draa country, and others to Riff and the North. Of their descendents, the richest and most influential made their resting-place at Wazan. By gifts and legacies, the house of Wazan became at length so powerful that the Shereef built a magnificent mosque, with five naves and gilt balls on the top of the minaret, and this he called Dar Demána, or house of safety.

Moulai Tazeb, the grandson of the Shereef who built the mosque, extended his religious influence to all Morocco by founding a religious order, which he knew how to turn to political ends. But he had to contend with the Sultan, Moulai Ismail, who was cruel and unscrupulous enough to baffle the ambitions of most men. But the foundations which Moulai Tazeb laid by forming the religious brother-hood of the Tóaima, his grandson Hadj el Arby, known as the Miracle-worker, was able to build upon. Hadj el Arby was father to the late Shereef who married the English wife, and who in 1884 was the origin of questions which took place between the Sultan of Morocco and the French Republic.

The Shereefs of Dar Demána, or, as they are better known, of Wazan, occupy the peculiar position that no Sultan can be proclaimed Sultan without their sanction. In effect the Sultans are subjected to an election ; for when a Prince is designated as successor to the throne, those who surround him and approve of his election draw up a mani-festo in his favour, and this document must be presented first of all to the Shereefs of Wazan, and if the Shereef writes his assent at its foot and affixes his seal the election is secured, because when sanctioned by such a high religious authority the Prince-elect is considered as Sovereign by Divine right.

The power of the Shereefs of Wazan became excessive, and the late Sultan, El Hassan, being a man of resolute temper, determined to carry further the designs of his grand-father against the authority of Wazan, and show the tribes in the North of Morocco that there was another dispensation to be reckoned with besides that which had associated itself with the Mosque of Dar Demána, and the religious brother-hood of the Tóaima. That some steps were necessary, if not

justifiable, cannot be questioned if there was to be any
Sultan at all.

The Shereefs of Wazan had arrogated to themselves a
species of high-priesthood, coupled with all the weight and
power of a feudal baron.   The description given me of the
election of the Sultan by the Shereef is as follows :

' It is a veritable consecration, which prevents any city or
tribe from opposing it.   When the message is read from the
pulpit to the public in the Great Mosque, and when the
notables of the Cadi, the body of Ullémas, the chief
governors, and Bashaws, pronounce the sacramental formula,
" Alah ensor Seedna !" (God exalt our Lord !), the people
confirm and corroborate the election with loud acclamations,
and the document, having been signed and sealed, is returned
to the Court.   From that moment the Sultan is legitimatized,
and the turbulent mountain kabylas, who repel when they can
his material authority, revere and venerate his high religious
state, and regard him as the true Emir Moummeen as the
Prince of Believers, the Sword of Islam.   His authority has
been confirmed by another authority more eminent, who
surpasses all the grandeur of this world.   But if the Grand
Shereef should refuse his consent, such action would carry
with it disastrous effects for Morocco.   The reign of Mulai
Soliman illustrates such a case, when the miracle-working
Shereef, Hadj el Arby, dethroned and replaced Sultans, and
the kabylas at his command rose in rebellion.'

That story reads like a page from our own history, when
Thomas à Becket made himself a terror to the King by the
forces of religion and superstition.

But it was not only the power of consecration which made
the Shereef a danger to the Sultan.   The religious order of
the Töaima is a mysterious order, which appears to have
copied its principles from those of certain Indian sects.   It
extends the power of its chief by secret emissaries to
Algiers, Tunis, the Sahara, and part of the Soudan.   The

emissaries are provided with a mysterious emblem; they transmit their sacred orders by word or by writing. When Moulai Ismail realized the danger to his authority from such an order, he gave way to an outburst of passion, and determined to destroy the founder of so dangerous an association. But the astute Shereef Moulai Tazeb succeeded in disarming the ire of the infuriated Sultan by addressing to him these well-known words, which history has transmitted and tradition popularized: 'Ye (that is, the Alawy Shereefs) to reign, and we (that is, the Edrisites) to consecrate your authority.'

It is to the trouble with the Shereefs of Wazan that most of the uncertainty and unhappy divisions which in the past have weakened Morocco must be ascribed. Such a state of affairs naturally stiffened the back of so energetic a ruler as El Hassan, and inspired him with the determination to strengthen and perfect the system of repression initiated by his grandfather and resolutely established by his father. He took the strong measure of publishing a firman, to the effect that the superior (viz., the Sultan's) authority should take cognizance of crimes, faults, etc., of all the persons of that district without distinctions of classes or categories, as well those who lived in the country as those residing in the city. Thus he humiliated the Shereef, and reduced him from a privileged magnate to a simple subject like any other. The Shereef found himself, not only under the jurisdiction of the Sultan, but of a simple Kaid, before whom he would be bound to appear at the citation of the lowest Moor.

The Shereef of Wazan had weakened his authority by indulging in drinking bouts. When sober, and before he acquired this fatal taste, he is described as a man of intelligence, and even of charm. The pious Moslems affected to ignore his weakness, and it was customary amongst them to declare that drink could not harm him—that champagne became pure gold when it touched his sacred lips. Disgraced and fallen, he bethought him how best he could secure himself against the Sultan's fīrman, and he went in person to solicit that protection which the French nation had frequently endeavoured to entice him into accepting, and which must eventually lead to complications, seeing that undoubtedly the French had their reasons for granting it.

The effect upon Moslems of the news that the Grand Shereef had placed himself under the protection of Christians was most extraordinary. To account for his conduct, a report was circulated that the Grand Shereef was no son of Hadj el Arby. But the kabylas thought to see in the Shereef's action the dawn of the time, prophetically foretold by Moulai Tazeb, the founder of the Order of Töaima, when the people of Moghreb (Morocco) will conquer the lands of the East—viz., Algiers and Tunis—expelling the Beni Sfar, the men of yellow race. According to popular belief, the Beni Sfar are the French. But enlightened opinion, taking into consideration that at the time Moulai Tazeb lived, in the reign of Moulai Ismail, the Turks ruled the Berber States and were constantly threatening Morocco, decided that they were the men referred to as 'the yellow race.' It remains to be seen what steps will be taken to realize the dream of conquest suggested by Moulai Tazeb's prophecy.

The present condition of the Shereefs of Wazan is that of vassalage to France. The eldest son, whom I passed while he sat in his tent at Ain Filfil, is represented as living entirely under French supervision. On the occasion that he came to Tangiers he was practically sequestered, and sent back with a guard of honour (*sic*) of Algerian soldiers. He seems to have inherited his father's taste for strong drink, and cannot be regarded as exercising much influence even in Wazan, where he resides. The two young Shereefs who live at Tangiers, Moulai Achmet and Moulai Alli, are the sons of an English wife. Their pretensions to the position of Shereefs is based on some clause inserted in their mother's marriage documents,

which was intended to give her sons priority; but the validity
of such a clause is disputed on the ground that no one can
inherit the rights of a Shereef unless his mother was a
Shereefa.

The younger of the two sons has served in the French
army, and may be considered to have acquired a certain
knowledge of the world, which, coupled with the infusion of
white blood—may render him less Moorish than the average
Moor. But both young men are well aware in what direction
their interests lie, and the elder plays his part as a devout
Moslem and a strict head of the religious order which has
been of so much service in the past to the House of Wazan.

In themselves, neither of the three aspirants would be
capable of offering as Shereef the slightest trouble to the
present Sultan.   But with the backing of France it is far
from improbable that they aim at greater things.

It is said by those who favour the pretensions of the young
men that the saying of Moulai Tazeb, 'Ye to reign, and we
to consecrate your reign,' has ended in effect with the
marriage of the late Shereef to an English wife, and that the
time is not far distant when the Shereef of Wazan will be
Sultan of Morocco.   It is not improbable that the first active
step taken by France in Morocco will be towards establishing
an independent kingdom of Fez, and placing on the throne
one of her own protégés of the House of Wazan.   This view
gains substance when we reflect on the work of Count
Chavagnac in the Riff country, and the drawing up of topo-
graphical surveys from Ceuta to Rabat by a French Captain
of Engineers, M. Levallois, and many distinct hints given
from time to time in the French press.

This is hardly the time or place to speculate as to the
future which awaits Morocco.   The cards are a strange
mixture.   Moslem fanaticism is a strong suit.   The value of
the Shereefs of Wazan depends on the hand which plays
them.   The effect of French intrigue may be to offend

Moorish fanaticism—always strong in the North—and in that case the very lives of the Shereefs of Wazan would not be worth much. People are reluctant to believe that the son of El Hassan can be as weak and foolish as some interested persons represent him to be. One factor which must not be lost sight of is the Moors' innate dislike to foreign interference in any form, and it may not be impossible to foresee the ultimate result of the Wazan French backing upon so excitable and easily prejudiced a people long before it comes to pass and to take steps accordingly.

Abd el Kader and the Kaid amused themselves by powder play; that is, they galloped their horses at a furious pace and discharged their guns as they passed us. It is an unmeaning sport, but Moors enjoy it.

Before noon we sighted the river Sebou, the largest and most important river in the North. It abounds with fine fish, notably the shad, which is the best eating fish in the world. The Sebou is a waterway which penetrates into the heart of Morocco. At about twenty miles inland it approaches a large lagoon, then it turns south, and shortly afterwards by an abrupt curve it goes north-east by the Marmora Forest, and breaks into three branches in the plains of Jamista, one leading towards Fez, and another towards Mequinez. If it be true that at sixty miles inland this river is always deep to ford even in the dry season, there is probably water available for navigation for 100 miles during eight months of the year. Passing through so fertile a country, it is amazing that no use has been made of this river. All kinds of romance attach to it, and one of the upper reaches is called the River of Pearls.

The whole of the land might be settled with a prosperous peasantry, and the transport could be put upon the river inexpensively and removed easily elsewhere. It is the fault of the English that they want to go into everything with a first-class outfit, regardless of expenditure. Whereas a

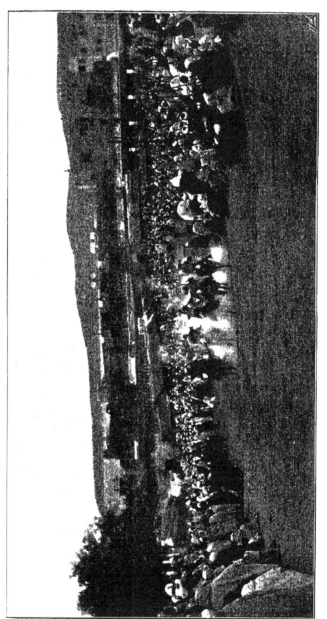

Mr. Cazalis Photo   Tangiers

POWDER-PLAY

railway requires bridges, a permanent way, and rolling-stock, a light draught steamer could 'run her nozzle agin the bank,' and pick up bags or baskets or skins of produce here and there wherever signalled, and carry men or animals, and burn oil or wood for fuel, and go somewhere else if no cargo were forthcoming. I would rather be given the Sebou to do as I like with than any railway concession in Morocco.

At the mouth of the Sebou is the town of Mehidya, whose origin is obscure, but the present ruins are Portuguese. It was built much as it is now standing to fall, as the base of the Portuguese expedition in 1515, which had Fez for its objective, and which terminated at the Battle of El Kasar. I believe the best approach to Fez* is along the River of Pearls. The bar at the Sebou is not formidable, and very moderate dredging and constant use would soon clear it. There is, besides, a small bay to the north of the lagoons, and probably the lagoons could be pierced at some point and used as a harbour.

The development of waterways would mean that a considerable tract of the best land in Morocco would be open to settlement. The tribes might give some trouble at first, but I incline to think that if the matter were undertaken on a purely commercial footing, and they were from the first encouraged to trade, and found that they obtained fair prices for their cattle and grain, and that the goods sold to them were of good quality, they would facilitate the enterprise. I met a man who could always travel alone and unarmed amongst them, and they said: 'We do not mind you, Christian. You bring us tea and sugar, and we get money by you. But as for the Sultan and his soldiers, we will kill them if they come here.' I heard an instance of a man riding alone, who came upon two of them in a narrow pass

* Mehidya is the nearest port to the northern capitals, the distance to Mequinez being 60 miles and Fez 103. See Meakin, 'Land of the Moors.'

who were fighting. They stopped fighting, and said: ' Let the Christian pass. We have no quarrel with him.' And after he had passed they went on fighting again.

After crossing the river, we rode along the black sand, which is still exported in small bags, and used instead of blotting-paper, and passed under the walls of Mehidya. Innumerable blue rollers flew in and out of the holes in the walls, to Mrs. Greathed's delight, who had never seen these lovely birds before. We pitched our camp near some ruins of old Portuguese forts on the shore.

Before we could buy anything in the town we had to see the Kaid, who was sitting on what was once a grand old portico to administer what he pleased by way of justice. He was a poor old man, and looked ill and wretched, and a glass of tea was brought to revive him. He gave us permission to buy what we wanted, and we walked on to see the chief sight of Mehidya—a wonderful city gateway in the Portuguese Arabesque style. It looked out across the wide river towards Laraiche and Mequinez. There was an air of magnificence in the ruin which spoke of distinct enterprise ages before we were born. The red colour of the stone and the simplicity of the design united in rendering it at once picturesque and fitting. From the outside it seemed exactly what one would expect to find at that spot.

But what a ruin the place was ! It sent the blood rushing through my veins to look at that splendid river sweeping through the most fertile land on earth, where thousands of happy, prosperous people might be living and made glad by it, and nothing there but wickerwork huts, a fugitive people, and this town like a rotten, worm-eaten nut at the end of it ! I seemed to see the worm-hole through which the last vestige of life had escaped in the empty window in the gateway.

They say the name Mehidya signifies ' replenished.' Those heaps of ruined houses with bits of tile sticking round the

last grand Bab! Replenished! With its marble step to
the North Port stained with the dung of the cattle driven to
shelter in what was once the Governor's palace and the
grand hall of the kasbah. Replenished! Its gaol replenished with fresh human victims from the country round
to increase the stink which comes through the narrow bars.

On our way back we went to look at the prison. It was
very full. Many of the prisoners had good countenances,
notably one old peasant, whom it seemed cruel as well as
insolent to put in irons.

CHAPTER XIV

MEHIDYA impressed me immensely with the Portuguese
period in Morocco, though afterwards at Mazagan and Saffi
I found more striking buildings and very interesting records.

The Portuguese were grand and romantic. They went to
war splendidly in velvet and lace, with inlaid armour and
ornamental arms. And what masters they were of the
engineering and navigation of their time! They reached
Morocco just when the Moors were declining from the spirit
they had displayed in Spain; and had they come upon other
terms their conquest would have been an unmixed boon.
But they failed, and they have left in Morocco only stately
ruins and the infinite harm caused by their perpetuation of
the crusading spirit. The ambition to wrest an empire from
the infidel had a certain religious grandeur about it, but its
practical effect was to intensify Mohammedanism and render
the Moors the most fanatical Moslems in the world, and the
result of the militant religion of Spain and Portugal is that
the Moors are imbued with a religious *esprit de guerre* which
could with the slightest encouragement be directed against
Spain or Portugal again.

Empire is only for those who can take 'broad views in
space and long views in time,' and to allow religion the pro-
minence of a question, instead of treating it as a part of the

civilization which belongs to it, is to jeopardize the balance of diplomacy.

It is a blunder to blame Islam for all the faults of the Moors. Islam has upheld the Moors betwixt heaven and hell, or at any rate maintained them in a singular position between Europe and Africa. While it prevented them from rising to the level of the advancing West, it has saved them from falling into the black savagery of the cannibal and Central African tribes. The faults of the Moors lie much deeper than a creed. They lie with facts which have rendered Mohammedanism possible and popular. The faith of Islam expresses a state of things existing in human nature which racial, climatic, and geographical conditions have encouraged. Mohammed found certain evils rampant. He either excluded them or placed them under regulation, and that he effected this proves his greatness. His human spirit probably quailed before the task of setting ' a counsel of perfection' before his followers, knowing that they could not accept it in sufficient numbers to give him the support he needed to extend his work. Though lessened, these evils have been handed on stamped with authority. What was in his time a great improvement is becoming more and more glaringly defective, and even offensive, as civilization elsewhere advances.

There is some truth in the remark I heard in Tangiers, that had Mohammed lived in more civilized times and in a more civilized country he would have been a very much greater man. But the question is, Would he have founded Mohammedanism or any other religion? He might have been a greater Luther or a greater empire-builder than we possess. The position in Morocco is that of a population on the margin of Europe holding fast to laws and customs which are absolutely abhorrent to modern humanity, and yet associated with the worship of the one true God, the Creator of the world.

In attacking polygamy or slavery, or working for their elimination, we must consider that these ancient evils would not necessarily disappear were Islam destroyed. Islam is one powerful truth allied with human imperfections. The faith did its work by stereotyping improvements which have worn thin, and the question immediately before us is whether the old bottle of Islam is able to receive the new wine of Western ideas and commerce.

It was not civilization, but a creed, which tore these people apart ; a creed was the rock on which both struck and foundered. If we are to blame Islam for the vices of the Moors, can we not with equal reason blame Roman Catholicism for the ruin of Spain and Portugal ? Religious teaching passed into dogmatic pronouncements, and became customary and traditional. There are Moors and Catholics who do not believe, yet who conform outwardly ; but neither of them can escape the moulding of national character inherited in blood and bones and the surroundings of life. We are apt to forget that in England the reform of the State and Church is always going on, and that we are always engaged in adapting our institutions and bringing them up to date. But the East is conservative, and I have met Moors who have lived for years in Europe, and while there assumed European habits. When I knew them in Barbary they were extreme Moors, and stronger in their opinions than those who had never left the country, as though the flood held back by artificial barriers had but gathered force for a headlong rush in the old course immediately opportunity offered. They knew how to be Western towards the Western, with that extraordinary adaptability of manner not uncommon among dark-skinned races.

It is the Oriental nature, so hard to fathom or describe, apparently accentuated in some respects by the infusion of black blood, which laughs at the West and despises it. We can but watch and note the tendencies. For instance, that exaltation which produced the religious literature of the East runs to seed in extravagances, resulting from a thirst to gain a reputation for sanctity. Much of this religion tends to madness, dancing and frenzies forming the ritual considered best calculated to attract the notice of the Divinity by devotees who are perfectly sincere, for these frenzies are a natural mode of expressing something which they have always had, but which we have not got. It is said that the Prophets had recourse to dancing, and Mohammed does not appear to have restrained his followers from similar indications of corybantiasm.

But there is a method in this madness which runs upon dollars. The 'holy fool' need not beg; the creature is supposed to have reached God and to be endued with the Spirit of God as he walks with vacant eyes, clad in rags and dirt. Delusion suits the Oriental temperament; instead of hypocrisy being hateful, as it is to the Westerns, it is in fact delicious. They are sincerely hypocritical. The missionaries' remedy is conversion to Christianity; but taking into consideration past history and the attitude of Christianity towards Islam, it is not so easy to see how such a change is to be enjoined upon any part of the Moorish people.

I heard of one missionary, who was a clergyman of the English Church, and who, having done his best to convert the Moors, withdrew from the field, feeling convinced that Christian missions to the Moors were a mistake. The law of the land is the law of the Koran, and that law forbids the preaching of another religion, and punishes apostasy with death. But the missionary saw that the chief obstacle lay in the nature of the people themselves, and that to attempt to attract them from a faith which had moulded them and made all the conditions of their life, would result in a compromise at best disastrous to the prestige of Christianity. Influences which begin before the child is born become stamped on his character in the harem, and never leave him

while life lasts.   Therefore, when a friend of mine asked the
missionary alluded to if he believed it possible to make a
Christian of a Moor, he answered: ' Frankly, I do not.   But
if you are to do it, this is the only way : You must burn all
their books ; you must catch them young ; you must squeeze
all the blood out of their bodies and grind their bones—
then, if you can make them up fresh, you may make them
Christians.'

How far the Moors, who are the grandest impostors in
the world, and scarcely possess the horror of charlatans and
mountebanks felt by us, delude those ' fonde people,' the
missionaries, I am not prepared to say; nor yet to say
whether or no the missionaries may be impostors, either
consciously or unconsciously.   But it was soon clear to my
mind that no man who was not a missionary could say that
he believed in a single Moorish conversion to Christianity.
The missionaries are interested parties ; subscriptions depend
on their making out a good case for themselves.   I have
heard it said that their lives are ' noble instances of devotion ';
that 'they have given up all to preach the Gospel to the
heathen '; and that they ' labour in the cause of Christ.'
But, on looking into the biographies of some of the missionaries as furnished by the serial which publishes an
account of their work, I found the following :

' It was during his apprenticeship as a woollen dyer in the
little town of Tillicouthy that the " grand change " of his
life took place.   After six weeks of deep conviction of sin he
was converted . . . while standing at his work, through the
instrumentality of a man employed in the same place.'
Another ' at sixteen years of age was apprenticed to the
Caledonian Railway Company, where he remained until
entering upon training for missionary work.'   Another 'was
brought to Christ when only eleven years of age, and soon
began to think of foreign mission-work.   She took up educational work, and in her various situations ever found oppor-

tunities of serving Christ with acceptance and blessing.'
Another, 'when only six, was brought under conviction of
sin, but considers that he did not believe to the saving of his
soul till he was about twelve years of age. The assurance of
salvation came later, as he was on one occasion crossing
Carlisle Bridge. . . . He had from childhood thought of
mission-work, and at one time thought of abandoning his
apprenticeship, but saw that it was wiser to finish his studies
as a solicitor first.'

There would be something pathetic in these stories if the
people who escape from being small clerks or Board school
mistresses, at the best, went out to travel with bare feet and
live on locusts and wild honey. But I found that not in-
frequently the first thing they did on reaching Morocco
was to marry—indeed, this was recommended—and picture
the result if one of these young ladies, 'convicted of sin' at
an early age, paired off with a young man assured of salvation when crossing a bridge, and the progeny they would
add to the population. On more than one occasion the
house the missionary lived in was described to me as 'the
best house in the town.' As they belonged to no denomina-
tion, it was difficult to see who set them their tasks or controlled their movements. They appeared to do very much
as they pleased, and to differ amongst themselves. At one
place I found them going for a picnic on mules and horses;
and I must say that I never saw them living otherwise than
at a far higher rate than the woollen dyer, railway clerk, or
Board school teacher would in England. Not that they
were satisfied. There were bitter complaints, possibly with
the hope of drawing from me a subscription to alleviate their
'wants.' As regards their means, or, rather, their salaries,
I felt some delicacy in making inquiries. But one man, who
was a banker, and on whom I felt I could rely, told me that
one missionary 'had managed to save between five and six
hundred pounds, and then he went home.' I conclude that

he was able to help himself by the sale of drugs, or the knowledge of some trade or profession, but the estimate given by one of the missionary societies states for a single gentleman and lady together, as equal to a married couple, 'about £220 a year. If there are children an increase in the estimate would be necessary. This does not include medical missions, hire of halls, etc.' The class of people enjoying in Morocco salaries of £220 and upwards, and benefiting besides by the rate of exchange, would find it difficult to earn half as much at home. Certainly, the curates of the impoverished Church of England would think it princely.*

The native sees at least two aspects of Christianity. The man who goes about with the name of Christ always on his lips is not necessarily the best exponent of Christ's religion.

---

* 'The following is an estimate of the average cost for a single lady living simply :

					£
Board and clothing, etc.	...	...	...	...	50
Rent ...	...	...	...	...	13
Teacher	...	..	...	...	5
Annual share of furlough	...	...	...	...	7
		Total	...	...	£75

'In addition there are expenses of the work and general maintenance and management of the mission, which bring the total cost to little less than £100 a year.

'The cost of a single gentleman, living simply, may on the average be estimated as under :

					£
Board and clothing, etc	...	...	...	...	65
Rent ...	...	...	...	...	13
Teacher	...	...	...	...	5
Travelling	...	...	...	...	7
		Total	...	...	£90

'This, again, does not include a share of expenses of work and adminis-tration, which brings up the amount to about £120.

'The cost of a married couple, living simply, may be estimated as equal to a single gentleman and lady together—that is, at £165, or, including expenses of work and management, at about £220 a year.'—*Missionary Report.*

The layman who furnishes an example is better calculated to impress the Moors than one missionary I met, of whom it was justly said that 'it would be difficult to imagine a man whose life and character were more at variance with the religion he pretended to preach.' 'All things are fair in love and war.' Perhaps the missionaries think so; but in no respectable business could such a maxim be adopted. It is the conduct of delicate matters which is worth half the battle. Of missionary methods the following account was given by a missionary, and taken down by a friend of mine, of a Christian marriage which they solemnized at Fez.

After telling of all the 'marvels the missionaries were working in dark Morocco,' of 'the deep love' incited by them, and their 'great popularity,' he went on to say that the wedding had been arranged about a year before it took place. 'The missionaries thought the man, who was "a very true Christian," ought to marry, as in all Mohammedan countries it is thought to be rather a slur on a man if he be not married. The woman came from Tetuan. She had been married to a Mohammedan Moor, who divorced her. But before she married him "the seeds of Christ had been sown in her heart, and he divorced her because she cried and was very unhappy. The Moorish husband was old, and the woman was *very unhappy*."' On it being remarked that the wedding, which was notified at home as a triumph, took place surreptitiously in Morocco, he replied that 'God worked in secret ways,' and that 'the seed fell in quiet places.' But it must be left to the missionaries to prove that the Almighty is not only sly, but needs their 'slimness' to accomplish His ends.

In one part of my ride I came across a missionary who spoke enthusiastically of a girls' school they had opened. I asked what class of Moorish girls attended the school. He looked taken aback, and said: 'Well, not the highest class.' But on my pressing him he said they were 'a low class.' I

asked what they would do when they had finished their
education. Would any respectable Moor marry them, and
would they wish to be married to Mohammedans? He
answered that 'in our work'—he pronounced it 'wuck'—
'it does not do to look too far ahead.'

It struck me that these girls were not likely to raise the
prestige of Christianity, which, sad to say, is low enough
—so low as to reflect badly on the civilization which is
associated with it.

Another feature in missionary enterprise which I regard
as mischievous is that, as there is very little discipline
among the missionaries, they go into the country preaching
what at best may be called their own doctrine, and making
their own presentment of the Christian religion. So that
we seem to be anticipating the time when many false
prophets shall arise, and say, 'Lo, here is Christ!' or
'Lo, there!' etc. It was difficult to say to what society
the missionaries belonged. There is a Scottish mission, but
not under the direction of the Kirk or Church of Scotland.
There is an American mission, but that seemed the hardest
of all to understand, for, instead of being under a bishopric,
it was involved in the consular affairs, one missionary having
been appointed temporarily to represent the American Consul.
But the Americans are noted for their irregularity, and
probably a missionary would suit the Government at Washington better than some of the Consuls who have been sent
out from the United States, whose characters were not of
the highest. Granting the validity of the command, 'Go ye
into all the world and preach the Gospel,' exception must
be taken to the audience to whom the words were addressed,
to the methods employed, and to the qualifying commands
elsewhere in the Bible. The natives who hang about
missionaries are far from being considered acquisitions in the
service of Europeans. The easy familiarity, which might be
excusable to our own poorer classes, is not the best rope by

which even they can climb to a higher level. Nature has
fixed limits which cannot be skipped. I remember when in
the South a missionary asked me if I was aware that the
black man was my brother. I replied that I did not admit
the truth of any such statement, 'but,' I said, 'just for the
sake of argument, we will grant it—the black man *is* my
brother. Now, would you like to have him for a brother-
in-law, because you may do so and welcome?' Will it be
believed that this graceless divine turned sulky, and actually
would not speak to me again after my generous offer of the
man he called my brother?

Missionaries may not intend 'familiarity to breed contempt.'
Allowance must be made for their early training and peculiar
expressions. They told me 'they liked to have all things in
common,' and probably they wear each other's clothes and
borrow each other's tooth-brushes. It would only be in
keeping with the manners of a woman with whom one has
a bare acquaintance, yet who subscribes herself 'Your sister
in the Lord.'

The section of missionaries most deserving of sympathy
was that which devoted itself to medical work in behalf of
the Moors. Could these people have separated themselves
from the religious peculiarities and fanaticism of the ex-
ponents of the Gospel, it would not be difficult to bestow on
them something stronger than sympathy.

The sufferings of these poor Moors would be enough to
touch the stoniest heart, but when they are expected to pay
for nursing and medicine and charity with the price of
apostasy, the enterprise is self-condemned. It is a sin for a
Moslem to hear anything against his own religion. One
Moor, of whom I saw a good deal, was for a Moor a very
good fellow. Charitable to his own people, kind to his
servants and family, the husband of one wife, and having a
good reputation in business both among Europeans and Jews,
this man spoke to me with great bitterness of the mission-

aries. He said: 'Let a man have any pain, or be put in prison and lose everything—it is all better than that he should change his religion. But these people come to the poor and those who have nothing, and perhaps, to make life a little easier, they do this thing, which is the greatest sin a man can do.'

I have heard it denied that the medical missions in Morocco are Christian missions, but when I cannot get a straight answer from people associated with the work itself, I turn to some of their publications, and in the journal already quoted from I find the following: 'Since Ramadan* a great many women have come (to the dispensary), and frequently they have been really attentive while I spoke to them. So often they look indifferent, and as if they were only enduring our words, *because they know it is our rule to speak to them before giving medicine.* When visiting one day, a stranger asked me some questions about the medical mission, and this led to my telling her the Gospel. Turning to her sister, she said: "And do Moslems sit and listen to that?" The answer was: "*They are obliged to, or no medicine would be given.*"' One of their tracts contains this passage: 'A most useful aid is the Medical Mission. . . . The medical knowledge among the people is generally almost nil, and disease is rife. . . . *Every opportunity is taken of preaching the Gospel to the waiting patients. . . .*' One woman missionary volunteered to me the information that she was 'allowed to expound the Gospel in the men's ward on two afternoons in the week.'

I own that I thought with pain of the suffering people lying there having added to their bodily affliction the mental torment of feeling their last shred of morality break down. How dire is their need of charity and help the pitiful expression in many a face one passes is proof enough. The following, taken again from a medical report, is a very true

* The Mohammedan fast.

picture : 'He comes again without audible petition or plea for readmission, his whole appearance uttering the silent prayer of abject want and intense need.'

The following extract from a report gives an even better idea of the methods employed to advance Christianity, or, as they say, 'to win souls to Christ':

One day last July we were called out to see a bundle lying upon the native burial hearse (which was used as a stretcher). It proved less inanimate than appeared at first sight, and was a worthy object for the Famine Relief Fund of India : a skeleton, with bones only just covered by skin. A gaunt figure, this Abd-es-Salaam ('Slave of Peace'). What a mockery was his name ! They had turned him out of prison on the previous day—turned him out to *die*. Corpses are never coveted. The poor limbs were contracted and powerless—would he ever speak again? His brother pleaded for his admission, but the hospital was not a mortuary. He was dying, and they knew it. When turning away to hide the tears which *would* rise, a voice one had not thought to hear commenced to plead, 'Oh, take me in !' That settled the question. If hearts were not adamant, there was no alternative. He might at least hear of Christ before he died.

He was a youth of some seventeen or eighteen summers, who had murdered a man in his mountain home, and for this crime had been imprisoned Life in the gaol meant being 'killed by inches,' instead of on the gallows. Though he was a murderer and in a dying state, we remembered that a 'dying thief' and murderer once entered Paradise with the Saviour. The brother, who promised to remain with him— twelve months in prison meant a loathsome case to care for—slipped off within an hour, and he was left upon our hands. When hearing of salvation for the first time, from the doctor, he asked 'Did you say, if I believed in Jesus, *I* could enter heaven?' An interest was awakened Three of the missionaries and a native Christian, from time to time, pointed him to Christ. Soon, however, he grew careless ; then, one day, woke up to know himself dying; and, oh, the wail ! 'The doctor says I am going to die.' At one time he said he would believe in Jesus, but the battle was raging fiercely now. How could the arch-enemy lose such a trophy? He must fight hard for this one at least, having been so secure of victory heretofore On Sunday the poor fellow covered his head with the hood of his cloak, careless and hardened. He did not wish to hear, yet he was drawing very near to the dark valley.

On Monday, as the missionary once more told of death, of life, and eternal life, he cried . 'Go *away* from me. I do not *want* to hear. I will *not* repent ; I will not believe. Go away.' That evening our native servant, when I was speaking to him about this case, said to me, 'Ah, but there *are* those over whom the Truth has gone for ever; his time is past; there is no more repentance for him.' Awful verity! Tuesday unconsciousness set in; on Wednesday he died—without God, without hope —a *lost soul* And although Jehovah was glorified in the proclamation of His grace, in this case it became but a 'savour of death unto death' to the perishing one. The prince of the power of the air won in *this* struggle Was it because of a tardy message; an insufficiency of messengers, as in our first losses in the battles in the South; few troops, and those late on the field? The 'Slave of Peace' had *never* heard of a Saviour who can regenerate and save from sin, even in *this* life, until he came to *die* His mother never sang to him 'There is a green hill far away.' His father read not in the evening hour and at family prayers, 'There they crucified Him.' And so he never knew, never had the offer until, hardened in sin, he came to meet its penalty, physical death, and found another, 'where their worm dieth not and the fire is not quenched.'

Even allowing for the natural chagrin of the missionaries at the escape of a convert whom they had captured under such favourable circumstances, and of whom they might reasonably have felt secure, there is to the mind of the average thinker a painful hopelessness for a Christianity which bears such fruit as this. One pictures the dying Moslem drawing his hood over his head to shut out the babel of three missionaries and a native Christian. 'Lost soul' and 'hardened sinner' though he might be, at all events he did not seek relief by apostatizing.

Another tract gives the following story, which throws a little light on the Mohammedan view of Christian methods: 'One day Mena's husband warned me. He said: "You know we all respect and love you. You cured my daughter; I shall never cease to be grateful to you for that. But we must all follow the religion in which we were born. So come to my house as usual, if you will, but not to speak of Christ." A day or two after this conversation the Imam . . . said: "What have you done to Mena and Salha? They refuse to go to the Zamea, and are praying in the name of Jesus. That is evil exceeding. Our women are poor and ignorant, and we have to govern their minds and hearts.

You know we did love you, but that love has turned to hatred. We shall do our utmost to uproot this faith implanted by you in the hearts of our women, and I have to request you to cease your visits to my house, unless you promise never to bring up again the subject of religion. . . ." The womenkind appeared to be seriously upset, and to have been, at all events, threatened with a beating. "What *shall* I do?" she exclaimed, with tears in her eyes. "Must I hide my faith, or give up my husband and two dear children? He will divorce me, or perhaps I shall be secretly murdered,"' etc.

It might be thought that the Mohammedans would engross all the time and strength of the missionaries, and all the means at their disposal; but this is not the case. They overflow with zeal to such an extent that they cast their eyes at Roman Catholics; and mention is made of the 'conversion' of an ex-priest and his baptism, by which it would appear that these people, who have no orders themselves, do not admit the validity of the orders of Rome, and yet cling to ceremonies. I came upon one man who devoted himself exclusively to the Jews. But I could not gather a very clear idea of the nature of his work. It seemed to be partly medical—though he was by trade a tailor before he became a missionary—and partly educational. I was told that he had never made any converts. I heard at one point on my travels that the Jews played on the missionaries, pretending to be converted. They then induce the missionaries, who, as doctors, approach the Moors very closely in time of sickness, to get outstanding claims settled. It was complained to me that the most refined torture could be resorted to in such cases. But I utterly disbelieve such a story—firstly, because I have no substantial ground for believing it, and, secondly, because the missionaries as Englishmen are not likely to behave in so devilish a manner. As doctors I believe they effect some good. I only regret that whatever good they may effect physically is outbalanced by the harm of their fanaticism, which at best only adds another disturbing factor to this already distracted land.

Medical work is a very paying business in Morocco, if the doctor be skilful and understands the treatment of the diseases common in the country. In the lagoons and marshes there is a good deal of fever, and an enlarged spleen is a very common and very painful ailment. A great many natives suffer from stone, and I heard of a German doctor who settled on the coast. Like most of the medical missionaries, he was qualified, but had not succeeded in gaining a practice at home. He made money in Morocco by doctoring the Moors for stone. He operated as much as he pleased on them, and when he had mastered the complaint thoroughly he went home to Germany, and rapidly rose in his profession as a specialist. He was not a missionary.

Sore eyes and various forms of ophthalmia are very common, but the scourge of the country is syphilis. This atrocious complaint is said to have been introduced into the country 200 years ago by immigrant Jews, and, considering the conditions in which the Jews lived, it is not unlikely. An immense impetus had been given to the ravages of the complaint by the introduction of low Spanish women into Tangiers during the last decade. Leprosy is to be met with, and sometimes of a highly contagious kind, and also elephantiasis. I heard in Morocco for the first time that it is believed that this disease is propagated by mosquitoes. Certainly Morocco is a mosquito country.

What struck me most painfully was the want of proper care for women at the time of child-birth. Whether Spaniards, Jews, or Europeans, there appeared to be no adequate nurses and few good doctors. The natives have their own ways, which are so truly barbarous that the marvel is how mother and child survive.

I have often wished that some society existed for providing

medical and educational missions which should be entirely secular. The preaching of Christianity does not consist in meeting fanaticism with fanaticism, neither are prayers which wind up ' in the name of Jesus Christ ' necessarily breathed in the spirit of Christ ; nor do I believe that the honest and sincere Moslem ' must go to the fire and the worm.' It is the promise of our Lord, who said, ' Other sheep I have which are not of this fold ; them also I must bring,' on which we rest. But when that time will be no one knows. He will do it Himself ; and perhaps it will not be till we have undergone some great change, or till the world, with its cruel discrepancies, its crippling incongruities, and narrow limits, shall have passed away for ever.

It is said there should be a distinct sequence—commerce, education, civilization, religion. But naturally progress rests with individuals who unite all four elements in themselves. Great religious and racial difficulties confront us in our Empire, which no scheme, plan, or system can eliminate or metamorphose, but which will yield before an individual. It is almost certain that opinions, if sharpened, become the power for starting the engines of war, as they certainly keep in repair those of oppression.

Religion, which can, and does, advance with man's advance, is man's best friend ; but we cannot transpose it singly. Our whole civilization is inextricably mixed with it. Whether it be a municipality, a colony, a school, a hospital, or a house of assembly, all owe something to the religion of the country. Instead of ' conversion,' I rely on results such as we can show in our Empire, which one of our noblest administrators has called ' the efficacy of impartial and uncorrupt government, of a bold development of the vast natural resources of the country, and prudent introduction of self-governing institutions, to heal old sores, to create new interests, and gradually to bring divers sections of the people to co-operate for the good of their common country.'

CHAPTER XV

WE rode on, leaving the sea and some smaller lagoons, we
turned inland and crossed the road which runs from
Mequinez and Fez to Rabat. This was the country of the
Beni Hassan, an Arab tribe, and very truculent. There was
a discussion amongst our Moors, which ended in taking us
off the road only to come back again. First Mehemmet
came to me with a tragic countenance, and, drawing his hand
across his throat, said that the people in these villages would
cut my throat unless I stopped at the Sultan's village close
by. This did not suit me, as I wanted to reach Rabat as
soon as possible, so I said: 'All right. I shall go on for
another hour or so, and if you are afraid when you get there,
you may go back.' Then the laugh turned against Mehemmet, and I found that the other men were quite willing
to go on.

At last we turned off the road going inland, and up a hill
on the top of which was a douar, where we camped for
the night.

Other travellers were before us, and the whole centre of
the douar* was taken up by a caravan of camels, about ten
in number. There were besides a herd of sheep belonging

* Village of Bedouin tents.

to the village, some goats, mules, and donkeys, and one mare
tethered to a tent by herself.

The douar was formed of tents arranged in a circle, with
their backs outside.   The little space between them was
blocked by thorns, and even when the thorns were removed
it was so narrow that a camel could only enter by being long
in the legs, while my pack-mules fairly stuck.   I had dismounted immediately on reaching the douar, and loosened
Conrad's girths while he grazed, and finding that we had to
camp inside, I led him through the enclosure.   He does not
lead very well, and I took him myself, because he is always
sure that I never jerk his mouth.   To my surprise, he stepped
through the narrow entrance and over the tent-ropes as 'to
the manner born,' and created quite a sensation among the
youth of the village.   There was a rush towards him; a dozen
hands were stretched out to take the bridle or catch hold of
the saddle or pat the horse.   Conrad accepted the admiration
and the welcome with great good-humour.   It is town Moors
whom he abominates, and he used to cause poor Mohammed
Jellally to sin many times in the early morning, by lifting
his fez by the blue tassel and flicking it away from him.
Mohammed ran to recover his fez, shaking his head and
saying that the horse knew he was the 'señorita's horse, and
could do these things'

From my horse the scrambling, howling crowd turned
their attention to me.   But not rudely, only in open-mouthed
astonishment, asking innumerable questions which I could
not understand.   One old man put out a bony hand to the
straw hat which I wore, which was not made like Moorish
hats of palmetto.   He held forth to the rest about that
straw hat, and at last ventured to feel the brim round with
his long fingers.   Then the crowd departed suddenly to
question the Kaid about us, and stand staring at us from
a distance.

Meanwhile they had taken Mrs. Greathed to see a little

wild boar tethered and treated as a pet, and asked her if that was what she ate.

As it grew dark, we took all our possessions into the tent, and it was fairly crammed. We had it well pegged down all round, for the Arabs are clever thieves, and will slip their hands inside under the canvas.

Each tent had a fire outside for cooking the evening meal. It was a strange scene—the tents all round, with the stars above; the camels, goats, and sheep, and these wild-looking natives, sheltering altogether. They had to send two miles for water, and it was very difficult to get any for our own use, though I offered as much as a peseta for drink for my horse and mule. Each tent had at least one savage dog, and what with these brutes and the camels and sheep we expected a disturbed night. But soon the light of the fires went out, the tents were closed, the dogs ceased to fight, and we slept soundly till daybreak.

The camels were the first to be up and away, and I was glad when I heard them go snarling through the thorn-bushes. As soon as they were gone, I took Mehemmet, who could speak a little Spanish, and went round the village.

Each tent had two compartments. In one side the inmates slept, in the other they plied their occupations. The headman of the village accompanied me, and he was very friendly. There were two women in one tent, engaged in that closest of partnerships, the grinding at the mill. In another a woman sat grinding alone, or, rather, waiting for her friend to return. I asked to be allowed to take her place. I was astonished to find what hard work it was. In the next tent a woman was weaving a white woollen material, like a very coarse homespun. She had no shuttle, but drew the thread through with her fingers, and combed it down into its place with a large comb. Other women in other tents were busy carding wool or winding it, and some were spinning. Outside one tent I found several hanks of rough, dark-brown

yarn.   On examining it, I found it to be the kind of palmetto
yarn of which their tents are woven, and which is drawn from
the brown fibrous casing on the palmetto.   These tents were
made of very wide material, similar to what we know as
cocoanut matting, but much stronger, thicker, and more
closely woven.

There was a tent standing by itself out of the regular
circle.   In this a tailor sat cutting and sewing jellabas, and
round him were collected the youth of the village engaged in
learning to read and recite the Koran and to write Arabic
characters with reed pens.   All the young men had gone out
herding cattle, or taking wool or produce to the town of
Rabat.

The old headman was so friendly and kind that I wanted
to make him a present by way of good-fellowship.   But I
had nothing very suitable.   Some cigarettes and a box of
matches were promptly taken from him by his pet grand-
child, who hung on his arm, and to whom he seemed able to
refuse nothing.   He wanted us to give him some of our
enamel hardware, but we could not spare a bit of it.
Mrs. Greathed had, fortunately, some safety-pins, and these
charmed the women.

I should have liked to stay much longer among these
people.   A more strange mixture of pastoral and industrial
life, with brigandage and murder, it would be difficult to
imagine.   These villages were always having fights and
attacking each other—either on the score of vendetta or of
cattle-lifting.   But the industrial and trading instinct was
very strong, and if a chance of military service were given
the young men, and they could be drafted off upon active
service for a year or two, I believe the restlessness which
makes thieves and robbers of them would wear out in time.
Their women were not veiled, and it struck me that they
were treated with great respect.

After many 'good-byes' we rode off to regain the broad

Fez road, along which, for how many centuries nobody knows, the caravans have passed carrying the gold, slaves and ivory of the desert down to the coast.

The approach to the city of Rabat, or rather Salli, in the light of the morning sun was one of the most beautiful things I have ever seen.

We were riding up a broad, straight highway, some fifty yards across, of sand so deep that no footstep could be heard. Either side was lined with a deep row of gray cactus backed by the overhanging branches of fig-trees in the brilliant green of spring attire. At the far end of the vista, where the blue sky dropped down to the earth, stood a dazzling white city of square houses and straight-lined walls, and domes glistening in the vivid light, while all along the road came the slow-paced camels with their noiseless, swinging stride, and heavy-laden mules and toiling donkeys, raising a little cloud of dust. Now and then a party of grand Moors, bound for Fez, rode past in high-peaked scarlet saddles, and dressed in dark-blue cloaks and fine white drapery, or the pointed fez of a soldier made one bright spot of colour far off.

For two miles or more my eyes were chiefly attracted to the city as it slowly rose before us. It was Salli of the rovers—Salli where Robinson Crusoe was a slave. There were vineyards on either side of the road, and nightingales sang most sweetly and doves cooed and complained.

Leaving Salli on our right, after passing the usual mounds of filth, we crossed the Bû Ragrag in a boat, and taking the Kaid and Abd el Kader with me, I rode to the British Consulate.

Mr. Neroutsos received me very kindly, but he did not give me much hope of being able to do anything for Abd el Kader. He advised me to apply to Sir Arthur Nicholson, but he feared that I had not ground sufficient to give Abd el Kader protection myself, and in all probability no one could be found on the spur of the moment who had the power to do so, either. He himself did not know of anyone. He called Abd el Kader into the office and questioned him a good deal, and told me that he was favourably impressed with him.

The next day we went to Salli, accompanied by Mr. Bensaade, his servant and the Consul's soldier. The sun was blazing, and it was very hot, which made the row across the water all the pleasanter.

The Bashaw was away, but inside the gate we were met by the Kalipha's soldiers, the Consul having written to him and asked for a guard for us, and under this escort we walked round the double walls and through the narrow, winding streets of Salli. Built by the pirates with money accumulated by sea-robbers, this town was one of the finest I had visited, and was kept in fairly good repair. We went through streets where one house after another was a palace, and I was told that the Moors living there are very rich by some means or other. There are no exports or imports, or any manufactures to speak of. No European is allowed to live in the town, or even to stop there for a single night; and the Jews are very closely confined to their Mellâh.

The town walls are in such repair that they look as though only recently built, and in the grand houses of the Moors are twisted columns and carved capitals borrowed from Venetian art. There is a special feeling of mystery about Salli, and the hostility displayed to Europeans increased the feeling that one was treading upon dark and secret ground.

We visited some houses and drank innumerable cups of tea, and some wine at the Israelites', and we went outside the city to sit in the Bashaw's garden. Even with our strong guard we did not escape being screamed at and cursed for Christian dogs that we were. Perhaps it was fortunate that we did not understand all that was said.

Children took up stones and threw them at us, and were whacked on the head by the soldiers. One man, who said or did something intolerable, was immediately chased up a side-street by both soldiers, and I heard him being beaten at the end by the servant who carried a stick.

In the soko we saw for the first time some of the 'braves' who live in the hills and wear their hair long as a sign that they are desperadoes and prepared for any devilment. They seldom come into a town, and their surprise and curiosity respecting us was remarkable. One was a dark man—he might have been a Spaniard. The other had fair hair, as fine as silk, and with a red tinge in it like burnished copper. They were so absorbed in watching us that they appeared to be unconscious of anything else. It was like the gaze of a wild animal, intent, mystified, alert. I felt that one could make terms with them, and reach a point very similar to that which it is possible to arrive at with most wild things. But domesticated these creatures would never become. They were wilder than hawks. Their courage I doubt, but not their craft, cunning, or treachery. Their faces were not brave, but thievish.

The oranges were delicious, and we had been short of them since leaving El Kasar. We sat in the soko eating one after the other under the shade of a mat awning, and the soldiers kept the crowd off us. Then Mr. Bensaade's servant brought some water in a pannikin from a water-jar which stood there, and poured it over our hands in a refreshing stream. In this market slaves were sold which the pirates collected in their ships from all parts of the Mediterranean, and even from the coast of Ireland. Very fine mats are made at Salli of the rushes which grow in great abundance outside. The Arabs use them for sleeping upon in their tents, and every hut I went into had its rush mat. But these at Salli were very large and of mixed colours— red, white, and blue—woven in very good and even intricate patterns, which the weavers appear to keep in their heads, for when we saw them at work they had no design to guide them.

About half of the Rabat imports go to Salli, for there is a large covered market where nothing but Manchester goods are sold. The shops were very good, and there was altogether a greater air of substance and wealth about Salli than any town I went into, Marakish not excepted. I wondered where the money came from, but I never found out. I suspect that the hill-men came there to do their shopping in preference to Rabat, which is more European.

While we were sitting in the cotton-market enjoying the shade, a little slave-boy of about seven years of age ran down from a passage in the bazaar to fill a little drinking-mug at one of the stone jars which stand at intervals to serve that purpose. He let down the small bucket, drew it up, but there was only very little water. The jar was almost empty. The expression of disappointment and dismay on the baby face was touching. Then a Jew—a young man—went and let down the bucket skilfully and poured into the little mug all he could get, encouraging the child with kind words to drink it and make the best of it. His manner was so gentle that the little fellow's face brightened, and he drank the small draught with gusto, and ran back to his master's house with a smile on his face.

The heat was great, and the sun poured through the trellis and the thin mats slung across the streets to make a shade. We went outside the city, to walk in the Bashaw's garden, through the north gate, and past the cemetery where the Christian slaves were buried; then down a hill to where a small stream met the Bû Ragrag.

It is up the long valley formed by this stream that the Bashaw's garden extends. It was laid out and planted by slaves, and is still maintained by slave labour. It was the richest and by far the best-kept garden I saw in Morocco.

We walked up a path under a grove of orange-trees whose petals whitened the ground.   Then we came to pomegranates bursting into flower.   There were sweet lemons, apricots, peaches, figs, and vines ; and a stream of the clearest water ran gurgling and sparkling like crystal where the sunlight fell upon it through the foliage.   We sat down to rest by a tank where the ground was green with moss and ferns, under the shade of a mulberry-tree, whose branches met those of a gigantic orange, and here we listened to the singing of the nightingales.   Our retinue was increased by the man who had the charge of the garden, and who was most anxious that we should see the whole of it.   That it was extensive we had already proved, but something must be allowed for Moorish exaggeration when he declared that it would take us three days to get to the end of it.

Salli, with its grand houses and foreign air, was built to be self-contained and for pleasure, judging by the gardens within the walls and air of old-time luxury.   The rift in history caused by the fall of the Moors and the recession of Spain, when each in turn became wrapped in the rigidity of fanaticism, was impressed on Salli.

The initial blunder was the failure of Christianity in Spain.   There was a time when, with a little breadth and statesmanship, Christianity *might* have won, or, at least, held its ground as an influence.   But—

> 'The Spaniard, when the lust of sway
>   Had lost its quickening spell,
> Cast crowns for rosaries away,
>   An empire for a cell.
> A strict accountant of his beads,
> A subtle disputant on creeds,
>   His dotage trifled well ;
> Yet better had he neither known
> A bigot's shrine nor despot's throne.'

And now Salli, with its streets closed to the infidel, lest their polluting feet should come too near their holy mosques and shrines (for there were streets through which we might not pass), and the narrow bitterness which shuts out Europeans, the forbidding hatred and contempt which shrouds all life and thought, was typical of the strongest and deepest, the most implacable, Mohammedanism.

And how proud they were! With what hauteur they swept past us in the streets, with a curse under their breath! I tried to picture what they must feel. They may no longer defy that mysterious force which lies behind in the regions beyond Spain. They dare not enslave the infidel or make him pay tribute as of old. Why? It is the will of Allah to afflict them thus, and they betake themselves the more frantically to their prayers, that the day may come when they may set their foot on us again.

The objects of Islam are twofold, and perfectly suited to the character of these people. Dominion comes first, and is the public object—the object for which every Mahdi arises. The second is a private object; it is to attain a state of ecstasy—not contemplative, but an exaltation of the feelings to the overpowering of the senses, a heart-drunkenness, a highly intoxicated sentiment, visions, the gift of prophecy, culminating at last in a state which we should put under treatment and control. It was inevitable that these two religions—Catholicism and Islam—both insisting on temporal power, should clash.

Dr. Brown, in his introduction to Leo Africanus, gives this account of the treatment which led finally at a later period to the expulsion of the Moors from Spain: ' Though all who wished to seek a home in Barbary were transported thither in public galleys at a charge of ten golden doubles a head, but very few could afford to avail themselves of that privilege. . . . Padre Bernaldez, the Curate of Los Palacios, disposes of them in a manner less creditable, though possibly his statement is an accurate account of what happened in some cases, " For," remarks this historian, "the Christians shipped the men, gave them a free passage, and sent them to the devil." Religion, nevertheless, sat easy on the Spanish Moors. Thousands had been more or less voluntarily converted by the liberal-minded Talavera and the more bigoted Ximenes, and, outwardly at least, performed the duties of their new faith. It was not till 1610 that Philip III., at the instigation of the fanatical Archbishop of Valencia, deported the remnants of the race which still conformed to the creed of their fathers, retaining as slaves a certain number to expiate their offences against his sovereignty by toiling in the galleys or dying by inches in the mines of Peru. In the execution of this *grande reso-lucion,* as the King termed it, about a million of the most industrious of the "Morisco" inhabitants of Spain were hunted like wild beasts and banished to Africa with every concomitant of barbarity. Many, indeed, were slain before they could reach the coast. The crews in many cases rose upon them, butchered the men, violated the women, and threw the children into the sea. Others, driven by the winds on the sandy shores of Barbary, were attacked by the marauding Arabs and slaughtered, despite their creed or their nationality; for a people who killed or enslaved every shipwrecked seaman, and every tribe of which was at war with every other, were not likely to bestow much esteem on castaways in Spanish garb, speaking Arabic with a Castilian accent, and whose previous history did not altogether clear them of the taint of renegadism. Few escaped maltreatment and robbery. . . . Many, disheartened with the coldness of their co-religionists in the cities, wandered into the desert and perished from privations and hardships which their life in Andalus had little fitted them to endure.'

It was these expatriated Moors who came to Salli, and to revenge themselves on Spain turned pirates, and made especial havoc of the Spanish shipping.*

* Budgett Meakin, 'The Moorish Empire.'

The principal pirate stronghold in Morocco was Salli.
All the coast towns became in turn the possession of Spain,
Portugal or France. Salli itself and its sister town Rabat,
and the city of Sla, a little way inland, formed for a time a
small independent republic. The tribes on the hills furnished
excellent recruits, but the good pay offered inducement to
all the mercenaries and renegades in Morocco who crowded
to fill the rovers' galleys with men of daring and resource.
Some idea of the Salli rovers' character can be gathered
from the description of the small port of Mehidya when it
was captured by the Spaniards early in the seventeenth
century—'a perfect kennel of European outlaws . . . the
offscourings of every port, who, like the squaw-men of the
West and the beach-combers of the Pacific, led a congenial
existence among the barbarians.'

In his interesting history, Mr. Meakin states very clearly
that the Moors learnt nearly all they knew of sea warfare
from Europeans, and to show how this was done he quotes
from a contemporary record, which gives an evidently faithful
picture of the times and manners:

'Ward, a poor English sailor, and Dansker, a Dutchman,
made first here their marts, when the Moores knew scarce
how to saile a ship: Bishop was ancient, and did little hurt,
but Easton got so much as made himselfe a marquesse in
Savoy, and Ward lived like a Bashaw in Barbary; they
were the first that taught the Moores to be men of warre . . .
till they became so dispyrited, disordered, debauched, and
miserable, that the Turks and Moores began to command
them as slaves, and force them to instruct them in their best
skill, which many an accursed runnagado, or Christian-
turned-Turk, did, till they have made these Sally men, or
Moores of Barbary, so powerful as they be, to the terror of
all the Straights, and many times they take purchases (prizes)
even in the main ocean, yea, sometimes even in the narrow
seas in England; and these are the most cruelle villaines in

11

Turkie or Barbarie, whose natives are very noble and of good
nature in comparison of them.'

Probably the principal ship-building of the Salli rovers was
done at Rabat, for I was shown a large, long, lofty hall, with
a floor sloping towards the water-level, where I was told the
ships of the Salli rovers were built. Yet the towns were
rivals, and often at bitter enmity with one another. The
market where the prizes were sold, and where most pirate
business was transacted, was at Salli. The prizes were put
up to auction, and the money evenly distributed among the
crew.

At Shellagh the best of the Moors exiled from Granada
established themselves, adding to the city many of the
buildings whose picturesque ruins are among the loveliest
things in Barbary to-day.

We left Salli by the 'Baker's Gate,' and I was told, as a
further proof of the lawlessness of the country, that on Salli
beach Kaid MacClean's horses were stolen. They were taken
at night from the camp, and kept in the hills for about a
fortnight, and then brought back and sold in Salli market.
But the most remarkable thing about the whole affair was
that the Kaid of the district could not recover them.

After Salli, Rabat had all the air of a modern bustling
town. We spent an afternoon buying rugs and carpets,
Moorish lanterns, and other curios of native manufacture.
The numbers of small shops where the various trades are
plied with unremitting zeal is astonishing. But the port of
Rabat suffers from a terrible bar, so that even when a ship
comes into the roadstead it is sometimes uncertain whether
she will be able to connect with the shore. The trade of
Rabat is gradually being drawn away to more favourable
ports, which emphasizes the fact that trade requires releasing
at the seaports first before any improvement can be attempted
in the country itself. It does not seem probable that light
draught steamers could cross the bar of the Bû Ragrag;

but if they could, the Berber or hill tribes, which come
down to touch Rabat, and terrorize the whole country of the
Bû Ragrag, would render a peaceful settlement of agriculturists extremely precarious. There is no country trade
from Rabat. In that direction there is stagnation. The
natives come into the town and buy what they want at the
shops. Thirty thousand pounds' worth of Manchester cottons
are absorbed annually in Rabat and Salli, only an inappreci-
able amount being sent out of the town. Sugar to the value
of £36,710 came in during the year, rather less than in the
previous year. Candles to the value of £7,206 comes next,
and tea to the value of £5,942. But the import trade in
every article is declining. It is difficult to account for such
a sudden decrease, but in the case of some goods, such as
Manchester cottons, it is generally believed to be in a great
part due to the high prices ruling in goods.

Spain no longer contributes to the Rabat market, and has
withdrawn her steamers. The river will not admit the sailing ships which can lie in the river at Laraïche. In the
year 1900 only one sailing vessel, a German, came to Rabat.
The difficulties of the bar may be understood from the single
fact that the large steamers of the London company visit
this town less frequently, preferring to tranship cargo at
Gibraltar on to a small steamer, which brings the accumulated cargo of several steamers to Rabat as it can fill up.

Ship-building of large barges or lighters is still carried on
at Rabat. The Sultan has two barges always in readiness,
in order that he may cross the Bû Ragrag when he goes on
one of those progresses through his dominions which carry
fire and sword among the tribes. But the present Sultan,
being a minor, for several years has left this time-honoured
custom in abeyance. However, when I was there rumour
was busy about his approaching visit. The barges were
being painted, and some of the cactus hedge was cut on the
further side of the river, to enable him to pass without

catching his red umbrella in the thorns.   These things were done as a matter of course, but no one expressed the least satisfaction or pleasure at the idea of the Sultan's coming, or appeared to look forward to it in the slightest degree.

In Rabat I met an old Moor who had been sixteen years in England.   He was able to chat quite fluently in English. He told me that Manchester was 'really a very nice place, but he liked Barbary better.   Nevertheless,' he added, with a friendly nod, 'the English are good people.   They do not push Moors about, like other Christians, and I think they are a kind people.   Yes, and I like them even better in England than I do in Barbary.   Barbary is the country of the Moors, you understand.   Yes, we are Moors here.'   And indeed they are.   This old man, as he walked about in his bundle of gossamer draperies, was a piece of unconscious comedy.   He and his colleagues presided over the Customs, and they agreed that it was so extraordinary a thing that a woman should come and walk about Rabat that they got up from their seats, or, rather, cushions, of custom, and came trooping behind me, causing a total cessation of business in the port of Rabat for the space of one hour.   I had to manœuvre round to get them safely back to their perches, which they were glad enough to reach, sinking with groans of fatigue into their cushions again.

Merchants in Rabat have the greatest difficulty in obtaining warehouses or space to store goods.   The Moors are so jealous of all Europeans that they will not lease properties to them, and purchase is absolutely out of the question.

The exertions of the Consuls have prevented the sale of slaves in the open street.   The sales take place in the yard of a fondak.   There we saw four black women sitting on a mat looking round apprehensively.   There were only a few men hanging about, and the bidding appeared to be very slack.   One woman had a little baby of a few months old in her arms.   The upset price for her and the infant was $20.

Their evident fear and uneasiness was painful. To buy them all and set them free seemed the only course; but a little inquiry and thought convinced me that it would be a mistake to do so.

The Moors who saw us enter disliked our presence. They even seemed to look a little ashamed of themselves. There is no doubt that a good deal of hideous cruelty is practised upon these slaves in a quiet way. There was a man in Rabat who was notoriously cruel to his slaves, and one day his female slaves got him alone, and between them cut him in pieces. Then they locked up the house and ran away. They made their plans very well, and must have had friends, for they were never caught.

That evening Dr. Kerr, a medical missionary, came with his wife to our camp, and spent about an hour chatting with us. We were camped outside Rabat, between the palace and the cemetery, and the kasbah shut us off from the sea. The prison was close by, and on one side a large mosque. We had a good deal of heavy rain in the night, and this, together with the noise of a midnight feast which was being held in the mosque, made sleeping difficult. The midnight service was on one occasion tremendous, and the babel became deafening when at some specially sacred moment all my Moors rushed out of their tent to howl the chant at the tops of their voices.

In the great barracks or gaol the Sultan confined a remnant of the M'zaab tribe, which he 'ate up' immediately on coming to the throne. The whole affair was a gross iniquity, and an instance of the total miscarriage of justice common in Morocco. I learned all about it later in my travels, but at Rabat I heard the fate of the unfortunate rebels. The prisoners numbered 400, but they were so cruelly treated on the way from their country, which is to the south of Marakish, that many of them were in a dying condition by the time they reached Rabat. Even to these no mercy was shown.   They were put in panniers on donkeys at the last, and soldiers walked beside them beating them with sticks when they groaned or cried out.   Then the wives came and camped outside the prison on the spot where my tent stood.   They were in a destitute state, but people did what they could for them, and they were very willing to work, so as to buy food to feed their husbands.   But life in a Moorish gaol is not conducive to longevity, and these men were broken in spirit by ill-treatment.   The close confinement, after the open-air life in the villages, told upon them, and the knowledge that they were imprisoned for life deepened their distress.   Thus they died off rapidly, so that at the time I arrived the women had gone away.   Only two prisoners remained alive within; and one poor wife remarked pathetically, 'Allah has forgotten to be kind.'

CHAPTER XVI

THE TOWER OF HASSAN—SHELLAGH

THE tide was not very high when we started with Mr. Bensaade to visit the Tower of Hassan, but the width of the river and its natural banks, and the view of the two rival cities on either side, made every yard of the little journey interesting and beautiful.

At the mouth of the river the bar was foaming; the white waves curling and riding on like horses charging a hill. The dazzling whiteness of the town of Salli showed above the soft line of a broad stretch of sand—the sand thrown up by the tide of years, which has deprived Salli altogether of a seaport, and left her dependent upon Rabat. On the other side the river-bank was rocky, and crags and huge sections of red rock had fallen into the water, and lay there overgrown with all kinds of foliage, from the hard gray masses of cacti and aloes to delicate ferns and creepers. There was a very beautiful pale pink antirrhinum which grew in the crevices of the rocks, and young wild vines threw their shoots with bunches not yet in blossom over the aloes and rocks.

We glided gradually over a perfectly clear surface of shining water, and then, as a gorge slowly opened, the magnificent tower came bit by bit into full view.

This ruin, incomplete as it is, offers a magnificent specimen of architecture in the style of the Alhambra—a finished and complete art, for which no better materials could be found than the red sandstone of Rabat and the tiles of Fez. The

lacework pattern of arabesque is thrown into relief by the
fact of the sandstone turning gray wherever its surface is
most exposed to the weather.   This gives an almost transparent appearance.   The richness, warmth, and depth lie in
the shadow, which remains of a warm red tone.   The Tower
of Hassan has never been completed, and the summit is
ragged and unfinished as the last builder left the last brick,
and suggests defeated aspirations and divided counsels.   I
am not aware of any record of the building beyond that this
unfinished tower is said to be a sister tower to the Girálda
at Seville, and to the Kûtûbiya at Marakish, and that they
were all built by Yakub el Mansûr (the Victorious) towards
the close of the twelfth century.

We climbed the hill from the water's edge, and it seemed
to me that I was landing somewhere from the quiet waters
of the Cam to approach those seats of learning which have
sent out administrators over an empire greater than ever
was that of the Moors.   I almost expected to hear the deep
sounds of the organ and the chanting of the choir of King's.
The spot was undoubtedly selected as a centre of learning
and culture, and dates from the best period of Moorish rule.

The predecessor of Yakub el Mansûr was his father, the
learned and pious Yusef II., who drew to his Court Averroes,
the last of the great Moslem philosophers, who ended his
days in honour in Morocco.   'For the last time,' says the
biographer of Averroes,* 'before its final extinction the
Moslem Caliphate in Spain displayed a splendour which
seemed to rival the ancient glories of the Ommiad Court.
Great mosques arose, schools and colleges were founded,
hospitals and other useful and beneficent constructions proceeded from the public zeal of the Sovereign, and under the
patronage of two liberal rulers, Yusef, and later his son
Yakub, science and philosophy flourished apace.   It was the
philosophic Vizier of Yusef who introduced Averroes to that

* 'Encyclopædia Britannica.'

Prince; and Avensoar, the greatest of Moslem physicians, was his friend.'

It is impossible to look at the Tower of Hassan without thinking of Averroes, and the part he must have played in founding this great University—arrested and incomplete— among the might-have-beens of history.   Averroes is best known as the great commentator on Aristotle.   He took up a position with regard to science which was identical with that of the New Learning in Europe, when it arose some centuries later upon the decline of monasticism.   The chief feature in his teaching was the separation between Catholic and philoso- phical truth.   ' The real grandeur of Averroes,' says the biographer already quoted, ' is seen in his resolute prosecution of the standpoint of science in matters of this world, and in his recognition that religion is not a branch of knowledge to be reduced to propositions and systems of dogma, but a personal and inward power, an individual truth, which stands distinct from, but not contradictory to, the universalities of scientific law.   He maintained alike the claim of demon- strative science, with its generalities for the few who could live in that ethereal world, and the claim of religion for all— the common life of each soul as an individual and personal consciousness.'

What wonder that this man, whose thought might be an advanced product of this new century, displeased the people of his time, that period of narrow scholastic orthodoxy ? What wonder that he was rejected by Islam ?   The ignorant fanaticism of the multitude was aroused, and at last, ' about the year 1195, Averroes was accused of heretical pursuits, stripped of his honours, and banished to a place near Cordova.   At the same time efforts were made to stamp out all liberal culture in Andalusia, so far as it went beyond the little medicine, arithmetic, and astronomy required for practical life. . . . When the transient passion of the people had been satisfied, Averroes for a brief period survived his

restoration to honour.   He died in the year before his
patron, Yakub el Mansûr (1199), with whom the political
power of the Moslems came to an end, as did the culture of
liberal science with Averroes.'*

Such was Averroes, the most prominent of the learned
men of Barbary in the days of the founding of Hassan's
Tower.   Morocco was then at the zenith of its fame as
a land of learned men.†   And the most interesting and
striking years in the history of the country are those
which begin with the reign of Yusef II., A.D. 1163-84, and
extend through the learned and victorious reign of Yakub el
Mansûr, the decline commencing under his son, En Nasir,
who, after sustaining severe losses in battle, is believed to
have been poisoned, 1213.

Yusef II. was a noble-minded and learned Ameer.   The
special feature of his administration was the delegation of
power to provincial Governors, whom he had the knack of
choosing well.   It was part of Yusef's policy to employ his
son as a Vizier or Minister, and this unusually wise
policy gave Yakub, afterwards known as El Mansûr, an
admirable training in sovereign affairs, so that his able
hand was felt immediately that he succeeded his father
Yusef.

Yakub was ' a tall, good-looking man of light-brown complexion, with ample limbs, wide mouth, loud voice, and large
dark eyes, clad always in simple wool.   The most veracious

---

* It is said that Averroes was imprisoned for a too liberal translation of
a passage which referred to Venus as a goddess.

† Dr. Brown, in his introduction to Leo Africanus, says : ' Fez . . . was
the seat of Arabic learning, to which students resorted from all parts of
Islam, and its libraries, as well as those of the city of Morocco, were
famous even in Cordova and Granada.   A fresh stimulus must certainly
have been given . . . by the arrival in Morocco of so many cultured men
from Spain.   The fact of such men leaving the cultured Courts of Seville
and Cordova to take up their residence in . . . Morocco shows that the
offers made to them by the African Sultans must have been of a most
tempting nature.'

of men, and the most elegant in language,' just even when the interests of his own family suffered thereby. His motto was, 'In God have I trusted.' Like several other Morocco rulers, he was the son of a Christian slave.

He began his reign in the customary manner, with the murder of his nearest relatives, and the liberal distribution of money from the treasury, but he had the courage to open the prison doors and to undertake a general reparation of injustices.

Though enlightened, he was an eminently popular Sovereign. The Arab historians wax eloquent in his praise. He was undoubtedly a great King, 'the most magnanimous in every respect. His government was excellent, he added to the treasury, he increased his power, his actions were those of a famous Sovereign, his religion was deep, and he did much good to the Muslim. May God have mercy on him by His grace, His kindness, and His generosity, for He is pitiful and loves to pardon.'

After this eulogy it is a little damping to find that Yakub's justice did not prevent him from administering 'the bastinado to anyone bringing before him a trivial question'; that his religion led him to 'revive the practice of the orthodox Kalifas of presiding at public prayer as Imam. Those who did not attend were flogged; those who drank wine were executed.'

Yakub was the contemporary of Saladin and of Richard Cœur de Lion. His strength lay in the combination of military genius with a taste for learning far ahead of contemporary Sovereigns. His son, En Nasir, inherited his father's respect for books, but he was less able or less fortunate as a general, and under him began the fall of the Moors in Spain. It is alleged that our King John, being in distress and unable to deal with his unruly Barons, turned to the Sultan En Nasir, and sent him an embassy to solicit assistance. The overtures were conducted by a priest, who

on his return was made Abbot of St. Albans; which is the
more extraordinary as John offered, in return for assistance,
to embrace Islam. The whole story is eminently picturesque. The priest had to pass through hedges of guards
and fine apartments till he came at length to the learned and
pious Ameer, who was diligently occupied in reading a book.

Rabat was built with the stones of ancient Roman temples
and with the labour of 40,000 Christian slaves, who earned
their freedom by completing the task, and were afterwards
settled as a tribe by themselves to the north of Fez, where
for some time they preserved their religion. Some historians
state that the town was built to commemorate the victories
of El Mansûr, and for that reason it was called Rabat, which
in Arabic means 'the camp of victory.' But taking other
matters into consideration, and the grand ruins of Hassan's
Tower and of Shellagh, it would seem that the intention was
to found not merely a military post, but a centre of influence,
which should be powerful and extensive on the pattern of
Alexandria, on which it was said the streets of Rabat were
modelled. 'Some,' says Leo, ' say that the reason why it
was built in this place was that King Mansor, possessing the
kingdom of Granada and a great part of Spaine besides, and
considering that Morocco was so far distant that if any wars
should happen he could not in due time send new forces
against the Christians, determined to build some town upon
the sea-shore, where he and his armie might remaine all
summer-time. . . . He caused this town of Rebat in short
space to be erected, and to be exceedingly beautified with
temples, colleges, pallaces, shops, stores, hospitals, and other
such buildings. Moreouver on the south side without the
walles he caused a certaine high tower like the tower of
Maroco to be built, sauing that the winding staires were
somewhat larger, insomuch that three horses abreast might
well ascend up, from the top whereof they might escrie ships
an huge way into the sea. So exceeding is the height thereof

that I think there is no more the like building to be found, and to the end that greater store of artificers might hither from all places resort, he appointed that every man according to his trade and occupation should be allowed a yeerely stipend; whereupon it came to passe that within a few moneths this town was better stored with all kinde of artificers and merchants than any town in all Africa besides, and that because they reaped a double gaine. . . . How-beit,' continues the historian sadly, 'after King Mansor's death this town grew into such decay that scarce a tenth part thereof now remaineth; so that at this present a man shall hardly finde throughout the whole towne fower hundred houses inhabited. . . . Comparing their former felicitie with the present alteration whereinto they are fallen, I cannot but greatly lament their miserable case.'

We walked all round the ground, several acres in extent, whereon were traced in ruins the plan of some vast building. A row of magnificent columns stood as though defying Time itself. There were the excavations for the baths, and again some fallen columns, and some stones not yet moved into their place.* The unfinished walls of enormous thickness were crumbling, and had become the nesting-places of crowds of hawks and blue rollers. I saw pigeons which had a nest in the tower, and marvelled at their temerity in rearing a family with such bad company all round. In old days the Moors bred pigeons with great care. Shakespeare frequently alludes to the Barbary pigeons.

The tower whence the muezzin's voice was destined never to call the faithful to prayer resounded with the shrieks of birds of prey and was the scene of incessant fights and many a cruel outrage. A small window, some 20 feet from the ground, had recently been walled up, but formerly it was possible to gain access to the tower through its narrow

* It is alleged that these stones were quarried and cut in Spain, and brought there to be placed in the building.

opening, and form some idea of the broad stairway within. But Christian curiosity led to the annoyance of Moslems, and evil people took refuge there, so the authorities ordered the window to be bricked up.

I went away by myself to think of all that this spot might have meant to the world had Islam realized its ideals, had it been able to compete with Christianity by civilized methods. And how nearly it had succeeded in attaining very real greatness! 'There is a tide in the affairs of men.' This was the high-water mark of the highest tide in Barbary.

In this 'camp of victory'—the 'uncongenial mixture of earthly needs and heavenly aspirations,' lies the weakness of Mohammedanism. But a religion propagated by the sword could not maintain an empire, and within that burning fanaticism there was no place for learning or freedom, though men might seek it wistfully—ay, and with tears.

Then, as we regained our boat and moved gently down the stream, and the tower with its ruined summit seemed to recede from our eyes, as its reflected image died out upon the water, I felt that deep silence which is itself a part of the East, and which a Western poet has felt and knew how to interpret as a sign of defeat :

> 'The tents were all silent, the banners alone,
> The lances unlifted, the trumpets unblown.'

Mr. Matteos, riding a pretty black Arab, accompanied us to see the ruins of Shellagh. I was delayed in starting, and went after them, taking with me the Kaid, who selected a different route, thinking to make up time by a short-cut. On the way my progress was impeded by finding half a dozen boys, who had caught as many young hawks and tied strings to their legs. They took pleasure in throwing the birds into the air and pulling them back with a jerk. This was intolerable, and I insisted, with the Kaid's help, in getting the birds given to me for 50 cents. Knowing that I had Moors

Mr Cavilla photo Tangiers

THE TOWER OF HASSAN.

to deal with, I would not take them for nothing, lest they should say I robbed them of their property, mercy being a quality they would not understand. But the Kaid fixed the price and I rode away with the hawks, and a fine time I had with them ! Never before had I had six hawks in my possession, and being on horseback made it difficult to negotiate with them. Had Conrad cut capers there would have been a scene.

I managed them by keeping all the strings in my bridle-hand, and having laid the birds on their backs in my lap, I held them down with the other hand. There they lay staring at me with the most impudent, defiant expression in their bold countenances. Blank amazement coupled with fatigue kept them quiet at first, but presently a leg was shot out, and my ungloved finger was caught in what felt like a small steel gin. I positively screamed with pain, and this was the signal for a sharp beak to be driven into the soft flesh of my thumb, and a concerted struggle of legs, wings, and beaks ensued. But I held on, for I knew the wicked tormentors, who were in hot pursuit at Conrad's heels, would have re-captured them in a moment if I let go. Thus it happened that I entered the beautiful gateway of Shellagh with an embarrassed mind, my one desire being to reach Mrs. Greathed and Mr. Matteos, who were waiting for me at the other entrance, and get them to mount guard over the boys while I let the hawks go. It was the nearest approach to hawking I have ever known. The flight of a hawk is peculiar; the bird is so light and made for flight. Opening one's hand and letting it go is like shooting, or the flash of a thought striking direct upon a given object. Five of the birds were, I believe, sparrow-hawks, but the sixth was a lovely bird, with gray or mauve on his head and back. His eyes shone like great carbuncles.

The ruins of Shellagh stand in a lovely valley within a wall, which creeps along the rocky summit of the hill, out

of which the action of a tributary to the Bû Ragrag has
carved a most fertile valley.

Tradition relates that when the exiled Moors reached
Rabat, this valley, containing the mosque whose tower still
stands intact, recalled Granada so forcibly to their mind
that they settled here and devoted themselves to repro-
ducing, as far as possible, the city which they loved so well.
The Moors consider it, though ruined and deserted, one of
their most sacred spots, and in the evening they ride out
with their little prayer-carpets to pray at the tombs. The
garden, composed of oranges, figs, and feathery bamboo, has
run riot. The dungeons are full of water and laid bare to
the light. Peasant women come there to wash their clothes.
In the enclosure where the Sultans are buried we were not
allowed to enter. Nature has reasserted herself, and where
once the crowd of humanity thronged the paved streets the
fertile soil has thrown up a wealth of beautiful foliage and
flowers, over which the bees go softly humming. In one
place a peasant had built a hut, and had a small patch of
broad beans and a few mealies. And this was not incongruous; but it is to be hoped that the ruins will never be
restored. Both their magnificence and their decay are parts
of history, and no restoration could make them half so lovely
as they are now, standing among the dislodged crags and
the wild growth of Nature in her most tender mood.

Shellagh apparently takes its name from Sala Colonia of
the Romans, though most probably there was an earlier
Phœnician settlement here. Leo Africanus who frequented
this spot, and saw it before it was ruined, 'was,' says an
historian, 'a most accomplished and absolute man. . . . As
Moses was learned in all the wisdome of the Egyptians, so
likewise was Leo in that of the Arabians and Mores. He
was not meanely but extraordinarily learned.' Leo gives
the following account of the city, and affixes a date which
is useful : ' King Mansor caused it to be walled round about,

and built therein a faire hospitall and a stately pallace, into which his soldiers might at their pleasure retire themselves. Here likewise he erected a most beautiful temple, wherein he caused a goodly hall or chapel to be set vp, which was curiously carued and had many fair windowes about it : and in this hall (when he perceiued death to seaze vpon him) he commanded his subjects to burie his corpes. Which being done, they laid one marble stone ouer his head and another ouer his feete, whereon sundry epitaphs were en-graven. After him likewise all the honourable personages of his familie and blood chose to be interred in the same hall. And so did the kings of the Marin familie so long as their common wealth prospered. Myself, on a time, entering the same hall, beheld there thirtie monuments of noble and great personages, and diligently wrote out all their epitaphs. This I did in the year of the Hegeira 915 ' (A.D. 1509).

It is a thousand pities that we have not this record. The white koubah, which contrasts with the red of the sandstone tower, was pointed out to me as the grave of the Black Sultan, who fell at the Battle of El Ksar, although another story says that Mulai Ahmed stuffed the skin of the dead Sultan and carried it in front of him to terrify the people of Fez. But there is nothing to show that all but his skin was not buried here.

Still stranger is a story of French origin, which corrob-orates the statement of an English sea-captain called Jack-son, who disguised himself as an Arab and obtained entrance to the dismantled and roofless burial-place of the Kings. He was shown two graves, which, he was told, were those of Roman generals. This statement was discredited, it being thought improbable that the tomb of any infidel would be permitted beside those of the Commanders of the Faithful. Yet the truth was even more extraordinary, for ' the mural tablet to the memory of the Sultan Abu Yakub Yussuf has a round hole close to the left edge, apparently from its

12

breaking the inscription, made after the marble tablet was erected. Through this hole there is a tradition that of old the Arabs were accustomed to put their hands and declare to the truth of any statement when a particularly binding oath was desirable. If the hand could be withdrawn freely, this was a proof of the testifier speaking the truth, but if he had told a lie a superhuman force prevented the perjurer from doing so. In 1880 M. Ducour, French Vice-Consul in Rabat, who was permitted to visit the tombs, put his hand through the hole, and fancied that he could feel on the reverse side of the stone something like engraved characters. Interest was accordingly made to have the tablet removed, when it was found that the surmise was correct, for, as the clearly-cut Latin inscription showed, the tablet had, previous to extolling the virtues of a Mussulman Sovereign, already recorded the merits of a Roman Proconsul. This was Aulus Cæcina Tacitus, Governor of the province of Betica, who had been recently promoted to the consulate, and the friend who reared the commemorative tablet was Septimus Carvillianus, a Roman knight.'*

Lovely as Nature has made it, history has clothed upon this spot the poetry of human interest of no ordinary description. While the people of the latest empire born in time were wresting from a tyrant the first charter of their liberties, here, between the mountains and the sea, men thought to conquer and govern, not by mere force, but by culture and science. They comprehended, as few have done, all the elegance and charm of which human life is capable.

> 'They say the lion and the lizard keep
> The courts where Jamsdyh gloried and drank deep,
> And Bahram, that great hunter—the wild ass
> Stamps o'er his head, but cannot break his sleep.'

They lay, under the pall of Nature, these great men by

* Vallentin, 'Bulletin Épigraphique de la Gaule,' 1881.

whose graves I passed, and I bent my head in gratitude to the flowers, whose faces looked up to the cloudless sky.

'I sometimes think that never blows so red
The rose as where some buried Cæsar bled ;
That every hyacinth the garden wears
Dropt in her lap from some once lovely head.

'And this reviving herb, whose tender green
Hedges the river lip on which we lean—
Ah, lean upon it lightly ! for who knows
From what once lovely lip it springs unseen ?'

CHAPTER XVII

LEAVING RABAT—DISAGREEABLE NATIVES—AYESHA—HOSPI-
TALITY IN CASA BLANCA, NATIVE AND AMERICAN—
TRADE OF CASA BLANCA

WE left Rabat with great regret, but Mrs. Greathed was
anxious to catch a steamer at Casa Blanca which was already
due. So the following afternoon we rode out of Rabat,
passing by the aqueduct, which some attribute to the
Romans and others to Yakub el Mansûr, and which, like all
old things in Morocco, was grandly planned and now in
ruins.

Early in the morning Abd el Kader left to return to his
village, very sore at heart, and I felt much for him, seeing no
chance for him. I had done my best, and was most grateful
to Mr. Neroutsos for the trouble he took in the matter.

Our way lay over a treeless plain, where crops of barley
seemed to grow well wherever the ground had been ploughed.
It struck me that a light railway run by mules could easily
connect Casa Blanca and Rabat. There were no bad rivers
and no serious hills to overcome. Casa Blanca might then
be improved as a seaport with a view to the Fez-Mequinez
trade, for goods might run overland cheaper than being
transhipped at Gibraltar for Rabat. It would also make it
possible for better trade intercourse, and tourists, who often
complained to me that they had no chance of seeing Rabat,
might manage to do so from Casa Blanca.

We were to have stopped for the night at a town off the

track, which is practically a hill-town, as Europeans do not go there, while the hill-men not only come down to it, but even stay the night. The difficulty was that we had two soldiers with us. I ascertained afterwards that the forest tribes (it is only eighty miles from the forest) have recently declared their animosity to the soldiers of the Sultan, and have proved it repeatedly by killing any one of them if they can catch him. The Kaid did not tell me this. He quietly denied the existence of the town, and when I pointed it out to him he assured me it was no town at all, only ruins, and that we should soon reach the spot Mr. Bensaade had told him of a little further on the road. However, I found the camping-ground was near a large douar, with a smaller douar close at hand. No sooner had we dismounted than a row ensued. At no point in my travels were the natives so disagreeable. They came out in great numbers, and were exceedingly nasty to the Kaid. To go away in such circumstances would be a mistake ; besides, it was interesting.

As they were 'bally-ragging' the Kaid quite unnecessarily, I went up to them, and, laying hold of the headman's shoulder and giving it a little shake, I asked him what it was all about. Rather to my surprise, he turned to me with a manner which was all civility, if not submission. Mrs. Greathed had said that the row arose because we were Christians, and, with her superior knowledge of the East, I had thought this was the case, but I saw then that there was something these people were afraid of. I told the man that I was English and was travelling, that I had no wish to hurt him, that I was a friend to the Moors. He still looked uneasy and anxious and very mistrustful, and not even when we bought things from them were these people really genial.

I walked down to the shore while the camp was shaking into order, and there I found a small bay, into which boats of four or five tons could easily enter at high-tide by the

channel of a small river. There was no sign of any fishing-
boats about ; only on the rocks was a hollow structure of
stones, from the top of which were a flagstaff or two. This
might be a saint's tomb, but it might also answer very well
for a signal-station. The next morning when I passed, I saw
a cave among the rocks and a slight track worn along the
grass towards it.

My belief is that these people are averse from the Sultan's
rule, and more or less on terms with the tribes. Whether
they do gun-running in that bay I do not know. That kind
of smuggling is done pretty openly at the ports, and it is said
that the Moorish officials themselves are interested in it.
Guns are the joy of life to these people, and at this place a
cripple boy had made a most ingenious toy pistol, which he
could fire, using an old Winchester cartridge for the barrel.
How he got his gunpowder I do not know.

The submission of the forest tribes to the Sultan depends
on religious fealty. They even go the length of choosing
their own Kaid, who acts as a judge or arbitrator in their
internecine disputes. Many times have different Sultans
sent troops to destroy these tribes, but artillery cannot be
taken into the woods, and the woods will not burn. These
tribes cannot be starved out, for they have in the forest large
spaces of cultivated land, where they grow fine crops and
herd cattle on rich pastures. They do not pay a peseta of
taxes, but they will make presents of their own free will, and
I believe if a Christian went among them speaking their
language, and accredited to one of their leaders, leaving his
soldier behind, they would behave with great hospitality.
No Sovereign would find them easy to rule. No Western
Power would have the same advantage that their Sultan has
of appealing to them for unity in religious belief. They
would prefer their personal privileges to any national pro-
gramme; and the excitement of internecine feuds, mixed
with the customary right to plunder the men of the plains

and sack towns if an opportunity offers, would be dearer to them than any scheme for the welfare of their country. But they love money next to their independence, also green tea, sugar, and candles, and these tastes offer commerce a very superior opportunity. The tribes possess a rude sense of justice, and they are open to a bargain. Were the country adjacent to them ruled with justice, firmness, and business perspicacity, they would be attracted to an alliance with any leading man who succeeded in winning their confidence and respect. They might be induced to enter his service, and form a useful body of troops or police elsewhere; but it would depend solely on the individuality of the man who approached them. As things are now, the worst of them get the best of it. A premium is put on good thieving.

The river was tidal, and after we had crossed it we had a long march against a fierce wind, which blew the sand in our faces; but we were obliged to go on in order to cross another small tidal river at the right moment. At last, the dust-storm being quite intolerable, and seeing some aloes, I called a halt, and had the tent pitched under such shelter as they afforded. It was lucky that we did so, for in a very short time heavy rain came on, which would have drenched us to the skin. When it was over, we had to pack and scramble across the river, which was not far distant, for the tide was coming up fast, and yet the river was running out, the reason being a bar of rock at the mouth of the river which the incoming tide had not crossed. The moment it did so the water would rush up the river with a vengeance.

Late that evening we reached a douar near Fedahlah, where Ayesha, the headwoman, received us very warmly in the absence of her husband. Ayesha was a relation of Abd el Kader, and news flies fast. We felt that the warmth of her reception was more than we either desired or deserved.

She wanted us to camp inside the douar, but it was particularly dirty and ill-kept. She feared lest our animals should
be stolen. When the men returned, they were alarmed at
finding us outside, but Ayesha exerted her feminine tact to
pacify them. She took my arm and led me away for a little
walk, and asked me a great many questions. Had I no
son? No. What a shame! Then I must have Ayesha's;
and immediately a little piece of mahogany she had on her
back was swung round and put into my arms. But the
baby, staring at my strange face with his round, hawk-like
eyes, set up a wail of dismay, and I gave him back to his
mother, who received him effusively, evidently much flattered,
for mothers are always the same. She came and sat in our
tent, and I gave the baby a piece of sugar, which fortunately
did not choke him.

Our start from Fedahlah was delayed owing to Mooleeta
having developed a bad back. The difficulty was smoothed
by Ayesha, who insisted on our having the better of the two
donkeys owned by the village. There was one horse, which
she strongly recommended; but we decided upon the donkey,
and Ayesha's husband mounted the horse and accompanied
us, taking a friend to sit behind him for part of the journey.
Ayesha in parting made us a pretty speech, saying that
though we were going away we should always remain in
Ayesha's heart. Her husband had just returned from fishing,
and presented us with six sea-bream, caught by a rod and
line from the rocks in a small bay.

It was a weary, trying march, the wind blowing very
strong, and occasional slight showers of rain. Mooleeta
delayed us several times by insisting on exploring every
village she saw in the distance, making off at full gallop,
with all the Moors except the Kaid in hot pursuit. By her
various antics and her love of a stampede, she had won from
the Moors the title of 'Mooleeta, the Racer.' They are fond
of giving names of this kind, and Mehemmet was called

Mehemmet the Good; why I do not know, except that he adopted a pose of extreme virtue, which I frequently found covered pecuniary transactions.

On the way we passed ruined townships. We were getting into the country of ruins, and there can be no doubt that the cruelty of the Kaids has diminished the population, which state of things extends through this part of Morocco and as far as the Sus country. The wind blew hard in our faces, and when Casa Blanca came in sight I told the Kaid to stay with Mrs. Greathed, and Conrad went away at a gallop. At Captain Cobb's house, whither my letters had been sent, I was received most kindly, and I accepted a kind invitation on behalf of Mrs. Greathed to put up there.

The tent was pitched inside the town, and when I reached it I found that the Bashaw had already sent his soldiers with the customary polite messages and the offer of a house. But the tent was up, and I wanted some dinner, and set to work to get it and to feed Conrad and Mooleeta. As I was watching a mutton chop, the soldiers returned with great swagger, bearing presents—two sugar-loaves, two packets of green tea, two packets of candles—and renewed the offer of a house, promising me at the same time a dinner, also guards to insure my safety for the night After the soldiers had departed, and all the green tea and one sugar-loaf and one packet of candles had been handed over to the Kaid, I went on cooking my mutton chop, not relying too much upon the dinner, and not knowing how late it might arrive.

Meantime the sun had dropped, and was gone altogether below the level of the town walls, sinking somewhere into the sea. I have observed that when the sun sets over or near the sea, there is a soft gray light after sunset, almost like our twilight at home. And I think this must be the reflection from the surface of the water of the light left in the sky.

I was taking advantage of this light to eat my chop in the

door of my tent, when, on looking up, I saw before me a
superb creature, who appeared like a vision. There, in that
pale silver light which lent mystery to the atmosphere, about
thirty yards from my tent, was a milk-white Arab steed,
whose tall rider was clad in a scarlet robe reaching down to
his burnished silver stirrups. His blue cloak was thrown
back, and hung in a long fold from his shoulder, disclosing
the fine white lining. A haik of the most transparent texture
was folded about his head, and framed the face with the
keen dark eyes, fine nose, and close-kept beard of an Arab
type. The horse's long white tail and mane were combed
to the last hair, and the scarlet harness embossed with silver
was beautiful and new. Beside this grandee there walked
on foot a tall officer, wrapped in a blue cloak, with high
leather boots of red morocco. This man was followed by a
troop of soldiers in long white cloaks and pointed scarlet
fez, who stopped abruptly at the word of command.

I left my chop, and called to the Kaid to know who this
dignified personage might be and why he came there. He
was the Kaid of the Bashaw's bodyguard, and he had come
to post my guards for the night. He rode solemnly round
my camp, posting twenty guards two and two at regular
intervals, and then, accompanied by his lieutenant on foot,
he rode as solemnly away.

When I had finished my chop, I sat by my camp-fire
watching the stars come out one by one. The wind had
sunk, and it was comparatively peaceful. The horses and
mules, tethered in a row just in front of me, were still
feeding, and the men in their tent lighted a candle, and were
busy telling stories and waiting patiently for the arrival of
the Bashaw's dinner.

Suddenly I heard the guards challenge someone, and the
answer rang out sharp and clear, ' Bashaw ! Bashaw !' As
fast as possible out of the darkness stepped the soldiers,
their white cloaks and pointed fez shining in the dim lantern

light behind two enormous trays with conical covers. Under
the first was a gigantic kouskous, and under the second a
savoury stew of vegetables and meat, with loaves of bread
set round it. The Bashaw sent me this dinner, and hoped
I should spend a good night. Bakshish, salaama, and departure. I sat down and made a hole in the kouskous, and
ate some of the stew, which was really excellent, and then
I summoned the Kaid to take it away, reserving for myself
a loaf of bread.

Soon after I retired to rest, but not to sleep, for the twenty
guards kept themselves awake by playing upon twenty instruments. There was the honest and humble-minded tom-
tom, but others were fifes, and never were fifes so shrill and
bedevilled. Tom-toms are never tuneful, so they are never
out of tune; these fifes squeaked and quavered and trilled
up and down and in all directions, getting wilder and more
wicked as the night wore on. Up to this point I had wished
again and again that Mrs. Greathed had still been with me,
but, knowing that she was tired, and that the travelling had
worn her somewhat, I was glad that she should have the
shelter of such comfortable quarters as those offered us by
Captain Cobb. The noise all night was trying, and it was
not till the sun rose and the guards departed that I closed
my eyes.

It was my intention to do what the authorities in this
place wished, for I felt that to attempt to please myself
would be fatal. The worst of it was that there was so much
variety in the advice given me that it was by no means easy
to see my way. I should have preferred camping outside
the town, but the British Consul and the Bashaw were
against this. The Bashaw pressed his house; the British
Consul advised a Spanish hotel. The house was dirty and
uninviting; the hotel was in the heart of the town, and I
should have been separated from my horse. To stay where
I was was not only uncomfortable, but I was to have the

nuisance of twenty guards every night. I thought it would
be as well to see how far the authorities would play their
game, so I started in the afternoon to ride out of the town
and camp near the cemetery.

As I was leaving some things belonging to Mrs. Greathed
at Captain Cobb's house, I was met by the Vice-Consul,
who had come down from the Consulate to tell me that if I
camped outside the Bashaw would send me twenty guards
—I, of course, to pay 20 pesetas, or as many more as I
pleased—but *he would not be responsible for my safety*.

I saw that it was nothing more than a dodge to get
twenty pesetas a night out of me. Besides, I suspected that
the soldiers were in league with the cattle-thieves, and some
of them looked raw and fresh from the profession, and
probably the Bashaw had more than an official acquaintance
with the thieves themselves. But this was the way the
Bashaw would get 20 pesetas. He would not be responsible, and the British Consul would take care not to make
him responsible, and I should lose my animals.

At this juncture Captain Cobb came on the scene, and
offered to put up my horse and mule, and take in all my
luggage, and myself into the bargain, and this offer I grate-
fully accepted. Subsequently Conrad, Mooleeta, and the
Kaid's old gray were kindly taken in by Mr. Butler, whose
stables were close by, and who allowed me to go and see
my animals whenever I wished. And so that evening found
me once more in company with the kind companion of
my travels, and under the hospitable roof of an Eastern
American we were in most luxurious quarters.

Captain Cobb has an acquaintance of some thirty years
with Morocco. He came to Casa Blanca almost direct from
Gibraltar, where he had taken his disabled ship, and with an
American's perspicacity he erected a steam-mill for grinding
corn. He was much interested to hear how many locusts
we had met with; and between Rabat and Fedahlah we had

passed a vast number of 'voet-gangers,' as they call them in South Africa.

The locust in this crawling stage is most destructive. They climb trees and walls, and will invade towns. They proceed straight forward on their march, and once, on making inquiry as to what they found in a lean-looking, little back-country town in Cape Colony, I was told that first they ate the people's washing which was hanging out to dry, and that then they ate their boots, and that, such aliment having refreshed them, they went on their way greatly invigorated.

Certain is it that very little is refused by them. But linseed, a crop grown only of late years in Morocco, generally escapes. Potatoes are devoured here, though I have heard they are refused elsewhere. Tomatoes, which were generally refused in the South, are eaten to the stalk in Morocco.

In Casa Blanca alone 700 dollars a day was paid for a month for locusts' eggs gathered by the natives and brought in to be destroyed. At first they were thrown into the sea, but they were washed back again, and the natives gathered them and resold them to the Government, which they could easily do, for many of the eggs were picked up on sand after rain, and consequently in as wet and messy a state as though they had been in the deep.

A great variety of grain crops form the exports from Casa Blanca. There is one called el dorah, which grows like a bamboo with a tassel at the top. The seed is excellent for fowls, and the natives make bread of it. It grows principally about Tangiers. Fenugreek is exported from Casa Blanca, canary seed, coriander seed, and maize. Linseed is increasing. Lentils vary in quantity, and go principally to France. Beans are a large export, though Egypt competes, the Egyptians getting into the London market earlier and better cleaned. The most important crop is garbanzos, or chick-peas. These are taken by Spain, but some are bought for France.

The cereal trade of Morocco is a valuable one, and could be increased were the peasants encouraged to settle and cultivate their land. In the neighbourhood of Casa Blanca much more is done than round Rabat, partly because more protection has been given to the natives, and partly because the people are not so unsettled by the proximity of lawless tribes. The thieving is no doubt very troublesome, for I did not meet anyone who had travelled much in this neighbourhood who had not lost a camel, or horse, or mule.

The chief trade of Morocco is that of great export houses, who buy the produce either direct from the peasants or in partidos (small parcels) from the small Jew traders. The great houses bulk the produce and find a market oversea.

Owing to the ravages of locusts, a check has been given to a trade which might have developed encouragingly, and even led to improvements in the ports. But besides locusts there is a blight which sometimes attacks the beans. It appears to come after a north-westerly wind, and the result is that the whole crop looks as if a fire had passed over it. One season the wind came late, and the beans escaped, but the peas were destroyed.

These blights, in addition to other drawbacks, render a trade dependent upon cereals precarious and speculative. As there is no prospect of any increase in the shipping, it would not answer, even with official sanction, to sink much capital in improving the port of Casa Blanca. The best policy would be to connect Casa Blanca overland with Rabat, and then improve the port. Freights rule very high, partly on account of the delay of steamers—too high, considering the prices of goods in the country; consequently the small importer, the struggling new man, suffers to extinction. But the established firms, which have commodious warehouses and capital to back them, charter sailing-vessels, or even steamers, as they require them, load them with Norwegian lumber or paraffin, and return them with a cargo of hides or cereals.

Such business can be done incidentally as part of a 'going concern,' but not independently. I heard of an American sailing-vessel which came into Casa Blanca with a cargo of Florida pine, which was immediately bought up by a large local house. Once a German attempted to import lumber, but the price was put down, and he was compelled to sell at a loss.

European traders now begin to find competition trying them, which is another evidence that the market has a very slight backing, that it does not expand, and cannot be made to expand owing to the oppression of the Government. It is practically impossible to find out what the population of Morocco may be. I have heard it said that it is somewhere between 4,000,000 and 8,000,000. Whether it increases or decreases is also as uncertain, but I believe there is little doubt that agriculturists diminish. There is a tendency to leave the land where their crops may be seized at any moment for additional taxes, and to crowd round towns where Europeans reside, and where they can live by picking up a trifle by doing odd jobs, and taking care to spend it before the Kaid can get hold of it.

It is quite impossible to find out the actual rate of profit made by the Moorish firms which trade between Marseilles and Morocco, and Manchester and Morocco. They buy goods to be delivered principally in Fez, and trade with the interior. They work more economically than the European houses, and therefore they can no doubt secure a profit, though they undercut in prices. They are very secret in their business, which is not to be wondered at, seeing how active the officials are in scenting out any Moor who can be squeezed for taxes.

But the Europeans compete amongst themselves in two ways, both as buyers and sellers. In times of drought and scarcity there are now so many buyers that the prices of cereals rise to figures which render the trade unremunerative. The Germans are sometimes reckless buyers. The Jews speculate in wheat and barley. As the export of these crops is prohibited, they buy to store, and sell on a rise in price.

So far as selling goes, the Germans have unquestionably laid hold of the cheap market. But this does not advance trade as it would in another country. Elsewhere the cheap market is made by encouraging people to buy who never bought before, and so extending the market. In this country it has acted chiefly by pulling down prices; people who bought before buy now, but they buy cheaper than before. As they have established by these means good relations with the natives, the Germans will, in event of any change taking place for the better in Morocco, be the first to benefit, and German trade will rise on the basis of the cheap market, which the British could not retain.

Morocco is not a country which lends itself to the compiling of reports. I never was anywhere where statistics or figures helped one so little. 'They wrote to me from Washington,' said Captain Cobb, 'to send them a report of the cholera. So I started out to see what I could do, and I met two Moors dragging a dead one. So I said : " What killed that man ?" And they said : " Allah—Allah killed him." I went a little further and met another, and I asked, " What killed that man ?" and they said : " Allah." So I came back, and wrote to say that I had seen two dead Moors, and the people said God had killed them, and that was all I knew.' What occurred in Washington when this report was received I do not know, but the account gives an absolutely just idea of some of the obstacles in the way of making reports, and the value of some reports when made.

CHAPTER XVIII

A RUINED TRIBE—A MOORISH FEAST—FRIENDLY MOORS—
MOORISH CHARITY—CHILD MARRIAGES—THE BASHAW

In Casa Blanca I heard about the tribe which was imprisoned in Rabat. Fortune smiled upon them once, and
sent them the singular blessing of an honest Governor
whose name was Shaaki. He levied taxes fairly, and his
people prospered so that none of them desired Protection.
Shaaki was very proud of this, and by keeping so many
of his people about him, and even encouraging others to
come and settle there, he obtained a large population who
were thus able to subscribe the legal taxes without difficulty. When destitute families from elsewhere arrived in
his Bashalate, Shaaki lent them donkeys for ploughing, till
they became prosperous.

As the Bashalate grew rich, other Moors desired to get
the Bashalate of M'zaab, and an intrigue was started to
induce the late Sultan to put Shaaki in prison. But Sir
John Drummond Hay getting wind of it, wrote the Sultan
a letter, so that Shaaki lived and died Governor of
M'zaab. After Shaaki there came a man as Governor who
ground the peasants and was probably the cause of the
rebellion. He had no doubt paid a large sum to be made
Governor of so populous and prosperous a Bashalate, and it
may well have been expected of him by the Court to raise
a larger revenue than Shaaki could be made to do—seeing
that Shaaki had won the respect of the British Ambassador.

13

When the Sultan dies the Government ceases to exist *pro tem.;* and this is generally the signal for rebellion and all kinds of lawlessness. In the general confusion the M'zaab tribe revolted in the hope of getting rid of their Bashaw. Probably they hoped to get Shaaki's son appointed in place of the man who had been set over them.

The Governor defended himself in his kasbah with ammunition which he had purchased himself. But his courage and resource did not avail him much, for the Sultan put him in gaol, where he is to this day. As soon as the Sultan felt himself strong enough, he sent an army into the country to punish the tribe. The rebels, hearing what was coming, fled from the district, taking with them all they could carry away. Those who had not joined in the rebellion saw no cause for apprehension and remained on their land in peace. But the troops, having received orders to 'eat up' the tribe, proceeded to do so. They burnt, they slew, they ravaged, they took hundreds of defenceless prisoners, who were treated with the utmost cruelty, so that a good percentage died on the journey to the prison at Rabat. Under such a government it is scarcely to be wondered at if the natives long for some other power in the land than His Shereefian Majesty. Subsequently young Shaaki was appointed Governor, and if the Sultan did not press him for money, he would be a fairly good Bashaw; but this obliges him to be hard at times upon the peasants. Neither has he his father's contented mind, but is said to be imbued with the Moorish love for 'making a pile.'

While I was in Casa Blanca, a feast took place—the feast of first-fruits—and the people held a kind of fair with swings mainly got up by Spaniards. Fathers took their children to the soko and bought them cheap fairings. The first-fruits consisted of walnuts, dates and raisins. Walnuts and dates should always be eaten together, say those who know what is good.

In Casa Blanca this feast is associated with the death of some old man who appears to have been a kind of Guy Fawkes in his day. At all events, he is held up to public execration, and boys and men go from house to house beating tom-toms and asking for money to bury this legendary offender. The better-class Moors indulge in much eating and drinking, and I was always tumbling over some servant or slave engaged in cutting the throat of a fowl in the middle of the street, which unlucky bird was to decorate the kouskous that evening.

One morning I was drinking tea with a friendly Moor, and trying to make the best use of such Arabic as I had picked up. I had a man with me to interpret; but whether one's interpreter is good or bad it is never quite the same thing as knowing even a few words for one's self, and I would rather make a mistake now and again with a little knowledge than be without it altogether.

As we sat on our cushions in an upper room, the Moor asked why I travelled in Morocco, concealing a smile as he spoke by peeping into the teapot. I said that I travelled to see the country and the Moors, in whom I took an interest, and also because I had learnt to love Africa down in the South. He seemed to understand my view perfectly, and to grasp the situation directly, asking me several questions about India, so that I wished I had had Mrs. Greathed with me, for she could have answered them far better than I did.

In common with most of his people, this Moor regretted that Morocco should be 'surrounded' by the French, while the Sultan was too young to cope with his many difficulties. To my surprise this man seemed quite alive to many things which might be done 'to make Barbary better,' and put his finger on the spot when he said that the great evil in his country was that 'Moors ate each other.' He pointed out in his own way the insecurity and confusion inside, and the outside steady pressure to which the country was subjected.

He referred several times to the French advance, from
Tuat to Igli—Igli to Tafilat.

But few Moors are either as clever or as enlightened as
this man. In talking to them I was sometimes amazed at
their ignorance. They are very astute in asking questions,
which they have a remarkable knack of arranging so as to
form a conclusive argument. To a Moor, Morocco is the
greatest country in the world. They do not believe that
France can compare with it in any respect, but she is a
nasty thing which they would like to drive into the sea and
drown, and it is a mystery to them why Allah does not do it
for them. Some of them have heard of the British Empire,
and they catch at the association with India, and at rumours
of prosperity in Egypt, which opens a vista of possibilities
for Barbary. Not that the Moors would submit themselves
to any outside rule. The world is divided like this—the
Moors are men, and their right place is on the top of the
world. They are the faithful and the elect of God. But
there are Christian dogs and Jews. The Christian dogs are
divided into many sorts, but the kind which the Moors object
to least is the English. They point out with charming
frankness that the English are very useful to the Moors.
They bring money into the country, which the Moors get
hold of. They have a gift for doctoring complaints—that is
why Allah sends them to the coast of Barbary. And besides,
certain English merchants have won their respect by neither
allowing the Moors to cheat them nor condescending to
sharp practice themselves. Even in Casa Blanca I heard
from Moors the term 'Consul Spinney's word,' and the
Moor who used it put his finger on his lips, signifying that
Mr. Spinney's word was as good as his bond. Not that
Mr. Spinney stood alone in this respect, but he was certainly
a grand instance of a man who made himself trusted and
respected by natives in a land where no son trusts his father,
and no father trusts his son.

Europeans may be sure that a Moor's heart is full when
his purse is full. He will never make a friend of a Christian,
but curiosity will carry him some way in asking questions
and listening to the answers, and he is the most hospitable
man on the face of the earth. They would sit asking me
questions for hours, till I became fairly exhausted with
giving simple accounts of what were really large problems.
But I knew that though they seemed to be learning the
questions by heart, and pondering over them, they would go
away unchanged in a single opinion or feeling; and all they
had heard had no other effect than the passing pleasure and
slight stimulant which a Western gets by smoking a good
cigar. But at all events I was at least a *good* cigar, and it
became almost a habit with some of them to ask me to dine
in order to enjoy one of these extraordinary talks, and I went
because they were certainly showing me a scrap of humanity
which was as novel to me as I was to them.

Of this I am quite sure, that no attempt at playing Moslem
will advance one in their confidence or esteem. But I think
it is a mistake to suppose that they dislike Jews more than
they do Christians upon religious grounds. On one occasion
a Moor first asked me if I were a Jew, and being answered
in the negative, he turned his head aside, and said : ' Nevertheless, I believe you *are* a Jew.' I told him at once that if
he disbelieved me I would drink no tea, and rose to depart;
but he called me back with many apologies, and I pointed
out to him that his sin (which Allah would remember) was
that he had doubted my word, and, like a naughty child, he
proceeded to make it up with me by putting extra sugar in
the tea, and patting the cushion for me to sit down upon.

The term ' The mad Christians,' which they apply to the
English, I at first mistook for contempt. I believe, however,
that from a Moor it indicates their belief that we are in some
way enjoying a certain amount of favour from Allah, which
makes us different from other Christian dogs, and naturally

we do things which cannot be judged by the same standards, which is why some of them adopted an indulgent and even solicitous tone in speaking to me, and overcame some things which otherwise would have shocked them.

'Does the date-palm grow in your country?' I was asked.

'No,' I answered.

'Do oranges like these grow in your country?'

'No.'

'But olives—it may be that they grow in your country?'

'No.'

'Allah!   But what *does* grow in your country?'

'Oats,' I replied with warmth.

'Otis?   Ah!'   Then they chattered among themselves, agreeing that oats were a weed. 'Otis' are of no account in Barbary.

By this means they have demonstrated that Morocco is a very superior country to England.   England evidently has nothing in it.   But suddenly they are confounded by remembering that the English are very rich and very strong. How *can* that be?   No dates—no oranges—no olives—and yet they are rich : where do they get their money from?

Someone suggests they get it out of their ships.   True! the English have many ships.   The French have ships, but they are poor ships; the English have *many* ships!   How many ships has the Sultan of England?   They *must* be many, for the Englishwoman says she does not know how many. But I—Omar—have seen all the ships of the Sultan of England.   They came to Tangiers.   How many were there? Well, it was in this wise : the son of the Sultan of England was in a ship, and so the Sultan sent all his ships to take care of his son, and they came to Tangiers, which was as close to Barbary as they could come.   They came in and said 'Bow!' and the Bashaw said 'Bow!' and the ships went away again to take care of the son of the Sultan of England. ' O son of a talking ass, how many ships didst thou see?'

' Well, there were—Wahad, thenine——' And the Moor
began to count on his fingers till he got to three, which he
called 'klatter.' He broke off to describe the size of the
ships, which digression drove the rest of the company wild,
for what they wanted to know was the number.

' Nobody knows how many there are ! The Englishwoman herself does not know how many !'

I said : ' There were, I believe, eighteen all told ; but the
King has a great many more ships than that.'

' Yes, we know that very well. He has ships which come
to Casa Blanca and take away beans; but they do not say
" Bow!" and what we want to know is how many ships the
Sultan of England has which can say " Bow!"' '

' Yes, truly ; that is what Moors wish to know, for it is
out of *them* that the English get their money.'

' Those which went with the son of the Sultan of England,'
remarked Omar, ' could all say " Bow!"' '

' Truly we believe thee ! The Sultan of England is a just
Sovereign, wise and merciful. He has many ships to make
his people rich, and he sends his son in them that he may
receive much wealth. Yea, he and his friends will return
with many presents and much tribute. It is well to be
friends with the English.'

In Casa Blanca there are a good many Moors who are
traders of considerable substance. They are charitable
according to their light, and consequently there are a great
many beggars—blind, halt, and maimed, lazy or needy.
Doubtless their histories would be worth inquiring into.
They form a kind of fraternity or society amongst themselves, and steal from each other with impunity, for no one
would heed their appeal for justice.

The wretched women, some bent with age, others merely
reckless, whose husbands divorced them or else were perhaps
rotting in gaol, had once been the fairly well-to-do inhabitants of some country village. Now, with every vestige

of self-respect gone, they fought and wrangled and cheated over the handful of blanquillo which we distributed after Friday's mosque. Amongst them I frequently saw children, but as a rule Allah is kind, and removes these poor little souls almost before they are old enough to know the very worst. But upon the back of some loud-tongued, swearing beggar mother a little infant may be seen, his head pillowed upon the dirty rags which partially concealed her person, and there it sleeps the sound and guileless sleep of a baby, with a face like a little angel's, in spite of the yells and execrations which rend the air around.

The dreadful evil of child-marriages was obvious in this neighbourhood. At Rabat I saw a child of ten years old being taken to be married. She was very much dressed and her face was elaborately painted. I do not suppose that actual marriage followed immediately, but a ceremony which consigned her to a certain bridegroom was gone through, and I believe he could claim her at any time. In Casa Blanca matters go much further; and it is not an uncommon case to see two children slapping each other, and find out on inquiry that they are mother and daughter.

A very worrying practice was that of putting children in irons for some trivial offence, such as playing truant. I have seen a poor little boy so heavily ironed that he could scarcely drag himself along. The sound of clanking chains is always a miserable one, but to see a child's limbs being twisted by them is most heart-rending.

I often passed by the house of the Bashaw, and before I left I went to take leave of him. He was a very benevolent-looking old gentleman, with a countenance such as a country clergyman in England might possess. But appearances were never so deceptive. He bore anything but a good character, and the unpleasant sound of someone being beaten was too common. I believe it is quite true that he condemns the prisoner brought before him to be beaten—

not to receive a definite number of lashes, but *to be beaten at his pleasure.* While the beating is going on he resumes his writing, which probably consists of adding up his accounts. When they are tired of beating the prisoner they ask the Bashaw if he has had enough. The Bashaw leans forward and examines the prisoner over his spectacles for a minute, and then says, ' You may go on—go on a little more,' and resumes his occupation. The awful state to which this callous cruelty reduced the prisoners was enough to demoralize any town.

I believe it was to this Bashaw that Captain Cobb was one day talking of the Far West. It is true that the Captain came from the Nutmeg State of Connecticut, where they are so rich in inventions that perchance you may buy wooden nutmegs, seeing that the country does not produce them, and gun flints, made of horn, so resourceful are the people of that province. But the Captain was talking of California. ' Where is that place ?' inquired the Bashaw. ' I guess you'd find it six thousand miles further west,' replied the Captain. ' I'd like to go to it,' said the Bashaw—' I'd like to go there to see the sun set.'

So spoke the Governor of the promising commercial city of Dar el Beida, otherwise known as Casa Blanca, who rules without aid of Mayor, Corporation, or Council.

Were the seaport improved by a mole from the rocks, a crane, and a landing-stage, Casa Blanca would develop rapidly. The element of trade is much stronger here than in other towns. The European merchants live in comfortable houses, surrounded with lovely gardens, where trees of heliotrope and masses of pink climbing geranium and blue idumea cover the walls, while the borders are full of larkspur, lilies, sweet-peas, carnations, and stocks. There are gravel-walks carefully swept, and even some attention is given to landscape gardening.

All this points to a large number of well-to-do Europeans

who have granted protection to a number of peasants, who form a prosperous foundation for trade.

Much might be done in finding fresh uses for some of the seeds grown in Morocco. There are some whose very names are unknown in the English markets and whose value is little understood even in Morocco. But the feeling is very decided that Great Britain is losing prestige in Morocco. Claims brought forward by the best of the merchant houses receive but scanty attention, and remain so long unsettled that business is becoming restricted through want of confidence. There is a misfit somewhere in the machinery which other nations have known how to prevent.

Casa Blanca's place in the merchant world is that of a seaport without ships, without wharves, without docks or landing-stages. On the occasion of a ship coming into the roadstead and sounding her horn there is a flutter and a commotion on shore. Lighters sail out to fetch the cargo and sail back again—if they can, and are not driven to the other side of the bay, some six miles out of the town. When, by good luck, they reach the shore, the cargo is flung out on the beach, and the lighter sails back again.

When there is no ship the town is rather quiet and time hangs a bit heavily. During my visit the tedium was relieved by the caprice of a mule, who learnt to pitch her voice exactly to the note of a steamer's whistle. She could deceive even Captain Cobb, and many's the time that Mrs. Greathed put on her bonnet and prepared to pay farewell visits prior to embarking, when she was stopped by the announcement : ' It's that blasted mule again, I declare !'

CHAPTER XIX

ON May 5 I rode out of Casa Blanca on my way to Azemour.
I missed Mrs. Greathed very much, and I was very sorry to
say good-bye to Captain Cobb, who had been the kindest
possible host, and in whose comfortable domicile I felt
myself back in the Far West under the Stars and Stripes
instead of in the circumscribed limits of an Eastern town,
with the barbarous rule of the Red Flag all around me. The
track was uninteresting. It dipped into a gorge and rose on
the other side with palm-trees cutting the sky-line; otherwise, except for locusts in the creeping stage, and for an
encounter with the late Grand Vizier, Sidi Moktar, the road
was dull enough.

First I met all the Grand Vizier's wives and his harem.
There was a strong armed escort. The women were about
forty in number, and very closely veiled. Each woman rode,
dressed in white, on her own mule in a Moorish saddle.
They looked like so many stuffed dolls, and were to me a
horrible sight, but quite outdone by the Grand Vizier. He
was a particularly revolting-looking black (or nearly black),
and had the audacity to pull his very handsome gray mule
into the same track or rut in which I was riding. He did
this deliberately; and, as Conrad hates a mule, I could calcu-
late in a moment what the consequences would be, and knew

that I should not care to interfere. However, Allah ordained
that just as this son of the Faithful was composing his vile
countenance into a disgusting leer, his mule shied—possibly
at my hat—and took him bundling and scuffling into the
palmetto scrub, so that Conrad never altered his stride.
Had I known at the time that this was Sidi Moktar—the
great man in disgrace—on his way to prison, stripped and
penniless, I might have been less angry. He had been dismissed from office and ordered to Mequinez, and as he was
escaping with his money and his wives, he was overtaken
at a soko and his money officially looted. The exact sum
is not known. There were seventeen mules loaded with
dollars, and as his captors were in a hurry, they contented
themselves with measuring the cash in muids. Shortly after
we had passed him we met about fifty camels and some
asses carrying the tents, mattresses, kouskous dishes, and
other camp fittings of the late Grand Vizier. In spite of his
ruin the whole thing had a sumptuous air, and I could not
help contrasting the life of such a man with that of the
oppressed, down-trodden, starving peasants as, bending
under their loads, they trudged along with their meagre,
heavily-laden donkeys.

My new muleteer was not satisfactory. He rode on a
mule and loitered with acquaintances. I rode up a hill,
and saw him in the distance smoking cigarettes, his complexion shaded by my parasol, to which he had helped himself. He was presently 'rounded up,' and feeling that he
had made a mistake, imagined that he could atone for it by
driving his mule hard, torturing the brute with a pack-needle
to make it go.

A thunderstorm was brewing, and I decided to camp at
the first village. Hardly was the tent pitched before the
lightning commenced, drawing patterns in the sky which
assumed all manner of colours—pink, violet, yellow, green.
The thunder rolled, the distant sea roared, and the rain

thrashed the roof of the tent, wherein I sat eating cold roast mutton and drinking coffee cooked over my spirit-lamp.

After a time the artillery in the heavens ceased, the clouds rolled by, and the moon came out white and resplendent. But the animals had not settled down, and hardly was I in bed when a stampede occurred, led, I believe, by Mooleeta. I never knew Conrad use his freedom except to come nearer to where I was. But Mooleeta was off, leading the Kaid's old gray, and stirring up the animals in the village. All my Moors got up and joined in the pursuit. Mooleeta was the first to be captured, but the Kaid went on, and I could see him in a moonlight which was as clear as day whirling round and round after his weird old horse, which looked as if it had stepped out of a tapestry, and screaming at it like a cockatoo.

The shortness of the first day's march obliged us to follow it with a very long one. We went through a country of low bushes about four feet high, which had been trimmed by browsing goats and camels. At intervals the ground was black with locusts. The natives were doing what they could to destroy them by sweeping them up, and either burying them or taking them away in sacks. We halted for lunch by a ruined waterwheel. Ruined kasbahs, and ruined rich Moors' houses were the camping-ground for peasants, who herded their cattle at night inside the spacious courtyards; ruined, roofless cottages stood in fields which had gone back to weeds; peasants of the most poor and destitute class were to be seen at work here and there. At intervals the Sultan has planted kasbahs or fondaks for the protection of travellers, but if people are starving, it is not to be wondered at that they thieve. The pitiful part of it is that no amount of industry will help them. At one time Captain Cobb had tried to introduce American ploughs. The natives were delighted with them, but the price—ten dollars—staggered them. He afterwards tried simple farm implements, but

with the same results. The natives were afraid to buy them.
Labour was cheap, for human life is nothing accounted of in
Morocco. But no one, even if he had the capital, would
dare to show he had ten dollars to spend on a plough.
Saints, Bashaws, Kaids, Sultan, would all suddenly remember
that they wanted a lamb, an ox, a sheep, or a carpet. If a
man had, by any chance, a few dollars, he dug a hole in the
ground for them and tried to forget them.

The muleteer wanted to go through to Azemour in the
day, which would have meant ten hours on the road; but I
would not hear of it, as I wished to keep my own animals
fresh. So after eight hours I told the Kaid that we must
stop somewhere. He recommended me to go to the house
of the Bashaw of the district, which we accordingly did.

It was a large house. The entire space walled in was
about 4 acres, as near as I could judge, but its condition
was ruinous. It was built by the predecessor of the present
Kaid, who was a rich man. The outer wall was some 20
feet high, and the great gate was guarded by soldiers. The
present Kaid's name was El Haîma. He was very poor, and
had to make what he could out of the peasants.

When the guards, who were sitting in the gateway, saw
me coming, they rose and ran inside to give warning; then
they returned and walked in with me.

The Kaid was sitting in an alcove doing 'injustice,' and
it thrilled me to think that I was standing where so many
wretched people had trembled, and that immediately behind
me was the court, where they were held down to be flogged
—flogged to death sometimes—because they had been a little
more industrious and intelligent than others.

The Kaid sat there with his rosary in his hand, for the
religious order he belonged to always carries a rosary. He
asked who I was and where I came from, was I French or
English. He read the letter from Sidi Torres, and was as
polite and smooth in manner as possible, but was afraid to

betray ignorance by asking too many questions. He was
deeply interested in the account which the Kaid gave him of
some sanitas which I had put on the Kaid's bad finger and
on Mooleeta's back. It was new to him that English people
were 'doctrinas' for horses and mules. The crowd of
guards which had collected smothered a laugh when my
Kaid told them of the care bestowed on my animals. The
Kaid remarked that English people were different to Moors.
They were a curious people; he believed they cared much
for trifles. By the way, was I a missionary? This displeased my Kaid, who had not felt that his finger was a
trifle, and who had no liking for missionaries, and, to my
amazement, he proceeded to give an account of my fortune
and estate, of the great dignity of my family, and the deep
anxiety which the Sultan of England himself felt as to how
Moors would behave to me in Morocco.

The Kaid was so fierce that they actually believed him,
and the Bashaw rose from his cushion in haste and some
confusion, evidently feeling that our pleasant chat was over,
and that he must exert himself if he meant to save his neck.
He walked away, carrying Sidi Torres' letter in his hand,
which he took at once to his Kalipha, timidly indicating
before he left that his horses and mules were here and there,
if the Englishwoman wished to see them. Of course, I
assented, and, accompanied by all the guards, went round
the two courtyards. Some of the animals were saddled, and
ready to start for anywhere at any time. They were none of
them of much account. The favourite horse was a fat black
—a cart-horse in front, but with bad hindquarters. The
guards admired it immensely; but my Kaid, who knew
what I thought, winked at me and said nothing, so of course
I praised it. Another was more the stamp of an English
hack, but would have sold well at £30 in the London
market. Yet another was there, lean and scraggy, with
a sore back. This the guards condemned, but it was,

nevertheless, a better stamp of horse than either of the
other two.

As we were leaving the courtyard the Kaid came towards
us.   He was more at ease in his manner.   He stopped short
and bowed, saying the usual 'Babbicum,' and handed me
back Sidi Torres' letter with a smile.   He laid a fat hand
somewhere under his chin, and assured me that he wel-
comed me with all his heart.   His voice was soft and
musical, but he would have spoken in the same tone had he
sentenced a peasant to have his throat cut.   I thanked him,
and went back to my tent, followed by all the loungers as
far as the gate.   Better manners no one could have had than
these guards.   Once satisfied that I was English, they
became almost confidential.   My clothes, especially my
hat, struck them, but from first to last there was nothing
rude or familiar in their behaviour.   It was most unlucky
that I could not talk to them.   My acquaintance with
Arabic only enabled me to catch what was being said
sometimes.

The evening was chilly, and it was getting dark, so on my
return I set the tea-things, and sat on my bed writing while
the water boiled.   Meantime, I saw a servant mounted on
a mule, with wide, gaping panniers, ride swiftly out of the
Kaid's house.   He was going to rob the peasants to get the
things from them which the Kaid would present to me.   A
big sugar-loaf, a packet of candles, and some tea arrived,
and were brought to my tent.   Scarcely had I thanked the
bearers for these than three poor hens and a score of eggs
were added to the accumulation at the door of the tent, and,
lastly, a sack of barley for my animals.

Tea was just finished when my Kaid introduced a stately
individual clothed in flowing white raiment, who carried in
his hands a small basin crammed with Moorish butter.   This
was the Kalipha or Deputy-Governor, who came to make me
welcome.   He nodded to me, and even smiled, but his

dignified manner and the sweep of his drapery seemed too much for me in my tent, where I sat on the edge of my camp-bed. He sat down on his heels, but I offered him a small stool, and he sat down on this, looking grander than ever. I offered him coffee, which he graciously accepted, and it interested him enormously to watch me make it. He was very silent, even reticent, nor would he give himself away by evincing surprise; but when he saw me light my spirit-lamp on the table he shot keen glances at the operation, and scrutinized me to make sure that his eyes had not deceived him. I felt very much like a conjurer giving an entertainment to an audience of one. He spoke in a short phrase or two to my Kaid, to whom all my ways were familiar, and who took a wicked pleasure in the discomfiture of his own people. The Kalipha said that the English had many things which the Moors had not, adding loftily that Moors did not require them; they were better without them.

When I gave him the coffee, which had plenty of sugar in it, he drew a long draught, smacking his lips out of politeness, and, finding it really good, his eyes brightened, and he settled down to really enjoy it. Truly Allah permits the Nazarene to know things which He conceals from Moslems. The Kaid agreed, and pointed out that friendship with Christians of the English kind was advantageous to Moors, for their cleverness and the way they cured people had nothing to do with religion. He himself had been cured by me, and yet I had not made him say any prayers or even listen to them. The Kalipha, on hearing this, said that he suffered from a pain, and laid his hand on his stomach. My Kaid ran forward to feel the Kalipha's stomach, and jumped back with a cry of alarm, and begged me to feel it also. In point of fact, the broad sash covered what I believe was an enlarged spleen. I was asked to prescribe, but, feeling that a course of treatment of some weeks would be necessary, I

14

demurred.   And what a pity it seemed !   He was a grand,
stately-looking man, with a face full of fire and energy, a
round head, a good nose and chin, a broad forehead, and a
scar below his turban.   He was a tribesman, and not a town
Moor.   I got out a little remedy which I thought might
relieve him.   He drank it off with an air of grand indifference, the Kaid standing over him and making a great fuss,
as though a troublesome child was being made to take a
nauseous dose.   Then I gave him two pills to take with
him, and, saying 'Salaama,' he rose and left me, walking
with the long stride and dignified manner of his race.
The next morning, before sunrise, and when it was still
dark, I saw him ride out in attendance upon the Kaid to
a soko some five hours away.   He sat his horse like a
Prince, and had far more the air of a Governor than the
Kaid.

The ride to Azemour was rendered unpleasant by a dispute
between the Kaid and my muleteer, Schaiba.   I could not
ascertain its grounds, but I gathered that it arose from the
Kaid taking a high hand with him anent his abominable
cruelties.   He had tied two fowls together, leaving them
each a leg apiece loose, so that they could struggle and
nearly tear each other's legs off.   He picked them up and
threw them about by the string.   I had seen this from my
tent, and, walking towards him, ordered the fowls to be
killed before we went on.   He was very sulky about this,
and muttered a good deal.   By the time I was mounted he
had raised a fury in the Kaid whose existence I never
suspected before.

The white walls of Azemour rise abruptly from the water
on the south side of the river.   It is curious, but all these
towns are built on the south side of their rivers.   The Um
er Rabia is famous for shad, and there were a great many
boats fishing.   The ferry was waiting for us, and we crossed
with less delay than usual.

In the town another dispute occurred between Schaiba and the Kaid. The former was determined to put up in a fondak in the soko, an evil smelling place, and the Kaid, who knew I always camped outside these towns, told him that I should do so here. Nevertheless, Schaiba drove his mules into the fondak, and came to assure me that this was the only place to put up. I had been riding by myself, taking note of the town, and not attending to what was happening. But, seeing this fondak before me, I called the Kaid, and asked, 'Why?' The Kaid replied in the softest and most mellifluous tones that the señorita could camp as usual outside the town if she wished.

After the animals had been watered and fed, I left the muleteers at the camp, and walked into the town with the Kaid, who took that opportunity of telling me that Schaiba was unbearable, adding the pious petition that Allah might leave him without clothes.

I was immensely interested in some of the old houses, which had devices stamped over their doorways. One which I noticed was a Maltese cross. Elsewhere was that unnatural emblem the crescent enclosing a star, which I suppose indicated that the house had been lived in by some of the Turks who in the eighteenth century came to Morocco.

The Jews are all very poor, and live in a crowded state, which must be very unwholesome. I found one who could speak Spanish. He was very civil, and invited me to his house. There was a movement in the crowd, and a young man, feeling his way because he was quite blind, pushed through the people, saying he had 'come to see the Englishwoman.' They laughed at him, but I was struck with his face. It was so intelligent and so bright that it was positively beautiful. I stretched out both my hands to him, saying, 'Feel the Englishwoman's hands.' But he knew very little Spanish. These people have no school and no hospital. This young fellow lost his sight after an illness.

Such Moors as I saw in Azemour looked at me with a very grim expression. The Kaid was several times asked if I were French.

This town is the last town of the kingdom of Fez. It is principally a fort, built by the Portuguese during their invasion in the sixteenth century. Once more I was struck with the fertility of the surrounding country, which might have made a prosperous town. What a number of well-to-do peasants might be living in that rich province of Dukalla! Along the river, as we were crossing it, I saw rich gardens, where life might be spent most pleasantly, while the town itself, situated at the end of a tidal river navigable for at least twenty miles of its course, could be made a collecting centre for the port of Mazagan, with which it might be connected with a light railway. I wondered whether a staple crop, such as cotton, could not be grown in that valley.

On leaving Azemour we appeared to turn inland, but a difference arose between Schaiba and the Kaid, which I settled by telling Schaiba to go in front where I could see him, and the Kaid to stay behind.

For the last stretch of the march we descended upon the shore, and there I saw the remains of the beautiful iridescent bubble called a 'Portuguese man-o'-war' lying on the sands, total wrecks washed up by the tide. I had seen them at Casa Blanca, but here they seemed to abound.

I remained at the camp until the tents were pitched, and then I rode into the town to call at the Consulate, where Mr. Spinney kindly invited me to dine. Later in the evening the Consul's soldier arrived with a complete dinner, most kindly sent by Mrs. Spinney.

The position of my tent was extremely windy; in fact, I had no peace or comfort, except at night, for all day I was plagued with flies and a gale of wind. But I was close to the sea, and my bath could be filled from the sea every day, which was very pleasant.

The Moorish authorities have prohibited the increase of the town of Mazagan by building. They say if people wish to live in a town they can go to Azemour, which is empty; but if Azemour does not suit them, let them come to Marakish. The natives get over the house difficulty by building themselves conical huts outside the radius of the town, so that my tent looked out upon more than one good-sized village.

Protection is viewed controversially here as at Casa Blanca. How otherwise could business be carried on? who would grow enough for export?—ask those in favour of it. A quack remedy, unjust in its very inception, open to corruption. Do away with it, and the Moorish officials will love us and be good, and the Sultan must 'do something'—say those opposed to it.

I find it is difficult to tell what is quackery nowadays, and it was plain to me that the East is so made that the Sultan is an essential part of it; that direct measures of reform are incompatible, if, as they must, they aim at the Court directly. The Court cannot reform.

Business in Morocco is very much what it was two or three hundred years ago, and consists of buying native produce and selling calicoes, and in the difference between gold and silver. There is no such thing as any corporation in the country to compare with the Hudson Bay Company, no mining enterprise such as De Beers. There is no bank or railway passing through the land, leaving everywhere the trail of facilitated and promoted schemes and commercial or industrial concerns bound up with themselves.

The bankers, who are generally called agents, buy produce, cereals, or hides. They ship it for their own account. They draw a bill on their consignee in London for two-thirds of the value of the cargo, and sell this draft to Moors who are requiring British goods. With the proceeds they go on buying produce. The bank sells a draft on Manchester;

the Moor buys it at 38½d., the value of the dollar being less than 36d., and the Moor sends a draft to Manchester for goods : the premium goes to the bank.

The Moors are now great importers of Manchester goods. The goods are shipped in the agent's name, thus giving him a lien, and rendering him secure ; but the Moors pay for them at once on their arrival, because it is to their interest to do so. I am told that this description of business is common all over the East, and that it is quite up to date so far as the East is concerned. But we are accustomed to look to railways, waterworks, tramways, etc., as among the opportunities of a new country.

It would be very difficult to say how much British capital is employed in trade in Morocco. It is said that there is not more than £100,000. On all sides I was told that the profits were not what they used to be, and many merchants seemed greatly disheartened. Nevertheless, Mazagan had increased in importance. It had captured most of the trade of Saffi and rivalled Casa Blanca, some saying that in time it would draw away trade from Casa Blanca as it had from Saffi. The large warehouses in Mazagan which were being erected seemed to substantiate the truth of these statements. There was considerable rivalry among exporters, and the Moors who brought in produce were often in great request. The exports from this port include almonds, both sweet and bitter, gum, walnuts, and cummin-seed.

It was impressed on me that one remedy for oppression lay in the Kaids and Bashaws giving a receipt for taxes. But I failed to see how any such measure, however just in theory, would prevent other injurious practices under a government which is open on all sides to abuses. For instance, M'nebbi, the newly appointed Grand Vizier, intro- duced the payment of taxes in French louis, instead of Moorish dollars. The way it worked was as follows : The Minister of Finance had a deposit of French louis. When the Kaids and Bashaws arrived to pay into the treasury their annual contributions of taxes or tribute, they went, as usual, to the Grand Vizier, who said : ' Go and buy louis ; all taxes are to be paid in louis this year.'   They went to the Minister of Finance, who alone in Marakish had louis to sell, and the Minister sold the louis at a premium of half a dollar on each louis.   This transaction positively raised the value of the louis in Europe.

The Jew is a factor in Barbary which cannot be disregarded, and the French understand that very well.   The position of the Jews in any country is singular.   They are not a class, but a people.   They have no country, and yet they are in nearly every country.   They are not heard as a people ; their great men rise as ' the voice of one,' and the cry is directed towards the whole world.   Perhaps more than any other race, they unite intellect and mental activity with strong energetic character.   For patience, determination, and dogged perseverance they are so remarkable that even the lowest of them offers a stratum on which something might be built.   This is the case in Morocco.   The Jews are actually part of the population, and though I do not believe that they feel any appreciable affection for the land of their birth, there is more homogeneity amongst them and a clearer conception of the wrongs which render the land difficult to live in and impossible to develop.   All nations have had a hand in moulding the Jewish character, and as their methods have been much alike, the Jew is in all countries similar. The hardest point in the Jewish character is his religion—a religion of fear and propitiation.   The orthodox Jew is no less difficult a subject to bring into line with modern affairs than is the Moslem.   Therefore it would be a dire calamity to depend too much upon the Jews in Barbary, because they are better educated, as they promised to become, and because they form, as they undoubtedly do, a medium between Moors and Westerns.   It is a curious fact that the Jews actually

present a concrete existence undisturbed by differences in
religious orders, free from the petty dominion of Shereefs or
saints, and with no tribal animosities. It would therefore
naturally be a temptation to select them for the grafting of
new forms in which the national life of Barbary might
develop.   Up to a certain point, the Jew would form a
very fair stick wherewith to train the Moor; but the
natures of the two races are distinct, and laws which
would benefit the Jews would not always suit the Moors,
and *vice versâ*.

The Barbary Jew will not fight, he has not pride enough
for decency, and his nerves are simply deadened.   The
Moor is eminently a fighting man, even the poorest is
intensely proud; they are very high-strung.   These differences render the Moors capable of things to which the Jew
can neither attain nor understand.

To the Jew the love of his own people has taken the place
of love of country, and after centuries of the most cruel oppression it would be expecting too much of human nature
for him, if given the chance, not to turn upon the Moor
and torture him in a civil and sociable manner, as Jews
know very well how to do; and such is their belief in
the effect of vengeance, that beyond a doubt, were they in
a position to wipe off old scores, the Moor would get scant
mercy.

There are amongst them some enlightened men.   Neither
is it strange nor wonderful that England has produced
not merely many distinguished Jews, but that in England
the Jews are less bitter and less antagonistic than elsewhere.   National life is not closed to the Jew in England,
and at once his character changes for the better, and he
becomes patriotic.   This feeling is so marked at times when
it might least be expected, that I believe the last race to
make a stand to save the Empire would be the Jews.   It
was in Barbary, and from a Barbary Jew, that I heard the

Ur Castilla prado Tangiers

A MOOR

strongest testimony to the value of Englishmen as administrators.

The Barbary Jew pedlar or small merchant is the hardest-working and hardest-living creature on earth. His past training has been such that to-day he can travel faster, live cheaper, and work harder than anyone else. Putting aside the saying that the Barbary Jew lives on an onion and a piece of bread in the morning, and a piece of bread and a radish in the evening, I have seen them travelling without mercy to themselves or their animals. They might have been made of bronze and with stomachs of flint. The consequence of this to trade is evident. He easily undersells all competitors, and yet he lives. Should he fail, he is indifferent to the disgrace. But he is not likely to fail. At any rate, he will enjoy a career of some years' duration, for he knows how to make one rope take the strain of another, like a spider's web. He will have used or abused his position which the credit of Manchester houses has given him, to get the 'cinch' on the Moors. His import trade has enabled him, by showing sufficient manifests, to secure Protection for a certain number of natives, and this is too profitable, too easy a blood-sucking business for him to rashly risk losing it by going bankrupt. He has a direct motive for underselling, because the larger his import manifests the more Protection he can give. It is said, however, that at last the British manufacturers have seen that they are not nursing their trade by injuring merchant shippers through giving credit to men who trade in an irregular manner.

The policy of the Jew is clear and even commendable, neither is there any policy in Barbary to withstand him. He gets the best education he can, he emigrates, probably to Brazil, and becomes a citizen of Brazil; then he returns to Barbary, and gets what credit he can to start business in a country which he understands better than anyone else. This is no case for reiterating the old truism that the true function of government is so to regulate the State that individuals may operate even against their will for the good of the State. For if Moors or Christians object to Jews, they should reflect that it is they and not the Jews who are responsible for the political and social condition of Barbary, where most things are going to the Jews.

The banking in Morocco does not promote, as it does in Canada, the development of the country. In Canada, if a man sees his way to a good enterprise—a pulp-mill, or saw-mill, or other industrial undertaking—the bank, after duly examining the business, will advance him money on easy terms. As his business succeeds and increases, all the payments are made through the bank, and perhaps the mill becomes the nucleus of a new township, where the bank does all the business so far as finance is concerned. In Morocco no one dreams of enterprise, no one has any scheme, industrial or otherwise. The Moors would say, ' The Christians are taking our country; we must stop them.' If a Moor makes money he is put in prison for it, and it is taken from him.

But at Mazagan there is a petroleum engine of English build, of 400 horse-power, belonging to an Italian. It grinds flour and makes macaroni callantita, vermicelli, and semolina, besides sawing imported timber into deals. It is capable of grinding 4,000 kilos of wheat per diem, and making 400 loaves of bread, which are baked in a large oven heated by dried palmetto-leaves, a load of which, weighing 50 kilos, costs fivepence. Imported from Algiers, the same palmetto-leaves are sold in Marseilles for 20 francs the 100 kilos. The export of palmetto from Morocco is forbidden, and so is the export of wheat, but this engine enables both to be exported in the shape of macaroni, vermicelli, etc. Wheat is cheap, owing to the prohibition, and the Moroccan wheat is especially suitable for these manufactures. The Moors are learning to appreciate macaroni, and there is sometimes so large a demand that there is none left for export.

But the mill at Mazagan, though it was the largest enterprise of the kind, is not the only one in Morocco. There was one at Casa Blanca and another at El Kasar. The mill at Casa Blanca grinds at about the rate of 700 pounds of wheat per diem. Previous to the erection of these mills, all the flour was ground either by women working at the old hand-mills or else by horse-mills, which turned out about 3 or 4 bushels a day. The stones used by the Moors are very soft, and the bread contains a great deal of grit. At Casa Blanca the Moors found that it paid them to have the grain put through the mill and sift the bran from it by hand at home. They appreciated getting the grain ground at a fixed price, without any portion of it being subtracted. In consequence of the popularity of the method, the old horse - mills were stopped, and their owners sent criers round the town promising that they would be honest in future if people would bring them their corn again; but the Moor, if he is turned, is generally turned for good.

In Mazagan I came upon a form of Protection which was new to me. It seems that if a native were seized by the officials and a banker came forward and said, 'This man owes me a considerable sum of money,' the man could not be put in prison. Perhaps for this reason the Moors have declared money-lending to be illegal. It interfered with their profits. But they go even further, and object to Europeans doing business on a large scale with Moors. A European once gave me an instance, saying of a Moor who had been recently put in prison, 'I have done business with that man for years, and I went and offered to pay anything he might owe for taxes, but the official said, "No; what I want is that you do not do any more business with him."'

There is a significant sentence in Mr. Spinney's consular report for 1900: 'However beautiful the crops may be, it is impossible that trade can improve until the taxation may be of a more lenient nature and the Arabs allowed to remain with some buying power.'

CHAPTER XX

MAZAGAN is a very interesting city historically, but its
appearance is modern, with several broad, straight streets
and a strong merchant settlement. The port could be easily
improved, and as the nearest port to Marakish it is likely to
become increasingly important commercially. Besides, it
has the backing of the rich and fertile province of Dukalla,
so that of all the ports I had visited it seemed the most
established and with the brightest future before it. The
feeling inspired by the place is one of hope, and the influence
of the West is stronger in Mazagan than in any place in
Morocco. If the Moors are ever to improve, if they ever
hear reason, it will be by listening to commercial proposals
from merchants whom they have learned to trust. It is
these men who are best calculated to give advice—men who
are too proud to be mean, too self-reliant to be cowardly;
men who are shrewd judges of character both by nature and
by training, and who all the time that they are buying hides
or beans are quietly taking the measure of the men with
whom they deal, and who are always ready to hold out a
firm hand to the native in time of misfortune.

I left Mazagan, having rearranged my transport, and
taking with me a native who could speak English and

cook, hoping that he would help me with Arabic. But I
found him unreliable, and I cashiered him on arriving at
Marakish.

It was at five o'clock in the evening of May 10 that I
mounted Mooleeta to begin the ride of 100 miles to
Marakish. There was a slight swelling on Conrad's back,
which began, I believe, by the bite or sting of some fly. My
heavy luggage went by camel, and I hired a pack-mule to
Marakish.

The road was somewhat monotonous, but the country was
fertile, and there were fine crops of canary-seed and barley.
After about an hour's riding we came to a most lovely scene
of rural prosperity. Broad acres of cereals stood in the
evening light, with fig-gardens flanking a collection of white-
walled houses and stores. It recalled many a spot in my
own home county in 'the leafy month of June,' as it used to
be before hard times set in for the farmers. The land was
particularly well cultivated, and I even saw a couple of
bullocks drawing a plough, as cultivator, between the mealies.
Outside the houses on a piece of grass lay four or five
camels, their drivers being busy with the large bales of wool
ready to be loaded up by daybreak the next morning for
Mazagan.

Ben Abbas came out to meet me, having been advised of
my coming. He was a stout man of some fifty years, with a
long gray beard, keen dark eyes, and a bronze complexion.
He was arrayed in spotless woollen drapery, and added to
his considerable stature by holding himself very erect. He
bade me welcome in the usual manner, holding out his hand
to me and kissing his finger-tips.

While he gave directions for the pitching of my tent I
rode round the camel-drivers' hut, and the hut which was
the school for the children of Ben Abbas and his sisters,
whom he had taken in with him to share his good fortune.
The setting sun shone over the crops of green and gold; the

white square walls looked comfortable; the gardens, protected by aloes, were full of fig-trees, well and evenly grown.
Moors moved about driving the cows up to be milked;
another was bringing up the mares for the protection inside
the walls. I could see a herd of fine sheep coming slowly,
all seeking safety for the night. Neatness and order pre-
vailed. There was no litter lying about, no weeds which
wanted pulling. There were black slaves, who looked
spruce and businesslike, and all moved without haste,
quietly, quickly and contentedly. What a change I
thought it from the poor tent and squalid douar! Yet
there were people who would do away with Protection. Ben
Abbas was nothing but a common peasant, a son of the soil,
and Protection had made a rich man of him.

Presently the big gates were thrown back, and I rode through
into a spacious, well-swept yard. Ben Abbas waved me to sit
on a new carpet spread under the shelter of a wall, where I
could watch my people unload. He posted himself near the
closed door of the house, where he commanded a view of the
whole yard, and gave orders to slaves and servants as they
passed. After setting down its burden my camel was sent
snarling and hiccoughing out through the gate. My horse
and mule were put together in a comfortable little corner apart,
but they are so painfully jealous of each other that they took
to kicking and had to be separated. The Kaid's old horse,
who usually took every opportunity of a stampede, had his
peculiarities pointed out to Ben Abbas, who grimly ordered
him into a walled enclosure, in which solitary confinement
the Kaid visited him and chuckled at his complete subjuga-
tion. Ben Abbas, seeing me interested in the animals, took
me to see his mules and one or two good horses.

Near my tent was a well, which was kept padlocked. It
was drinking water, and suggested the usual difficulties of a
dry country. The underground granary was opened to fetch
up the barley for the animals' feed. It was musty, but the

animals ate it. I noticed that the barley brought for my
animals was perfectly sweet.

Suddenly my camel reappeared. As the huge creature
strode into the yard I thought he would catch his legs in the
ropes and tie the tent round his person with me inside it.
But Ben Abbas was equal to the emergency, and had him
promptly driven beyond the cows, but where I could keep
my eye upon him from the tent; not that I desired to do so.

I made some tea in my tent, when the usual presents
arrived of sugar, tea, eggs, etc. Milk was brought me from
the cows, and a sheep was being slain. Scarcely had I
thanked my host, when the never-failing tea equipage was
brought, the kettle and brazier being posted outside my tent.
I arranged a blanket on a provision chest as a seat of
honour, and sat myself on my bed. After a little delay Ben
Abbas sent his son with a message that he could not come
himself. The son was a young man of about five-and-
twenty, with quiet, dignified manners, who looked at me from
time to time in open-eyed astonishment, and indulged in a
quiet, irrepressible chuckle. He had slipped his feet out of
his slippers and left them at the door of my tent, and he sat
on the provision chest with the hood of his jellaba carefully
folded round his face—a dark, handsome face of Arab type.
A black slave girl awaited his bidding with regard to the
kettle, and I called the Moor who could interpret to come
and stand at the door of the tent. The interpreter was in
some respects an advantage, but I found that I immediately
gave up trying to understand for myself. On the other hand,
I could express more through him.

After a few remarks, I learnt that there is no river in this
land, which is felt as a great drawback. There are wells, but
evidently they know nothing of water-storage, except what
they catch in a tank from the roof of the house.

The young man's name was Abdullah, and he was anxious
to assure me that he and his people liked the English very

much. I asked why, and he said rather timidly that they were a strong people, but they did not push other people about. There were so many of them, and many countries belonged to England. To my astonishment Abdullah asked about the Transvaal War. Was it finished? He expressed great vexation, clicking his teeth and shaking his head as if a wasp had stung him. He expressed himself to the effect that the Transvaal folk were a useless folk, who did not know where their own interests lay. Then he asked me who and what they were. I explained to him the origin of the Boers, and how it was they came to make war on the British, to all of which he listened breathlessly. But his eyes kindled and his face flushed when I described the aged Sultana, whose people's griefs were her own, and how all her millions of sons of all races and creeds rose up of their own accord to take her part and fight her battles. How some sent their sons, and those who had no sons sent money, and those who were too old gave means to the young. I told how eager the Indians were to fight for their English Sultana, but how the Sultana said 'No, this is not your fight,' and how then they sent money and horses and guns, and came to care for the wounded British, and carry them out of the battles to places of safety. Abdullah drew a long breath and nodded his head. He sat thinking for a few minutes, and then he said, 'It was very good of the English not to make the Indians fight.'

I gathered that he supposed we should have driven them into the trenches and kept out of it ourselves, and I suddenly saw a fresh piece of wisdom in restraining the dark races.

Then Abdullah asked about my new Sultan. He spoke of it as a great change from the Sultana. He wondered how the English would like it. He was not so sure as others had been that a Sultan would suit the English people so well. I told him of the King's goodness of heart, and of the new Sultana's care for the sick and suffering, and instanced her

15

visit to the wounded soldiers at Netley. This struck Abdullah most of all, and he referred to it again and again, adding, 'In my country it is not so.' At the mention of war he raised his hands and shuddered visibly. These people are quite different to the hillmen; they are a gentle race of industrious agriculturists, the very best material for a despotic Government to grind and oppress. And ground and oppressed they are to extinction, except when they can get protection. Then I told some tales of the Transvaal War—of the soldier who stayed by his wounded Kaid all night on the battlefield, and kept him alive by holding him in his arms, and of Kaids who had saved the lives of their soldiers at the risk of their own. 'Why do they do such things?' asked Abdullah, and I told him why.

Time passed quickly; it was growing dark; I lighted a candle, and still we talked on. I was giving an Arabian Night's entertainment of a new kind. Abdullah sat opposite with his mouth slightly open, showing his dazzling white teeth, looking from me to my interpreter, putting in a question with sudden nervous quickness, or uttering a half-suppressed exclamation. His eyes glowed and burnt; his manner betokened a strong effort at self-control; I sometimes thought he would burst into tears, but he mastered himself as these high-strung Moors do. He spoke of how his people were taxed over and over again, unless they were protected, and how all that they had worked for was snatched from them, so that, instead of becoming better off, they became poorer and poorer and died. He asked me if the people from India came to England, and I instanced the natives whom the late Sultana kept always with her. Abdullah had drunk some tea, and when I had finished he gave some to the interpreter, and then a glass to the slave-girl at the door. As we talked she drew nearer, and I shall never forget the dark eyes which devoured my face when I spoke of the dead Sultana's care for *all* her people. She was about fifteen years of age, probably of a West Coast tribe. Her skin was as black as ebony, but she was born in the household of Ben Abbas. We discussed the prohibition of exports, of which he was not in favour, saying that then people would die of want more often than they did. I pointed out that the rise in prices would be counterbalanced by an increase in supply, and he caught eagerly at this idea and worked it out for himself, concluding by saying, ' Yes, these things are good for those who work and take advantage of them.'

The talk had lasted an hour and a half, and I was getting very tired, so I sent my interpreter away, and, getting out my writing things, I waited for Abdullah to leave me. He lingered a little while watching me; then he arranged his drapery and rose, saying ' Salaama ' as he left me.

His departure was the signal for the appearance of covered dishes containing stews, kouskous, and bread. I partook of some of these viands, and sent the rest to my men. I felt that the effect of staying at Ben Abbas' could only be compared to a public dinner with speeches.

Ben Abbas and his people are early risers. Before it was light the calves were calling for supplies and the slaves and servants were passing rapidly to their work. Ben Abbas was on the scene, delivering orders in the tone of a general. The cattle, obediently and in order, trooped past my tent to go to their pastures with their several herds.

Scarcely was I dressed, when the inevitable tea-tray arrived again, brazier, mint, and all. It was carried straight to my tent for me to make tea for myself. I invited Ben Abbas to join me, but he excused himself; coming, however, and sitting on the provision-chest, so that we could talk. I had never made Moorish tea before, but I did my best. I know it was not a success, for my Moors, who took the remainder to enjoy it sitting in a row against the wall, made wry faces, and carried off the pot to doctor its contents in their tent. I was secretly immensely relieved that Ben

Abbas would not have any. I believe that his religion forbade his doing so.

He said again that he was very pleased to see me, and that he hoped I should come again, when he would be equally pleased to see me. He liked the English. They held to their word. They did not take things away from people. The Italians also were good. God be thanked, Ben Abbas had been protected for fifteen years! An Italian protected him and took nothing from him. His brother lived there with him, but in a separate house. We talked of locusts and petroleum, and presently Ben Abbas withdrew.

Tarts shortly arrived, and a large dish full of rolls made of paste and honey, fried in olive-oil; another large dish of paste laid in layers, with a pond of melted butter in the centre. I had been eating porridge and fried eggs, the porridge being especially delightful because of the beautiful milk with rich cream on it. I ate a small quantity of the tarts, and sent them to my men, who cleared out the dishes in no time. Then we struck the tents and rode on our way, Ben Abbas accompanying me to the end of his property, riding on a fat chestnut mule in a high scarlet saddle.

Once off the land of Ben Abbas, we came to ruins again and locusts marching with the wind. In Casa Blanca I had heard of a new way of using the fungus for destroying locusts. Instead of sprinkling it over the locusts, by dipping one flying locust into it the 'voet-gangers' were persuaded to eat it. They are notoriously ravenous, and when one has eaten the fungus and died of it his brethren devour him, and so on.

Leo Africanus describes the 'extreme dearth of corne, especially in Mauritania, caused by locusts.' But he quotes from another old writer's account 'Of an huge and pernicious companie of Locusts in Africa, which, after they had wasted the country, being drouned in the sea and cast up dead on the shore, bred a most woonderfull pestilence both

of man and beast.' Fifteen hundred corpses of 'lustie yoong
gallants' were carried out of the gate of one city owing to
this plague. The account is substantiated by Francis Alvarez,
a Portuguese, who advised the Ambassador to go in a religious procession, with relics, etc., 'and all we Portugals
sung the Litanie, and appointed those of the land to lift up
their voices aloud, as we did.' The locusts were caught
and conjured to depart; moreover, they were requested,
admonished, excommunicated, and finally given three hours
to depart into the sea, or to the desert, the mountains, or the
land of the Moors, so as to let the Christians alone. As the
locusts failed to be impressed, the birds of heaven, the beasts
of the earth, and all sorts of tempests, were summoned to
scatter, destroy, and eat up their bodies. These strong
measures were taken in the presence of a few locusts, who
had been caught in order that they might hear the admoni-
tion pronounced in behalf of the absent thousands, after
which they were given their liberty and allowed to depart.
'It pleased God,' says the pious writer, 'to heare us sinners
. . . while towards the sea there arose a great cloude with
thunder . . . and continued for the space of three howers
with much raine and tempest, that filled all the riuers, and
when the rain ceased it was a fearefull thing to beholde the
dead Locustes, which were more than two yardes in height,
upon the bankes of the riuers, and in some riuers there were
mighty heapes of them, so that the morning following there
was not one of them found alive upon the earth. . . . Many
of the inhabitants said, these Portugals be holy men, and
by the power of their God they have killed and driven away
the locusts; others saide, especially the priests and friars
of those places about, that we were witches, and by the
power of enchantments hade driuen away the said creatures.'
The treatment seems to have been popularly resorted to,
and the 'Portugals' must have made a good business out
of it, for we read of 'great reuardes' being offered them,

and they travelled from place to place to ban the locusts and bless the land, at the request of the people.

According to Alvarez, the most severe visitation of locusts came from the fertile province of Dukalla, where I then was. And certainly, judging by the immense numbers of 'voet-gangers,' it would seem that something in the soil and climate of Dukalla, and possibly in its abundant crops, makes it an attractive breeding-place for these pests. Nevertheless, the description given by Alvarez bears a somewhat suspicious resemblance to the Book of Joel, in which the condition of the land, owing to pests and war, is represented as worse even than Barbary : 'That which the palmer worm hath left, the locust hath eaten ; and that which the locust hath left, the cankerworm hath eaten ; and that which the cankerworm hath left, the caterpillar hath eaten.' But the prophet did not spare the people. Instead of judging the insects, he judged 'the inhabitants of the land,' and summoned them to repent of their evil ways in those touching words which are a very touchstone of sincerity : 'Turn ye even to Me with all your heart, and with fasting, and with weeping, and with mourning ; and rend your heart, and not your garments, and turn unto the Lord your God : for He is gracious and merciful, slow to anger and of great kindness, and repenteth Him of the evil.' Then, in return, comes the promise of plenty and peace : 'And I will restore you the years that the locust hath eaten.' This whole book of three chapters is a gem of poetical descriptive narrative, and there is no trace of the vulgar superstition which overlaid monkish teaching, and out of which priests and lawyers knew how to do a good business.*

* The idea that animals were subject to legal procedure died hard. In the fifteenth century Alvarez's treatment would have been held to be mild, for pigs were sentenced to be burnt alive or hanged. They were summoned, and put in the dock, and in one instance, when a sow was sentenced to be hanged for having killed a child, her pigs only escaped on the score of 'youth and bad example.' The subject was even open

That evening we stopped at the house of a Kaid who had been muleteer to the Sultan. His kasbah was in a neglected state, and the yard, when I rode through the gate, was full of Jews who had come in for safety on their road down to Mazagan, so I asked to be allowed to camp elsewhere, and was taken through ruined walls to the yard where the Kaid's horses and mules were stabled, and this I had to myself, save for the animals and the watchman, whose hut was in one corner.

In an unaccountable manner the Kaid had heard that I was coming, and had hardened his heart, believing that I was a missionary. No sooner did he find out his mistake than he deluged me with gifts to make up for his chilly reception. I wished to understand the matter, but had no opportunity for doing so.

The court was about 50 yards square, and when the inevitable stampede occurred the men borrowed my lantern and raced after the thundering hoofs. The wind was roaring, and the noise was magnificent. The sky was clear, and the moon and stars shone brilliantly. Conrad was quiet, and Mooleeta had not been able to get loose. I fully expected that in one of their turns the animals would charge into my tent, and I pulled the mackintosh sheeting over me wondering what it would feel like to have a cavalry charge go over one in bed.

Just before we reached this kasbah, the mountain which is called the Green Hill, and which is not far from Marakish,

---

to discussion. A treatise written by a lawyer defending the prosecution of animals has survived, and it is interesting to note that he commences by congratulating the people of England that they have not to deal with locusts, which in India are three feet long, and whose hind-legs are swords. Then he goes on to thrash out the subject. 'Must animals be tried? Have they committed crime? Must they be defended? Yes. Before what tribunal? The Church.' And he concludes with giving reasons why animals should be excommunicated. The last prosecution of an animal in England took place in 1740, when a cow was hanged.

was visible across the plain.   It rose up as Table Mountain
rises out of the ocean, and with a little cloud hanging
midway between its summit and the plain.

That day we crossed a dry plain, where the pools of winter
rain were shrinking fast.   We watered our horses at a vast
empty soko, where there were many wells, and the dryness
of the country was attested by the clouds of blue pigeons
which came there to drink.

During the march the pack on which I was riding suddenly
swung round, and I found myself quite unexpectedly on my
back on the ground, still holding my parasol over my head
and the reins in the other hand.   A peasant who was passing
stopped and said something consolatory.   To a Moor it is a
disgrace to be thrown, and this man, with Moorish courtesy,
meant to salve my mortified feelings by saying that I rode
well, and that the pack was to blame.   This made things
worse, for it was the Kaid who had put on Mooleeta's pack,
and my fall hurt him more than it did me.

My Kaid had established himself as my grand vizier.   I
had no claim whatever on his services further than as an
escort, but he chose to exert himself in every department,
and the time came when he even cooked my porridge.
When I was in a fix, if I said to him: 'What shall we do
now, Kaid?' the Kaid would answer: 'The señorita will
think of a way, and the Kaid will help her'—and so he
always did.

The fall shook me somewhat, and I decided to get twenty-
four hours' rest at our next halt.

This happened to be at another Kaid's, and he was out when
we arrived, so that my tent could not be pitched.   I went on
foot in the direction he was expected to come, and sat down
on a hillock, most of my Moors coming with me.

In course of time Kaid Ser Oti appeared.   He was riding
a fine black mule, with a black slave in attendance mounted
on another mule, and a train of ragged guards on foot.   He

had been out making the people destroy the locusts, for the Sultan had recently declared that the Kaids should be fined if they did not exterminate the locusts.

Kaid Ser Oti was very gracious, even friendly. He chose the spot for my tent himself, said I need fear nothing, and that he would see that I had everything I wanted, and he hoped I would stay and rest as long as I liked.

As soon as my tent was pitched I lay down, when to my astonishment Ser Oti came in person. He sat down, and we talked for twenty minutes. He was very sorry to hear of my accident, and again pressed me to stay and rest. I admired his vineyards and maize crops, and the good culti-vation of his land. He asked where I had seen the last locusts, and we talked about that. His reputation was good among Moors as a merciful Kaid. He exerts himself to make money by farming his land, so that he does not squeeze the peasants much. He is a strict Moslem, and spends some hours every day reading the Koran and studying.

Outside the walls of his kasbah is a small colony of Jews, who make clothes for the country people. They came and begged of me.

Ser Oti sent me down a dinner that evening, and the next morning, soon after daybreak, he rode out, and told my men in passing that he was going to make the people kill the locusts. The petroleum I had recommended would be too expensive. Doubtless imported oil would be; but I thought with regret of the wells in the country itself which no one might touch. Later one of his servants came to know what food I would like, and what I would take for dinner.

I rested until the sun declined. The heat was very great, but I enjoyed a bath, and in the afternoon felt so much refreshed that I decided to proceed.

Before leaving the Kaid's a large black scorpion was killed in the men's tent, which probably would have stung one of them that night.

We crossed the plain by the highway from Mazagan, and
then commenced to ascend some hills. I suppose we climbed
three or four hundred feet, and then our road was joined by
the highway from Casa Blanca and Azemour, which is the
direct road between Mequinez, Fez and Morocco city now
that the tribes have closed the other route.

I was surprised to find date-palms growing so high up.
The land was very dry, all the winter water-courses being
dusty. The sparse crops of barley had been blighted by a
wind, and the peasants seemed to become poorer and poorer.
Then the country flattened out into a plain, and I saw that
we had reached one of those plateaus common in Africa.

We fell in with some Jews bound for a soko, and I decided
to camp at the first village and attend the soko.

We were how in the Bashalate of another Kaid, who was
said to be extremely cruel. He had no less than five tribes
under him, so greatly were the numbers reduced. The people
were very wretched. Starvation had stunted and aged them,
and I was told that in the last year or two many had died
from having 'too little to eat.' They were emaciated, and
clad in scanty rags. 'A village of the Sultan,' my Kaid
called it; and verily His Shereefian Majesty had cause to
be proud of such a village. The small conical huts were
thatched to the ground and fenced with thorn-bushes. But
there was a bareness about them that was striking—no mat
to sleep on, no cooking utensils, no implements. The spirit
of the people seemed broken. The nearer I drew to Marakish
the more miserable became the people. Once I mentioned
this to a Moor, and asked why the people were so much
worse off in the South than in the North, and I jotted down
his answer, which was as follows:

'Marakish is Sultan—Sultan is many Kaids. Kaids snake
out other Kaids and go take 'em prison. Fez is mosque,
and mosque no snake out Kaids. Fez Kaid is Kaid always
—all same Kaid. Sultan Kaid-snake come say: " What do

dat Kaid? Take him prison. Make me Kaid; I pay so much." Then they take Kaid prison, and Sultan take his money, houses—all whatever he have. Sultan take money from Kaid-snake, and make Kaid-snake Kaid. And snake— he go to people, and say, " Pay me this—and this "—everything they have he take, because he promise Sultan he pay so much money make him Kaid.'

This is, I believe, a true statement. But the mosque, though preferable to the Sultan, is not a perfect rule. For instance, if a rich man dies, the mosque claims two-thirds of the property. Of the remainder, an allowance is apportioned to the wives and concubines, and a fair annuity paid to the head-wife and the sons or heirs. Thus the mosque has accumulated an enormous mass of property, which pays no revenue.

The Kaids of the Sultan have no mercy. Instances are far from rare when, on the death of a great man, his entire property has been seized, and the wretched wife and children, and all the other wives and concubines, and his mother, if he has one, are driven out to beg, work, or starve. No Kaffir tribe I came across in the South practised such barbarity as this.

Before retiring to my tent, I told my Moors that I must start early the next morning to make up lost time. Consequently the Kaid was up before daybreak; but the others had no intention of moving, and consequently I started, leaving my camel behind instead of its preceding me as usual.

On arriving at the soko and finding it a small and uninteresting affair, I decided to ride on, and at 9.30 we reached a group of fig-trees near a pool and a ruined tower and some huts.

I dismounted and lay down under the fig-trees, and, looking up at their twisted old branches and brilliant foliage, wondered how many thousands of travellers, on various errands, had in the course of ages rested under them on the old trail between Marakish and the seaboard. They were still arriving and departing all around me, with their long-maned, long-tailed horses, and ambling mules with high-peaked saddles, and camels with their drivers riding upon asses. I led my horse to the pool to drink, and brought him back to the shade of the trees, but the camel was a long time coming, and a Moor arrived who said he had seen both men and beasts in the thick of the soko. When they came at length, I made it quite plain to them that in future they were to start at my hour and keep my time, which they accordingly did.

The abject condition of the peasantry baffles all description. Bare life was left them, and very barely that. None were clothed, save in a few tattered rags huddled round them for decency. The little tricks of finery, such as brooches, were all gone, but now and again a woman wore a rosary round her neck made of some native seed or bean. Their faces were so sad; not even the children had a smile. Their chief hope lay in flight to some less cruel Kaid. This consisted in waiting till the harvest was partly reaped, thrashing as much of their grain as they could carry, and decamping quietly.

At this pool there was a family on the wing. They had a mule and a poor ass. The man seemed about forty years of age; there were three little boys and their mother. Their objective was Mazagan, where they would probably add another hut to those outside the town, and the man would start as a water-carrier, while the woman would take whatever work she could get. The parents looked very grave and anxious. I think they feared me as a spy, and thought they would be detected and brought back when they had hardly started. They kept well away by themselves. The donkey and mule were turned loose, and the packs were hung high up out of sight in a fig-tree. They were still there when I left, and I believe they meant to travel at night.

. When we went on, over an endless plain, where numbers of mules grazed, which I was told were the property of the Sultan, I saw twice crossing the road two fine specimens of the large yellow spider, with a body as big as a mouse, which my people told me was so venomous that its bite would kill a man. But the odd part of it was, none of them wanted to kill these beasts, their reason being that they had never hurt them. I found afterwards that the Moors have some kind of religious scruple about killing even reptiles unless attacked by them. This is their notion of mercy. But to their pack-animals they are inconceivably cruel—so inconsistent can religion make people.

CHAPTER XXI

'THE shades of night were falling fast,' when I heard the
boom of the gun-fire at Marakish. My little Mooleeta was
leading the cavalcade at a rapid amble, and we were going
merrily along over a perfectly level road, like the gravel
' sweep' to the suburban residence of some civic dignitary.

Our stopping-place for the night was a village of conical
huts, called M'nebbi, and soon after we arrived a Kaid and
some foot guards swaggered into the enclosure, who were on
their way to Mequinez from Marakish.

The talk was all about the new Grand Vizier, who started
in life as a peasant born in this village, and the people
seemed to entertain some faint hope that they might be left
a little more to live upon in consequence.

That night I scarcely slept. Not only did dogs bark, but
cats howled and my guards talked. At length, when I fell
asleep, I was awakened by a stealthy sound fidgeting with an
enamel plate which stood on the provision-chest. Naturally,
I thought of scorpions, and wished that my bedstead had not
been set quite so close to the side of the tent. I reached for
matches and struck a light. For precaution, I tied the neck
of the sack of barley containing the morning's feed, and put
it outside the tent. I searched for the scorpion, stick in

hand, till the candle burnt low. Then I walked round the whole camp, found the guards sleeping soundly, and so back to bed. Later in the night further experiences led to my discovering that the scorpion was a large, lean black cat with eyes like live coals. If there is one animal I dislike more than the pariah dog, it is the pariah cat.

The heat the day before had been very trying on the road, so we made an early start. I sent on the camel with the tent and kept the baggage-mule, while I made a hasty breakfast of coffee and hard-boiled eggs. Then we rode on, the stars above shining with a flinty look, and the moon with every appearance of debauch. It was deliciously cool, and I thought of the old Scott motto, ' Best riding by moonlight.'

As the light of dawn crept over the sky, I could see the rugged peaks and several features of the range of hills, which crossed our trail at right angles and shut us off from the plain of Marakish.

The ground was evidently highly mineralized. It had little or no top soil, but a quantity of silica or alabaster in a crumbling state lay on the surface. The subsoil was very hard, and the red colour betrayed its iron nature. The hills were probably 700 or 800 feet above the plain, and behind them rose the lofty and magnificent Atlas, whose peaks were outlined in snow against the sky. The Atlas reminded me of the Rockies seen from far off.

There was no doubt in my mind that the watershed from these hills would provide irrigation for the vast plain we had passed over ; but I felt uncertain as to the crops which might be grown there. The perpetual barley and maize struck me as insufficient for such a rich soil and fine climate. The fact that the date-palm grew on the hills which we climbed from Ser Oti's was an indication that subtropical vegetation would flourish with proper care. I wondered whether tea would grow ; how far the altitude was corrected by the latitude; what could be done for wind breaks. I saw some very rich dark soil in the hollows between the peaks on our last ascent, and in some of these narrow sheltered valleys it seemed to me that tea would grow, though of what quality it would be impossible to say. The habit of the natives of turning their goats loose has cleared the ground of vegetation and made the country more barren than it would be by nature. Besides, they have cut down every bush and tree for charcoal and kindling-wood.

But whatever crops, whether tea, coffee, or cotton, might be grown further back upon the plain, the part of it reaching from five to six miles from the base of the hills is undoubtedly as rich in minerals as it is poor in crops.

The silica was 'float' from the hills, and not an outcrop or surface rock on the plain. The plain appeared to be first clay shale, which nearer the hills became harder, till it was a strong slate, suggesting coal of some kind. There was abundance of ironstone; in fact, iron appeared to be a general feature everywhere. I noticed a hungry-looking gray rock in places, carrying quartz. Quartz appeared in boulders, but never in seams of any consequence.

Thus we entered the narrow gorge by which we were to pass through these hills, and I dismounted to walk in order to enjoy the scene at my leisure; for Mooleeta is of an ambitious nature and likes to get in front.

These hills contain an old gold-mine, which the natives speak of as the buried treasure of the Christians. But when I asked about it, my Kaid put himself into a state of fuss and agitation, first assuring me that it was useless for me to think of going there, as it was difficult to find, and we might spend weeks hunting for the spot; and, secondly, that if we reached the place we should never find the gold, for that the way to find it was a secret. But he was quite clear that gold was found there, and said that he had seen it.

What he had seen was evidently coin. I think it is quite

possible that the natives know of this gold deposit, and have some means of working the mine, which they do in secret; and possibly they coin gold pieces there also. The Kaid said they dug it out of a hole in the ground. Whether it is alluvial in some creek, or quartz, and they smelt it, I do not know. What struck me most in the ore I picked up was that there was a mixture of metals. In one piece I saw pure native copper, the outside being ironstone, and a seam through it of gray mineral rock, very fine, which probably contained silver, or the commonest mineral of the country except iron—antimony.

The Moors have no idea of separating minerals. I saw copper which I feel convinced carried other minerals, probably a percentage of gold. The 'native gold' (or gold represented to me as native gold) was very rich in colour and soft; and if, as it seems only reasonable to suppose, it is to be found in dust in the streams, it must be very fine, delicate dust indeed. The first thing necessary would be to ascertain what coal underlies the clay shale, for all the ore I saw was smelting ore, and the silica would make an excellent flux. There may be refractory ore in the country; but the copper that I saw was the simplest and easiest rock, requiring only the cheapest treatment.

The transport might be made during the summer season, and by the road I came, on wheels. There was nothing to prevent a team of mules taking a spider at full gallop most of the way. The hills certainly afford an obstacle; but there the spider could be packed upon a camel, and its contents on another camel, and deposited the other side of the hills. But all the transport necessary for initial mining purposes might come up on waggons to the entrance of the gorge at very slight cost.

To me the chief interest in the scene lay in the fact that this stony track—no better than the dry bed of a river some 20 feet wide—was one of the greatest trade routes known

to history. Left as Nature made it, untouched by the hand
of man, for centuries upon centuries before such great high-
ways as the Canadian Pacific Railway were dreamt of, merchandise came down from the heart of Africa and from the
East along this road. I was planting my feet where the
rocks and blocks of marble were polished by the spongy tread
of the great carrier of the desert. I had been through the
Rockies on the top of a freight-car, and I should have liked
to have ridden through this gorge on the back of a camel.
By this route Christian slaves were carried to Marakish;
their wounded feet had dyed these stones as, weary and sad
of heart, they stumbled on under the Moslem lash. And
from Marakish the black slaves had been taken to the coast
in fear of the strange world which lay before them, and turning sad eyes backwards to the lofty range of the great Atlas,
which shut them out from their homes for ever. What
stores of ivory, of spices, and perfumes, had passed through
this narrow way! and still the most wonderful thought of
all was, that it was the road to Marakish itself, the approach
to the heart and centre of one of earth's greatest empires—
an empire which still held out in its last stronghold against
all the science, diplomacy and civilization of Europe.

'This poor country!' grumbled Si Mohammed, who was
sorely tried by having to lead Mooleeta and sit his own pack-
mule, Mooleeta enjoying the opportunity of teasing the pack-
mule by biting her tail, which caused her involuntarily to
kick, though usually a well-regulated creature and not given
to flustering Si Mohammed's nerves. 'This poor country!
It never get no chance. India get railways; its people they
come to England and enjoy the Jubilee. China, she get a
chance some day. But this poor country never get nothing
—no railway—no——' But at this point Mooleeta rushed
forward, with consequences so dire to Si Mohammed that I
could not even explain to him that the country's very wants
were its chief fascination.

The heat was becoming intense. At the end of the pass
I mounted Mooleeta again, and rode till I called a halt, not
near the water, but a quarter of a mile from it, on the top of
a hill, where there were a few bushes, and a little dry grass
for the animals to graze, and from which I could enjoy the
landscape surrounding Morocco city.

Words fail me to describe the beauty of that view.
Doubtless all the previous travelling had tuned one's mind
to enjoy this last scene, and appreciate the various associations which made it of unique and incomparable interest.
But the mere physical conditions were of no ordinary loveli-
ness, and I lay with my back against my hold-all and wished
that I could find some hermit's cave in the rocks and live
there. I thought how interesting it would be to turn from
one's books to this wonderful Nature, and from Nature to
human nature as the travellers on the road showed it to one
—the merchants, the camel-drivers, the pomp and show of a
great man's retinue, or the fugitive whose ' life was given him
for a prey.'

All that day I remained in the shady retreat of my tent,
watching the scene before me of Morocco city, lying in the
centre of the plain beside the river Tensift, and half hidden
by the palm-forest, with a background of snow-capped
mountains guarding it from the rest of Africa. That forest
is said to have been planted accidentally by an invading
army from Tafilat, who brought dates with them for their
commissariat ; and, when besieging the city, threw away the
stones, which took root and grew, affording an instance of
the accidental benefits of war. The city was partly hidden
by a haze, and its dark-red colour made it difficult to trace
the outline ; but towering above all other buildings there
rose the shaft of the great Kutubíya Tower, surmounted with
those golden balls about which so many tales are told.

In the evening we went on a short distance to a village.
The sun was ' lifting the day ' into the sky when we left on

16—2

the following morning for Marakish.   But mists hung round
the hills, which made them look like Scottish moors, till the
delusion was broken by the rays picking out with pure gold
a feathery palm-tree here and there.   The bases of the
mountain, and much of the city also, were hidden, and we
plunged down into the plain, and into a deeper mystery than
before.

'Honour the date-palm, for she is your mother,' was one
of the sayings of the Prophet, and these palms drop their
fruit for travellers to gather it who approach the city.
Moors can never resist dates, and at every soko they rushed
for dates.   These Marakish dates are not to be compared
with those from Tafilat, but they are a commodity good
enough to eat, and form a large item in trade.

After riding for about an hour in the forest, we came to a
bridge, a quarter of a mile long, across what is at certain
seasons a wide river, but was then a swamp with a narrow
stream in the middle.

I could not have seen the palms to greater advantage.
The rising sun struck them low down, and left their waving
tops dark against the sky ; the golden tassels of their
blossoms were hanging down, and the green of the lower
leaves, as they swept to right and left, were turned to every
colour, from emerald to a soft gray.   Presently we left the
palms for olives—dark and yet so light—pomegranates,
with their flashing, scarlet blossoms, and mulberries, whose
fruit was already ripening.   These were the celebrated
gardens which stand in the palm-forest.   Down a long
green vista I caught sight .of a white tower and dome,
sharply defined by the morning light.   It was the Jumna
Mosque.

At last we entered the city by a low dark archway, so low
that we wondered how the camels managed to enter at all ;
but the walls were lower in places than the mounds of filth
to which donkey-drivers were adding the contents of panniers.

The day had gone by when Marakish sought to defend itself.
How crumbling it all was! The mosques and towers were
very grand, but over all was the same mournful air of neglect
and decay ; and the people, hurrying on their business,
seemed indifferent alike to the past and the future. What
had become of the life which planned and raised the city ?
What kept it going ?

I made my way to Kaid MacClean's house, and sent in my
letter. He kindly sent a servant with me to assign me a
house. It was a lovely old Moorish house in the heart of
the city, with curious circuitous streets approaching it.
Inside it was like an enchanted castle, with rooms and
galleries, staircases and cupboards, where one least expected
them to be, and for a day or two after my establishment
there I was still exploring it and finding fresh surprises—
here a new pattern in arabesque, there some fresh tiles, or a
window with an iron grill, or a cupboard curiously devised
to look like a shuttered window ; or I opened a door which
I had not seen before, and found myself in a new room.
The people who built that house understood the pleasure
and comfort of life. It contrasted above all things with the
huts of the peasants and my tent. It was delightfully cool,
and so beautifully quiet that one might be miles away from
any city.

After breakfast I went out to deliver my letters of introduction, and in the afternoon I received two Moors who
came imploring me to put up at their houses. They drank
tea, which I took care to let my Kaid make, with plenty of
mint, and one of them, failing to persuade me, carried off my
horse and mule, together with my Kaid's horse, to his own
stables. I thanked the Moor for his hospitality to my horse,
and he said he would care for it just as he would care for
me if I accepted his house.

Here in Morocco city the moth and rust corrupt, but they
do not disfigure. Time only tones and lends a pathetic dignity

to all things. The East would not be half so fascinating were it fresh and new. Even the dust, or mud, or rags, are touches useful to the picture; and when anything is renovated it is unseemly and disastrous, like the 'piece of new cloth in an old garment.'

I understand now why true lovers of the East are so tolerant of the East, and why they give their support to the tottering fabric. It is so easy for the West to see the faults and defects, but unless the East can mend itself, one trembles to think what Western fingers would do. Then, the East *must* see the defects in the West, but is too polite to remark on them. I felt sometimes that that exasperating politeness would be the death of me! It is positively a power, but it probably deprives us of more than we can imagine. Reform may have to come—from within, that is, on Eastern lines, it must come, with infinite patience—but the strength must come from without. How can such a thing be explained? The child must teach the father, viz., inspire his heart.

The first day after my arrival in Marakish was one of feasting—for the entertainments provided for me were tremendous. I will give an account of one feast, and leave the reader to imagine the rest. We sat on cushions on the floor as usual, and, after water had been poured over our hands by a slave into a brazen dish, the courses opened by a large dish of fowl stewed in olive-oil garnished with olives. A loaf of bread was given to each person; our host, who sat by my side, tore up the fowl with his fingers; and we dipped pieces of bread in the oil and transferred it, or a morsel of chicken, to our mouths with our right hands. We also picked out olives, and my host soaked pieces of his own loaf in the oil, and held it up to my mouth, which I was obliged to open for the reception of the delicate attention. Then the fowl was dismissed, and another was brought, this time stewed with onions. In time this was replaced by mutton, boiled with almonds and apricot kernels. The inevitable kouskous was brought in, and I hoped this would finish the repast; but it was followed by the forequarter of lamb and potatoes. Then a compound of green vegetables, mashed together and boiled in oil, was set before us. And this was followed by several dishes of cakes, made of paste and honey, fried in oil, and a large bowl of orange marmalade made with cinnamon. Then fruits were set before us, and water was again brought to wash our hands, this time being greatly needed, for they were very greasy. Two rose-water sprinklers were set before the host, who went to work to make me wet through with the scent. Incense was then brought in, and handed round, so that each guest might hold his chin over it and let it curl up his face. I found it too strong to be pleasant for my nose. Then the host stood up, and held his trailing draperies over the censer—a practice very desirable as a disinfectant, I feel sure. Tea was then served to us, and I was particularly pressed to eat a most choice delicacy—a rare and curious thing—which proved to be a small biscuit with 'Huntley and Palmer' stamped on it! The Moors called these biscuits 'cakes,' and appeared to find them delicious. Tea was followed by coffee; and then I took my leave.

Kaid MacClean was starting for England a day or two after my arrival in Marakish, and I did not have much opportunity for seeing him. Perhaps no European knows Marakish so well or understands the operations of that most corrupt and iniquitous Government as this Scot, who, being a Lieutenant in a line regiment at Gibraltar, left the Queen's service for that of the Sultan twenty-five years ago. At the time that he accepted the billet the father of Abdul Azziz was Sultan. El Hassan was an enlightened and intelligent man who, had he lived, might have effected a good deal for Morocco. His policy appears to have been, first, the conquest of the unruly tribes; then the fortification of the country against a foreign enemy; lastly, the improvement of the country itself. He had proceeded so far in this work that,

after much fighting, he was able to travel with a strong
escort through most of his Sultanate, and the power of
Wazan was broken.   The coast towns' defences were
repaired, and European engineers were engaged to build
modern forts.   He also purchased heavy guns of the most
improved pattern and mounted them at Tangiers and Rabat.
Apparently he believed firmly in the power of Morocco to
stand alone.   On the other hand, it is difficult for us to
gauge the obstacles which he must have had to encounter in
the introduction of any modern improvement.   Whether he
realized that it was a mistake to reject the proposals of Sir
Charles Euan Smith, how far the failure of the Embassy was
due to insufficient patience on the part of our Ambassador, I
do not know.   One trifling incident points to a difficulty
inseparable from dealings with Moorish officials.   The Sultan
ordered a bridge from England for the river at Azemour.
He died before it was erected, and it lies now in the Custom
House of Mazagan.   It is this awful lethargy in the official
Moors which must have been sufficient to break the heart of
an energetic man like El Hassan.   There is only one way of
conquering this difficulty—by quiet, dogged tenacity and
invincible patience.

The soldiers whom Kaid MacClean has drilled were there,
and they are more drilled than it would be possible to
imagine of Moors.   This alone speaks volumes for the
endurance and optimism of Kaid MacClean.   His personal
courage cannot be questioned.   At that Court he has seen
the very worst of the Moors, and must know better than
anyone the devices, the corruption, and intrigues, which make
up the official life of the country.   Yet Kaid MacClean is
absolutely sincere when he says, ' I *like* the Moors.'

He is a middle-aged man, but his enthusiasm, which
borders upon recklessness, burns so fiercely that one wonders
what he can have been as a younger man.   In Morocco there
is an ample field for his energy.   He is credited with being

the chief friend of the Sultan. His official position is not sohigh as seems generally supposed in this country; but he brings to bear on the Sultan and his Court the strength of a mind educated and trained in the outer world, which they fear, but of which they are ignorant.

It was very interesting to find a Scot befriending the unfortunate son of El Hassan, and speaking of him in such high terms. 'The Sultan is good—he is a good man. He is young, but he is good—thoroughly good. Give him time —he must have time—and he will be all right. Time is what Morocco wants.' He dwelt on the fact that the Sultan had controlled the tribes of which France complained, and spoke of the loyalty of the Filalis. But he declared that the Sultan's presence was necessary at Marakish, for that if he went away the tribes would think he was deserting them. I referred to the state of the people, and the Kaid agreed that it was 'bad.' 'What could you expect,' he said, 'with each little Governor setting himself up to be a Sultan on his own account?'

Was it only part of Kaid MacClean's cheery optimism that he scoffed at the idea that the Sultan was restricted in travelling by the hostility of the tribes? 'He can start now and go anywhere. Of course he can!' If this be the case, the condition of Morocco is more solid than I believed. But as I looked at the crumbling and stately ruins, with the Kaid's plea for 'time' ringing in my ears, I thought he was answered in the words of Gobind, 'And the parrot said to the falling tree, "Wait, brother, till I fetch a prop."' There was in it that touch of bitter irony with which the East abounds.

Then Kaid MacClean offered to play to me on the bagpipes. Dressed as a Turk, he walked up and down with the pipes, but they were possessed with a 'dour' spirit. They yelled and shrieked, but utterly refused to respond to 'Cock o' the North,' and at length the Kaid laid them down.

The most interesting figure in Marakish was Kaid M'nebbi,

an intelligent, ambitious, and unscrupulous man, but not without a policy for the future. M'nebbi began life as a servant in Marakish. As a common soldier he attracted the notice of Ba Ahmed, the late Grand Vizier. The latter, finding him intelligent and useful, made him a prime favourite, and placed great confidence in him. Thus he had the advantage of seeing the inner working of a Grand Vizier's mind, and also the privilege of getting to know most of Ba Ahmed's private transactions. Ba Ahmed was fortunate in dying Grand Vizier, but after his death M'nebbi approached the Sultan and opened the eyes of His Shereefian Majesty on many points. The result was that several marks of favour were bestowed on M'nebbi by the grateful Sovereign. He became Minister of War, and just before I arrived in Marakish he had been made Grand Vizier in the place of Sidi Moktar.

But what excited and worried the people of Marakish was not M'nebbi's promotions, but the unusual number of imprisonments, deaths, and dismissals which had taken place one after the other in a few months.

There was the late Grand Vizier, Hadj el Moktar, who in Ba Ahmed's time was Minister of War. He was related to the Sultan El Hassan by marriage. Both his uncle and nephews were about the Court, though the two boys fell into disgrace with Ba Ahmed. So far as I could gather, there was no charge whatever brought against Sidi Moktar, but he was dismissed, robbed of all his money, and sent to prison at Mequinez. The Governor of Marakish, Ben Doud by name, was seized, dragged out of his house by common soldiers, and despatched to Tarudant. The rumour was that he had been so roughly handled that he died on the way.*

I once said that I was sorry for Ben Doud, and this produced a storm, for he was a most unpopular Bashaw, owing to his odious cruelty. He used spies to ascertain how much

* Ben Doud survived his imprisonment, was released, and sent to El Kasar in an official capacity. Perhaps he surrendered his money.

money the people had; then he trumped up cases against them, took their money, and sent them to prison. He seems to have been feared and detested beyond the power of words to express. 'If he be dead, that is good; if he die dragged in pieces, what did he do to people who are in prison now? He is finished with, and if the soldiers should kill him there is no more use for him.'

Ben Doud's sister had married Ba Ahmed, and it was by reason of this connection with the Grand Vizier that Ben Doud went on undisturbed in the amassing of wealth. His riches were believed to be enormous, and it was said that the Sultan wanted them. To the great chagrin of all concerned, not a dollar was found in his house, nor would Ben Doud divulge where it was hidden. Many were the surmises as we sucked tea out of glasses and listened to the gurgling of a stream in the garden of orange and heliotrope. It was said that Ben Doud had placed all his money in European banks, but others disbelieved the story. The most generally accepted theory was that it was concealed in Ben Doud's own house. I asked how so large a sum of money could be hidden, and only one person know about it. For a moment my question was regarded as too simple to require an answer, but at length one Moor kindly undertook to explain: 'A man when he is rich can put his money on two mules at a time. He goes away to where he knows he can hide it. Perhaps he takes one slave, perhaps two, with him. He puts the money safely in the place with the help of the slaves, who make it all good. Then he kills those two slaves, and comes home without them. Yes, what good are they? They would talk some day, and all that man's trouble would be as nothing.'

Some commiseration was expressed for the Master of the Horse, Lyashi Ulad M'boh. No one seems to have had any complaint against this man; but he was dragged from the sanctuary of Sidi Ben Slieman and tortured to death by having his hands slit open and lime rubbed into them. It was said that M'nebbi objected to him on the score of having been snubbed by him in his early days, when, in the service of Ba Ahmed, he was sent on errands. Another report ran to the effect that this exceptionally cruel death was due to his having married his brother to a black slave who was desired by a most exalted personage. These were the most remarkable charges, but there were many others of less account. Many of the country Governors and Kaids were dismissed, and their Bashalates given to others, who paid heavily for the office.

M'nebbi, however, had already taken the wise line of making himself popular by encouraging the Sultan to spend money, and some traders were jubilant at the large orders for velvet, silks, and similar rich materials, which came from the Sultan's house.

All the relations of Ba Ahmed were turned out of office and banished, their places being filled by insignificant people or friends dependent upon M'nebbi. The offices of Vizier were for the most part abolished and absorbed into the Grand Viziership. This seemed to point to the centralization of authority, and might tend ultimately to improve the administration. M'nebbi, whatever his origin or history, was evidently a strong man, and he stood now in people's eyes as one who had triumphed, for those enemies who were too powerful to dismiss had 'died.' He could reckon upon certain support. There was the Kaid Aissa ben Omar, a powerful man on the coast, credited with understanding the wants of the merchants. I heard that, barring Sidi Mohammed Torres, this man was the 'finest Moor in the country,' and that he had come to the conclusion that squeezing had reached its limits, and that, if revenue is to be made and private fortunes retained, other methods must be sought. All 'friends of the Sultan' contrive to amass money, but M'nebbi must be alive to the fact that credit cannot be supported on boxes of French louis locked up and concealed, and that some fresh veins must be tapped for profits which the dead and ruined peasantry cannot yield. No one could make better suggestions than the Kaids of some of the coast towns, who must be weary of the merchants' complaints. Respecting improvements at the ports (the expense of which would fall upon the Nazarene), several could no doubt speak as to ways by which such changes could ultimately be treated as milch kine of the faithful if they had English to deal with, and not French or Germans. There are, besides, other ways of raising money, such as the sale of concessions—if M'nebbi could find anyone in England to buy them. These things have been done elsewhere. What is wanted in this direction is a little strengthening of Moorish credit. Capital will not flow into a country with so powerful a nation as France threatening interference. Matters were resolving themselves into a struggle between M'nebbi and France. It was a stupendous task for a man of M'nebbi's limited education and experience to keep France at bay! He could look to Kaid MacClean for advice in military matters, and the latter would be grossly ungrateful if he did not mean to support to the uttermost the independence of a country where he has risen to honours and fortune. But the Kaid is not a diplomatist, far less a statesman, and his position is that of drill-instructor to the troops, and not Vizier.

There was pointed out to me an elderly Moor called Sid F'dool Gharnit. Round this man circulated all manner of tales of French intrigue. So far there was foundation for them that Sid Gharnit was the friend of Dr. Linares, and Sid Gharnit appeared to have few friends among the Moors and very little prestige.

Of Dr. Linares, I was told that ' he is the cleverest man in all Morocco.' He is believed to have rendered much valuable assistance to the French Government during his

five-and-twenty years' residence in Morocco. He was first
medical doctor to the French military mission to the
Moorish Court. He is said to have been the confidential
adviser of the French Chargé d'Affaires at Tangiers during
Sir Charles Euan Smith's abortive mission. About seven
years ago Dr. Linares was appointed French Political Agent
at the Sultan's Court, and another doctor was sent to the
military mission.

CHAPTER XXII

WHEN Kaid MacClean and M'nebbi, the new Grand Vizier, were starting for the Court of St. James, Sid Gharnit was appointed Grand Vizier *pro tem*. The Embassy and its object were the constant theme at many a feast. So was French aggression, and so was M'nebbi, and so was Sid Gharnit.

M'nebbi was regarded as a resolute man of uncommon energy, who would take strong measures. Such a Vizier, it was said, would be very displeasing to France.* If the scheme of France is to split up Morocco by reviving the kingdom of Fez, a powerful Grand Vizier would be an obstacle to her policy. It was considered that the continual unrest at Tafilat rendered the presence of the Sultan at Morocco city imperative. The tribe at Tafilat is the Filali, the loyal Shereefian tribe on whose fidelity the Sultan depended to save him from the open rupture which was apparently all France needed for an excuse to invade

---

* I was surprised to find the following reference to M'nebbi's discomfiture at the hands of Sid Gharnit in a despatch in the *Times*, dated August 5 : 'Although it makes but little difference to Europe who is Grand Vizier in Morocco . . . this crisis has been considered as a battle royal between British and French diplomacy. . . The French are as anxious as the English to have a tolerably firm and stable Government in Marakish.' This despatch was penned after M'nebbi had saved himself from Sid Gharnit.

Morocco itself. Meantime fighting between the French and
the Moslem tribes so near to the holy city of Fez had
created a profound distrust in the minds of pious Moslems.
Other causes less obvious disturbed the northern tribes.
The presence of the Sultan at Fez to quiet the disorders was
demanded. There was a bitter feeling against the Shereefs
of Wazan, and the temptation of the looting of Wazan in
revenge for the support the Shereefs were credited with
giving to French designs might any day offer sufficient
inducement for a descent of the Berber hordes.

It was courageous in M'nebbi to leave the country and
start on his mission to the Court of St. James, in itself an
action not likely to be pleasing to France. But the move
was a popular one with the Moors. M'nebbi had powerful
friends among the Kaids all through the South of Morocco,
and in a policy which showed the slightest independence of
France he would be certain of reckoning on the support of at
least one powerful tribesman in the North. But the game
M'nebbi was playing was certainly a dangerous one. He
might never be disgraced, for he has powerful friends who
could represent his case to the Sultan favourably in spite of
any statements of an adverse character. But M'nebbi might
die, as people do in Morocco; and when he dies the chief
interest will be to see who disappears with him. It will be
another ruin the more, another milestone on the downward
path. But he is strong and resourceful, and ready to oppose
steel with steel. He knows, and has known from the beginning, all the forces arrayed against him, and has sat down
and counted his chances. With all the fighting spirit of his
blood M'nebbi will fight for his life. He knows the odds.
He is racing against time, for every day brings the dis-
integration of Morocco nearer. The sands are running
fast.

Whatever M'nebbi's shortcomings, whatever his pros-
pects, no one regretted Ba Ahmed. Public opinion

unanimously condemned him. 'He was a bad man; God took him!' was the mildest expression. He was second Vizier to the late Sultan El Hassan, on whose death he saw the opportunity for his own advancement by proclaiming Abdul Azziz, a mere boy with a long minority before him, during which the Grand Vizier could do as he liked.

The elder brother of Abdul Azziz was in disgrace at the time of his father's death. He had been appointed Governor of a province, and his father was displeased with his expenditure. This was sufficient excuse for Ba Ahmed to pass him over and proclaim the younger son Sultan at Fez. The mother of the elder brother was of the Rahamna tribe, and she made an effort in behalf of her son. She sent her handkerchief to the headmen of her tribe and summoned them to arms. This was the origin of the general insurrection which followed on the death of the Sultan, and which Ba Ahmed suppressed with so much cruelty.

It was part of the policy of Ba Ahmed to keep the present Sultan in leading-strings. He treated him as a child, gave him toys to play with, and shut him up so that the people should not see him. It is said that he encouraged the boy in vicious practices, which have told heavily against his constitution. But the Sultan's mother is a Circassian, and her influence has been steadily exerted in the opposite direction.

Now and again I heard remarks of a scathing nature passed upon the Sultan; but this was more frequently the case at some distance from Morocco. There he was regarded with pity as too young and inexperienced; and a veil was drawn over his objectionable tastes and his tendency to European amusements and dissipations.

A certain mystery is intentionally allowed to cloak Abdul Azziz. He is a 'dark horse' to most people, and no one knows what he will turn out to be. He very rarely appears in public, possibly owing to the state of his health.

Since the death of Ba Ahmed efforts have been made to

educate him, encourage better feelings, and awaken the
intelligence he is said to possess. Very varied accounts of
him were in circulation. One represented him as a highly
nervous, hysterical youth, in terror of the Powers, and
especially of France; another, as a hardened debauchee,
given up to the Spanish dancers, to whom he had been
introduced by the French; another, as a young man of
extraordinary ability and the highest character, holding
remarkably sound views as to government, with a winning
manner and engaging appearance, who had indeed been led
astray by that arch-fiend Ba Ahmed, but who was only too
ready to break with old ties, and whose one ambition was to
see his people happy. While one account represented him
as completely under the thumb of the French, another
described him as entirely English in all his sympathies, and
caring to hear about nothing but England. Some people
assured me he was mad, others doubted if he were alive, and
a missionary sympathizer described him as 'a young man of
truly Christian ideas, of whom the missionaries have great
hopes.' But on reflection it was difficult to associate
Christianity with anything I heard of the doings of Abdul
Azziz. There was also a report current that he meant to
marry an English wife. He has undoubtedly great curiosity
as to the many inventions which Kaid MacClean has brought
to Marakish for his enlightenment.*

Both Christianity and the English wife would be courses
fraught with disaster, and may be dismissed. His figure is
a sufficiently pathetic one without them. Probably never
has the red umbrella shaded a more worried head than that
of this poor boy, whose position is none the less difficult
because of the multitude of counsellors offering contradictory
counsels, and not averse to using pressure. He has the

* I have already referred to the Moorish gift for appearing Western
towards Westerns. Abdul Azziz appears to possess an unusual share of
this gift, a not unfavourable sign.

Oriental nature which adheres like a limpet to the position of ruler; but Morocco is all the while slipping away from him. It is not a rock, but sand, that he is clinging to. Doubtless, in fits of depression and in boyish waywardness Abdul Azziz may appear distracted. The echoes which reach him from the outside world are of Sovereigns living in the hearts of their people, on firm thrones in Christian lands, and, Moslem though he is in his blood and his bones, he must envy their estate. That he has times of exuberance, of jealousy, and suspicion, when he glories in proving that he is Sultan by indulging his caprice, who can question? He has been shown some of the wonders of the Christian world, such as fireworks and photography, and life in our cities by the cinematograph; and amazing it is to see camels gravely and sedately marching along with the frames for pyrotechnics loaded on their backs. It is said that he photographs well, but there is a touch of Orientalism in the camera, with fittings of pure gold costing some £2,000. That he is attracted by the fearless (perhaps reckless) nature and robust personality of Kaid MacClean is very natural, but that he would always submit to the guidance of Kaid MacClean is another matter. It is not impossible that he has inclinations towards taking an English wife. He has learnt a little English, and he may flatter himself that Western standards and Oriental conduct could embrace and form an object-lesson to the world as easily as he can switch on the electric light into his crumbling old palace. But I do not believe he would ever be permitted to realize any such dream. It is only one of his 'Christian ideas,' which the missionaries may overreach themselves by building upon. A man who at twenty-one has three wives and many concubines, and has lived through such a boyhood, is not likely to possess Christian ideas or to secure a decent European for his wife. Whatever amelioration of his people's lot, whatever civilization comes into the country

during his reign, will come borne upon commercial treaties
devised between Moors and merchants, which treaties it
will be his duty in his people's eyes to try and divert and twist
to the advantage of Moslems and the supremacy of Islam.

Hope for Morocco does not lie in starting questions or
propounding theories. If the rulers cannot see that it is to
their interest to govern well, they will not do so. The Moors
are an acute, cynical-minded people, with very loose inclinations, and I believe them to be incapable of spiritual ideas.
The more I saw of them, the more was I struck with the
baldness and matter-of-fact stamp of their thought. They
are utilitarian in their views, and Unitarians rather than
unbelievers in religion. Among the peasants I found gentler
thoughts, and even the poetical feelings of the mind which
are independent of physical needs. But it would be a
thousand pities to repeat in any form the error of Spain and
Portugal, and raise a religious question in the East. The
missionaries have established themselves in Marakish; I was
told by one of their body (or bodies, for they are many, and
apparently at variance with each other) that they were 'very
busy' and 'getting on famously, though not so well as in
Egypt.' I asked what made the difference between Morocco
and Egpyt, and, to my astonishment, I was told that 'in
Egypt there were already signs of a coming fight—the preliminary clash of arms.' I was relieved to learn shortly
afterwards that steps for the restriction of missionaries had
been taken in Egypt by the authorities. It is not Christianity which is to be feared, but the methods employed,
and the various disputes to which the missionary enterprise
of independent sects leads.

One day when I was at a feast the conversation turned
upon politics. They asked each other what was happening
in China. But no one had any idea. I was asked if it was
true that the Chinese wanted to fight the English. I said
it was true so far that my Sovereign had sent a force under

a capable and trusted General. At this they seemed well
pleased. It would serve those Chinese right, for it was a
very foolish thing for them to wish to fight the English, and
proved how little alive they were to their own interests!
People should keep the peace with the English. There were
a great many nations now who never were heard of before.
Who are these Chinese to give trouble ? At one time there
were only Moors, and Romans, and English (and the whole
company began counting on their fingers), and Spaniards,
and Portuguese, and French—but the French are not of
much account. Now there are so many more nations that
it is quite difficult to remember their names. There are
these Chinese, and the Moscows, and Russians (here someone suggested that the Moscows and Russians were the
same, and a dispute ensued ; then we went on again),
Italians, and some say there is a people called Swiss; but
there was some doubt as to whether they were of equal importance with the Chinese—or the Transvaal folk, who were
giving the English so much trouble. It was generally agreed
that the world was a better place before the existence of
these upstart nations. Someone asked if these people were
all Christians. I said the Chinese were not. Many of them
were Moslems. At this they were amazed, and greatly put
out that their fellow - Moslems should wish to fight the
English. They could not understand it, and declared that
someone should be sent to tell them to desist.

Fear of France provides a form of moral torture for the
Moors. That the faithful should be humiliated as the
French know how to humiliate is unspeakably galling. It
is their lives—their souls—which are jeopardized. The
agony is all the greater because they feel their weakness.
These proud people are like dumb creatures in a cage, waiting to be devoured by their natural enemy. The points they
dwelt on with regard to the French were two—their rough-
ness in handling people who could not help themselves, and

the light value they attached to keeping their word. I
pointed out once that these characteristics were furnished by
some instances among Moors. There was silence for a
moment; then the answer came: 'You are English; the
English are not the French; nor are they Moors, but
friends of the Moors. To everyone his nature.'

During my stay in Marakish I heard a great deal about
French intrigue. It was said that the French paid better
for information than any other nation, and that they had
their spies even in the house of the Sultan. Certainly
Moors lend themselves very easily to become spies. At
one feast at which I was present there was a man who
listened intently, but he never said a word. I noticed that
he made signs as though he were deaf. The host must have
known who he was, but I could not learn his name. When
I asked, 'What is that man called?' the answer was, 'It
does not matter what anyone is called who comes to this
house; they are all distinguished people.' I believe the man
was a real Moor, and not a European inside a Moorish dress,
but never have I felt before what the cultivation of a gift for
spying can produce. The man had a trick of appearing
absorbed in his own reflections, a dreamer lost in contempla-
tion. But if anyone who happened to be speaking on political
matters dropped his voice suddenly, not all his Moorish
power of self-control could prevent a tortured expression
of distress twitching his features, and he would change his
position—lean forward to take another handful out of a dish,
or half rise to rearrange his jellaba.

No doubt Morocco is full of French agents—Algerians and
others—well supplied with French money. It struck me
that the report concerning the aims of the Wazan to obtain
the Sultanate was intended to draw the Sultan and his troops
North, so that the tribes beyond the Atlas might be induced
to fall on the French. 'Why does not the Sultan send an
army to keep France out?' But the Moors knew that the

moment the tribes rose France would seize the opportunity
to come down on Morocco with a heavy hand, and a state of
anarchy, rebellion, and disorder would spread from one end
to the other of Morocco, tribe fighting tribe and sacking
every town.   It was to save themselves from this awful state
of affairs that the Moors were ready to grasp at any straw.

Many Moors were ready to accept any terms from Great
Britain, on whom they looked as a possible friend, because
her Moslem subjects in India were contented with her rule.
'Morocco is a finer country than India ; why doesn't England
take Morocco ?   Let England take Morocco, and do with it
whatever she will, for the English are a merciful people.'
These and similar words were repeated to me over and over
again.   Hatred of the Christian was distilled into hatred of
France.   In their eagerness to save Marakish from becoming
'like Tangiers,' they would have accepted us with railways
and any other invention, trusting only to our abstention from
interfering with their private affairs.

For this reason the mission of M'nebbi and Kaid MacClean
to the Court of St. James's created enormous interest.   More
than once I was asked what the mission meant to do.   I said
they were Moors, and they ought to know.   Could they tell
me what it went for ?   Then one began to explain : ' The
Government is doing its best to keep out foreigners, because
the more they come the worse it is for us.   The object of
the present mission to England is to keep out foreigners.
When the mission gets to England and the English Sultan
sees the horses and the saddles which are sent to him as
presents, he will be ready to do whatever the Sultan asks.'
'And what will the Sultan ask ?' I inquired.   'He will ask
the Sultan of England to become his agent to speak
to France and tell her to let Barbary alone.   Moors would
like it if the Sultan of England became their agent.   They
would never try to make any conditions.   But what does it
matter if there are conditions ?   He may find out afterwards

that we did not agree to them, and that he has not got all he expected.'

I must own that the blood went to my head at the thought of my Sovereign making this discovery. But I merely pointed out that the Sultan of England could never become the agent of any people who were not his own people, or of any country where he had no interests.

'Well, then, let him take Tangiers. What has Marakish to do with Tangiers? It is full of Christians, and Moors hardly ever go there. It is by Tangiers that the French would get into Morocco.' I pointed out that France was never far from the Atlas, and already within striking distance of Fez and Marakish. 'What is it you want, then, before your Sultan will speak to France?' ' You must go back,' I said, 'and look at the Euan Smith treaty. We should want something like that, for without great interests England does not act.' 'What, the man with the flag!'* A pause. Then in a gentle tone of explanation : ' Railways will never answer in Morocco. They are very nice for Europe, like many other things which Englishmen bring here. They answer for a time, and then get out of order, and because no one understands how they are made no one can make them go again. That is how it would be with railways. Believe me, it is for the good of English people that the Moors do not wish for railways. Then as regards telegraphs—they would be quicker than the couriers, worse than the posts! The more these things come into the country the worse it is for Moors. Before people had couriers, those Moors who had money could go on and make a little more; but now there are these couriers, who bring letters up for everybody—everybody knows all about the prices, and Moors cannot make money.' I said it was not so in Egypt or in India, which was under British rule, and yet the people were generally better off.

'The great thing,' said the Moors on another occasion, ' is

* This refers to Sir Charles Euan Smith's hoisting the flag in Fez.

for people to keep their religion, and to get justice. The English are a just people, and if justice be there everything is there. There is nothing so good as justice. In this country there is no justice. Moor eats Moor. Every man is trying to do something against another man. Everything that a man has is wanted by others. Things were never so bad as they are now.' I said it was always darkest before dawn, and this had to be repeated more than once. 'That is true,' said the Moor, 'but in this country there never has been any dawn. There is no light; it does not come here.' I said its absence should encourage people to make it light. 'It is the will of Allah it should be dark.'—'We have a saying that God helps those who helps themselves.'—'That is true; but in this country no one knows who will intrigue against him and take from him all he has. Before they were so impoverished the Moors were very strong and *able* to help themselves.' Then, after a pause, he burst out: 'What is it makes England so strong? It is her justice; because they have justice and equality, and because they are kind to people of all religions—that is why England prospers.'

I wanted to give him some idea of public life and how people served their country for love of their country, and not for making money. He was visibly surprised. 'Human beings are never contented,' he said. 'Money, if it had a voice, would speak to those men and say: "Take me! I must circulate. Do business with me!"'

On one subject I was frequently questioned both in Morocco city and in many other places by various Moors. Our government of India seemed to impress them immensely, but they wanted to know a good deal more of the details than I could tell them. Where they get their ideas from I cannot imagine. But one Moor laid it eagerly before me that the English had fought the French in India and beaten them. One feature which interested them intensely was the variety of religions under British rule, and I was

questioned closely as to religious rites, of suttee, of the
Parsee Towers of Silence, as to the burial by the Red
Indians, and of Bechuana chiefs. Cremation shocked this
Moor very much. English forbearance went much too far,
in his opinion. He shook his head at the Hindoos and held
up his finger, and at last reached the bottom of all things
by leaning back and exclaiming: 'Even the Christians don't
do that !'

I asked him when he was a little more composed what
his objection was. He said: 'When a man dies, it is like a
sleep, and if when a man is asleep he has a very bad dream
that someone burns him, when he wakes up he will feel very
bad, and not be himself for some time to come. He will be
unhappy without knowing why.'

He asked with ill-concealed horror if it was true that the
Christians buried their dead very close together in a deep
hole like a well. I explained to him that in our burial-
grounds our dead were buried side by side and singly, and
that we made our graves a certain depth for sanitary
purposes. 'That is well,' he said. 'I think it is a good
plan, and so deep the jackals will not scratch them up.'

On one point the Moors of Marakish are very tenacious.
They believe their city to be the largest in the world.
Excellence in many things is described by size. They flatly
asserted that Marakish was much larger than Paris. (In
point of fact, one can easily ride round the outside of
Marakish in three hours.) Paris is a small town of no
account whatever. Even Moors who have been there, if
they are not French in sympathy, insist upon Paris being
a small town as compared with Marakish, and 'very like
Tangiers.' But they say it does very well for French people.
They were very anxious that I should admit that Marakish
was larger than London. I said, 'No, it is not larger.'
So, with Moorish quickness, they hurried to declare that
Marakish and London were both the same size, adding that

it was not wonderful that London was so large, because England belonged to India.

They asked me very often why I came to Morocco, and then what I thought of it. On one occasion I deplored the wretchedness of the people. 'It is true,' was the answer, 'that the people are wretched; but you do not know what they are like. If they were not made wretched they would be fighting the Sultan. That is the only way to govern these people.' I said I did not agree, and that their words reminded me of some Moslems who objected to English rule in Egypt, but who had been proved wrong. 'The people there are happy and prosperous and busy making money, which no one may rob them of.' A large piece of kouskous was politely put into my mouth. The Moor sat back with his hands hanging gracefully. He stared out into the garden, where the water gurgled and the shade fell from orange-trees and vines, but he said nothing.

One day when I was sitting in a merchant's store some wild-looking tribesmen called Dutts came in. They were struck at the sight of me, for I did not wear Moorish dress, and asked my Kaid who I was. Then the headman straightway invited me to go back to his country with him, and said he would take care of me. I asked what I should do when I got there. 'Walk about everywhere,' he answered, 'and see what a fine country it is, and enjoy yourself.' My Kaid was wild to go, but the merchant objected, saying we should be killed by hostile tribes on the way. I wished to accept the offer of the tatterdemalion, but just then I felt it would not assist the purpose I had in hand. So I accepted his offer, saying that I would go to his country some day, but that first I must go home and see my father. This arrangement suited all parties, and certainly I should like nothing better than to visit the Dutt country.

These Dutts smelt of attar of roses, with which they had come into Marakish. Their camels were 'loading up' that day. They were busy sewing bags as we talked, in which to pack sugar as a return cargo.

The town is at its pleasantest early in the morning. Some little sweeping is done and water-carriers do a little primitive watering. Camels which arrived overnight lie in the various soks while their burdens are being arranged for sale. Country people stroll about ready to sell wooden spoons, hats of palmetto, or rugs of their own sheep's wool.

One morning I rode out of the Dukalla gate through the leper quarters outside the city. The leprosy did not strike me as the same as that I had seen in Robben Island. At all events, I saw no cases which looked like the terrible tubercular leprosy. Dirt and confusion, coupled with utter neglect, reigned supreme, and the lepers seemed to go about just as they pleased.

I was glad to ride on to the olive-gardens beyond Bab el Khames, and left the main-road to Mazagan by a narrow lane turning sharply to the right below the slaughter-ground of the city, the scent of which was suffocating. This track followed the course of a stream in a deep channel. Palms overhung it, and, turning down another lane, the olive-groves commence with vines straggling over the trees, and blackberry branches half smothering the pomegranates, for which Marakish is famous. These gardens must be very old, for the olive-trees remind me of ancient hornbeams in an Essex park. Their trunks are twisted and hollow, sometimes forming a frame through which the distant landscape can be seen. Whoever plants a young tree does a good thing; but these, with their branches meeting overhead, are like old people or old friends: if one goes, it can never be replaced. There the voice of the nightingale never is mute, and the blackbird whistled and doves cooed, and the water from some of the thousand springs which enrich that plain gurgled and lapped against the roots of the ancient trees.

Very fine crops of lucerne are grown here by irrigation, and excellent food it made for my horse and mule as a change from so much green barley.

One morning, as I was riding out of Bab el Khames, the familiar clanking of chains struck my ear, and, turning in the direction of the sound, I saw a string of camels strangely loaded.   Each camel carried two natives.   They were prisoners being taken under a strong escort to the Sultan's prison, where they were to be confined for life.   I followed them, desiring my Kaid to find out who the prisoners were. One was so heavily ironed that the links were round his neck as well as round his waist, his wrists, and ankles.   He seemed scarcely able to sit upright.   They looked about them with eager, anxious faces, and I have not the slightest doubt that they were a very desperate and bad lot.   The camel-drivers rode behind on donkeys, and the guards rode horses on either side.   I must own that when I saw the counte-nances of these prisoners every scrap of pity died in me. Malice and all imaginable cruelty was stamped on their faces, and one, at least, looked a dangerous lunatic.   They came from Dukalla.   Suddenly, on seeing my Kaid, the Kaid in charge of the prisoners called a halt and rode forward, greeting us very cheerfully.   He was the Kaid of Kaid Ser Oti, and these were prisoners from that Bashalate.   I did not care to ask what they had done, so with many ' Bara caloufigs' and ' Salaamas' we separated.

The camel—the fast-walking camel—is the ' rush freight' of Africa ; and no one who has seen the caravans streaming into Marakish from the Draa, from Tafilat and the desert, can fail to admire those huge beasts, which make those long journeys with almost mechanical regularity.   It is a comfort to the burdened mind to see the camel with a supercilious expression on its curved lips walk away with all one's camp baggage as though it were unaware of having anything at all on its back.   Camels and camel-drivers are a race apart, belonging to each other and inseparable ; and what a lot of the work of the world they do, and do it as it can only be done! On one occasion my astonishment and admiration for the 'rush freight' of Morocco exceeded all bounds, for I saw the driver milking his beast outside a house in Marakish. He milked the camel into a wooden bowl and sold the milk. She was a huge white creature, with a little white one running behind her. Railways may carry milk, but they do not make it. Even the Canadian Pacific Railway would feel its spirit broken by such an achievement as this.

During the first part of my stay in Marakish the conduct of the Kaid of Glawie was much discussed. The Bashalate of the Kaid of Glawie extends as far as Skoora to the borders of Draa, and he wished to establish his authority over Draa. His rule in Glawie is firm, even severe, but has good points about it, for it is said that a trader can go through Glawie with a basket of gold, and no one will harm him. The Kaid has no wish to interfere where nothing is to be gained to advance his main object.

Now the caravans from Draa, which represent an immense trade, pass through Glawie on their way to Marakish. The route they follow is one of the main routes to Tafilat and the regions beyond. The caravans are very large, consisting of sixty camels, and they bring dates, attar of roses, lead, tanned leather of the choice Fillali kind, almonds, and spices. They discharge in Marakish, and go back with Manchester cottons, tea, sugar, and candles.

The tribes called generally the Draa thus own the most important trade. They are several distinct tribes, such as the Dutts, Aits, Ottas, but they are called the Draa, which is the name of their country; and, though the caravans may come from Timbuctoo, the trade is called the Draa trade.

The Kaid of Glawie wishes to rule this people by force, and compel the trade which passes through his country to pay tribute, and when I reached Morocco city the trade had been brought to a complete standstill and business was stagnant because the Kaid of Glawie had seized and robbed an immense caravan. The loss to the trade was very heavy, but the daring of the Kaid and the fact that the Government of Morocco took no steps towards compensating the traders created such a feeling of distrust that caravans had ceased to go and return. How far the Government itself was at the bottom of the Kaid of Glawie's action, to what extent high official personages might benefit by the piracy, no one, of course, could say. It would seem as though the desire to get money by some means or other was driving the officials into very dangerous courses, for in the present instance, though the country people who sold the produce of almonds, dates, etc., would suffer, the results of crippling the trade would make themselves felt down to the coast, and even to the Manchester houses in England. But this fact would be no deterrent to the Moors.

The idea of pillage and piracy as legitimate methods of business lies at the root of all their affairs, and I have heard sedate and plump Moorish merchants refer with a smug satisfaction to Mohammed's rule, that all nations who did not embrace Islam were to pay them 'tribute.'

There is another explanation of the Kaid's conduct. He may have been authorized to use these means to enforce the submission of the tribes, which have never been more than nominally under the rule of the Sultan. The Moors say they know how to deal with their own people. Certainly, they never use kid-glove measures. The tribe at which the Kaid aims is a large and powerful one, and therefore it is possible that he was acting under secret orders from the Sultan, who meant to reduce their independence.

Glawie is only a short distance from Marakish, and the Kaid's kasbah commands the pass in the mountains through which all the caravans must go. While I was in Marakish a party of English ladies and gentlemen who arrived started to ride to Glawie, where, I am told, the scenery is very fine.

These wild tribes are at so short a distance from Marakish that they may at any moment come down and loot the city if the handful of soldiers cannot keep them at bay. When the late Sultan died the tribes came down, though I am unaware whether any of them came from Draa. I believe they were the tribes in the vicinity, and they looted wherever they went. In Denmat the whole town was sacked, women were carried away by force, and Jewesses were put up for sale. All this was done, not for political reasons, but because the people believed that the temporary vacancy of the throne afforded them a chance of securing wealth by shorter methods than those usually obtaining; but the fire was lit by the Sultan's wife of the Rahamna tribe for her son's sake.

Marakish is the spot where one feels the Moorish bone in the country; but the skeleton is very slight. The country is the tribes. The attempt on the part of successive Sultans to rule Morocco as a whole has resulted in a skeleton of authority, whose bones the tribes break when they please. The Moors suited for administration are very few, and mostly enjoy some form of protection. If they offend the State which protects them, they lose protection. Even these men, if they were called upon to serve in an official capacity, would find it almost impossible to resist the customary methods of pillage in the collection of taxes. The best hope appeared to me to lie in increasing the use of the Amînas, or heads of trades, to collect taxes. But corruption is in the blood and bones of the Moors, and will probably only assume another form. Hitherto the Kaids have had the example of many saints whose tombs dot the land, whose lives afford an excuse for, and supply an argument in favour of, robbery and violence of all description; and if a course of conduct be justified by history and religion, what is to restrain a man's inborn inclination? Certainly not an indigestible religion or the scholastic arguments of a political economy totally alien to his country.

It was sufficiently apparent that one of the objects of the mission to Europe was to take protection off its hinges if possible. But the Moors are so exceedingly difficult to do business with that the question arose continually in my mind whether, if protection died a natural death, it would be possible for Europeans to live in and trade with Morocco. Once remove the necessity of a benefit from a Moor, once let him feel that he is free to act as he pleases, would even the best of them be any longer loyal or trustworthy? It is so difficult for Europeans to approach Moors commercially that they invariably employ the agency of protected natives or Moorish Jews. The caravans which travel to and from the desert can only be negotiated in this manner; nor could the trade with the desert be altered in its essentials in the same way as the internal economy of Morocco itself.

To put a case very simply. I wanted a servant in Marakish, and a friendly and excellent Moor offered me his slave, who was thoroughly trustworthy. I accepted the offer, agreeing to pay the slave a peseta a day, explaining that I could not employ the man as a slave. Brahim came, and I tried treating him as a servant, and failed completely. Even the payment, part only of which went to his master, was unavailing. I handed Brahim over to the Kaid, who addressed him as a slave, and hinted, to my intense disgust, that Hadj Absalom and the bastinado were within reach. The Kaid's treatment succeeded, and Brahim improved forthwith.

There are many other matters which are similar. It would take an Englishman years to fully grasp the utter unreliability of Moors in general. It is a most rare thing to find a Moor who is not working his mind on a double thread. One thread is his negotiations with you as he knows you wish them to be; the other deals with all manner of details, and is his chief solicitude; for he hopes to twist it round the other in such a way as to be able to rob you in every direction. A Jew has a better understanding of business. His

18

view is to promote business; and he is alive to the fact
that unrestrained robbery tends to the ultimate destruction
of commerce. Therefore he will be content with a liberal
percentage, and come back hoping for further employment.

I do not say that the Jew is a better man than the Moor.
That has nothing to do with the present case. But the Jew
has a better idea of business. If a Moor travels, and has
been to Europe, he learns a good deal about business. He
does not return a better man, but, generally speaking, he is
more reliable commercially. If people would only realize
how much commerce signifies, how the basis of a sound and
legitimate trade does more to advance civilization and promote peace than all the intrigues of decorated and starred
diplomacy, or the labours of missionaries to the heathen,
then surely we should display more anxiety for the commercial instruction of our youth, and for the abolition of
tiresome old treaties, which were an achievement in our
grandfathers' time, but which suit the modern requirements
of trade about as well as old sailing-ships and mail-coaches.

The travelled Moor is sometimes very astute. I met one
such in Marakish, and he took me on the roof of his house,
and said: 'Now, as you like travelling, I will show you
Marakish. That tower is called the Kutubíya, and there is
the Jumna Mosque,' etc. 'Now,' he said, 'do you see?'
He was in fits of laughter, the tears were running down his
cheeks; but I could not see the joke, so I asked him, 'What
is it?' 'Why,' he said, 'you are a traveller, and when I
travelled that was how people talked to me. They showed
me towers and bridges, and said that's what they are called,
and I went away and forgot the name and what they were
like. I cannot understand why people should travel for that;
I travelled for business, and that I did not forget. Business
is the only thing worth travelling for. If I want to see
towers and bridges, I can see them here, where I don't want
anyone to tell me what they are called.'

CHAPTER XXIII

CATHEDRAL towns and the influence of the Church in
Europe created many of our local markets, and so a saint's
tomb in Morocco, especially if there is a spring beside it,
and an endowment for the maintenance of ropes and skins
wherewith to draw the water, will conduce to the collection
of Moors and to the doing of business. Prayers and business
travel very well together in Morocco. A Moor would as
soon forego his reputation for piety as appear without
clothes. They are fond of dress, and display no small taste
in it, and it is much the same with religion.

In the Sok el Abd, or slave-market, in Marakish there is a
saint's tomb, and this market, in common with the Khames,
and apparently all the others, invariably opens with devotion.
The chief auctioneer leads the prayers, and his fellow-
auctioneers, standing round him, decently and reverently
make the responses.

One evening I was sitting in the slave-market in Marakish.
The slaves had been brought in and put in their separate
pens. Some came most unwillingly, brought by other slaves
or by servants, and in one case I saw positive force used.
It was a girl of some dark breed from the interior, and when

18—2

I asked why she was so truculent, I was told that slaves
hated the sok. I believe they dislike the publicity of the
sale. In this case the girl, who looked very naughty, to say
the least, objected strongly to the removal of her veil, and it
was forcibly dragged away from her woolly head, displaying
a countenance which did not recommend her. Meantime a
certain amount of sweeping had been effected, and water-
carriers came in to lay the dust by a pretty liberal sprinkling;
otherwise the trampling of the slaves as they paraded round
with the different auctioneers shouting out their prices would
have caused too much dust for the public.

I had taken up my seat on a stone bench, with my back
to a corridor, and my Kaid stood beside me. The auctioneers
hurried into a semicircle, and at that moment the travelled
Moor, who had been to Marseilles and Mecca, and who had
taken me on to his roof to show me Marakish, entered, walked
up to me with a 'salaama,' and sat down by my side. We had
often talked about religion, and he always maintained that
the law of the Prophet was entirely good, point by point.

Then prayers began. The head-auctioneer praised God
who made the world. Amen. Who sent the Prophet whose
name was blessed. Amen. Then he cursed the devil.
Amen. Then they all lifted up their hands, and with closed
eyes fervently prayed God to bless the market, and make
things go straight, and give them good sales, that they might
make plenty of money. Amen. The Hadj by my side
folded one hand devoutly over his face and joined in the
responses.

Hardly was the last amen pronounced, when the auctioneers
rushed off to fetch the slaves out of the pens, pulling the
veil off this one, adjusting the shirt of another, dividing
them up into lots, rebuking a mother for not having wiped
her baby's nose, and ordering the children to take somebody's hand; if one showed signs of being troublesome,
they took it themselves. Yet the poor things were as a rule

subdued enough. I marvelled at their painful submission and remembered the lash. I regarded it as the worst possible sign, the hopeless woe of people who accepted bondage.

At last they started. Then the Hadj, who had been watching me intently, asked: 'Do they have slaves in England?' 'No,' I answered. And then the yelling of 'Thenine! thenine!' (two dollars) for a little girl of seven, who looked entirely Moorish; of 'Klatter! klatter!' as the prices rose; and 'Asperah! asperah!' (ten dollars) for a girl of sixteen, apparently from the West Coast, 'a baby for a dollar,' began loud and fast. Some were sold in lots—a mother and three children, or two or three boys and a girl.

In the Moor's short question, and my still shorter answer, how much was hidden! All the difference between the East and the West; for the keynote of the East is conquest—conquest for slavery. Then the Hadj asked the Kaid, who, of course, told me afterwards all he said, why I came to the sok, since I had no business, and if I thought the Moors were fair and upright in their business transactions. The Kaid said the Englishwoman went wherever she pleased. He could not himself always tell why, nor yet what she saw to interest her. But that is the way with Englishwomen. They think about things which Moorish women do not trouble about. As to the Moors, the Englishwoman was good, but it was not easy to deceive her. This last was a home-thrust, as there had been a little matter which the Hadj tried to explain. The Hadj was at all times anxious to impress me with the piety of Moors, as a proof that all they did was right, and far better than the rest of the world.

I never doubted the sincerity of this man's intensity of Moorish religious feeling. No Moor is ashamed of religion; it covers the people's character as the flowers cover the ground—not put on, but growing out of it. This man made his religion a careful cult of the best that he knew and that

his instincts led him to believe, and he expressed himself
with persuasive grace and charm and without fanaticism.
His arguments were directed with a skill that bordered on
casuistry, balanced by quaint touches of philosophy. But
how entirely his opinions were steered by his instincts, and
how completely mere argument would fail in altering his
principles, I saw, not by a sudden flashlight, but with steadily
increasing certainty.

It happened that a slave was being sold that evening who
interested me extremely. He was a very fine specimen of a
coal-black man. He was tall, with a well-shaped peppercorn
head, and he had the bearing and manner of a Prince. His
age was against him, for he was full-grown, and boys fetch
the best prices. I tried to discover his origin, but in vain.
He seemed too frightened to speak much. He came from
the interior, but a very long way—I should think from
Central Africa. The auctioneers objected to my asking if he
had been a slave for a long time, declaring stoutly that he
had. From the uncertain manner and dejected, hopeless
air of the man, I think his position was fairly new to him.
He was very resigned and patient, and I felt a strong wish
to rescue him. His price was 8 dollars, which I could
have afforded, but the difficulty was what I was to do with
him afterwards. The moment I bought him he would have
been free ; but I was leaving the country in a fortnight, and
how could I in so short a time teach him to be a free man
in a country where it is difficult even for the men of the
Moorish nation to protect themselves against oppression?
Not only would they have taken advantage of him and
cheated him, but he would have become reckless, and have
learnt, by associating only with the lowest classes, all the
worst Moorish vices. The slave-marks on his face I could
not obliterate, and probably the best fate would be that he
should be kidnapped and sold as a slave again. This very
often does happen, and the adools are adepts at making out

papers which the English Consuls, if appealed to, have the greatest difficulty in disproving. To send him back to his own country, if it could be done, would probably be to send him back to be murdered, for in all probability this man's story was not unlike that of Joseph, whose brethren sold him to get him out of the way. What profit is it if they slay their brother and conceal his blood? Better sell him to the Ishmaelites.

I remembered seeing, in a corner of the sok at Tangiers where strangers were allowed to camp, a party of freed slaves. They were natives of Sus, and were devout Moslems, having made the pilgrimage to Mecca. They were the most idle vagabonds imaginable, without a redeeming point, clad in dirty old rags, and the women wore silver ornaments. It was bare humanity, without a vestige of grace or charm. They supported themselves by carrying water, begging, and doing odd jobs, but did as little work as possible, and they were the recipients of a dole raised in England for freed slaves. That had probably attracted them to Tangiers. But they never stayed anywhere very long, and they did not look as though anyone would desire their neighbourhood. As I looked at them, a feeling of such hopelessness came over me that the best I could wish for these people was that they might be kidnapped and enslaved again, and made to wash and to work. When I saw the man, who was the husband of the two wives and the father of the vulgar, impudent, and generally detestable offspring, hurrying to his prayers, I remarked to my Moor that all devout Moslems were not men, but brutes who badly needed a master. He reflected for a moment, and then replied much as follows : 'A man was once a good Moslem, but it came that all he had was taken from him. His wife may starve, his little children they die. It came because he had something that he was put in prison. When men saw what happened to the good man, they said : " If that bad thing comes to a good man, what may happen

to me? I will not trouble. I will eat and drink; I will not
work hard; I will enjoy myself, for to-morrow we die."' If
Islam fails to provide freedom for the free and to protect
the most devout, what hope is there for a freed slave and
outcast?

The trade in slaves is not the successful business it once
was; the Moors are not so rich or willing to give the prices
they used to do. The Arabs buy them chiefly in the Soudan
in exchange for merchandise. There is always fighting going
on in the Soudan, and as soon as the Arabs come with merchandise from Timbuctoo and Senegal, the tribes sell their
prisoners for goods which the Arabs have brought. These
Arabs at one time bought their goods in Mogador; but
since the French have opened up the country Mogador has
lost the greater part of the trade with Timbuctoo, though it
is still the centre whence slaves are dispersed. Akka is the
great centre of the caravan trade; ostrich feathers and ivory
are purchased there.

Timbuctoo and the Soudan do not furnish half the slaves
in Morocco. Many slaves are born in the country, and in
times of famine children of the peasants become slaves. If a
case arises in which the father of a child is a free man, and
if he recognise the child as his, then the child is free. But
such cases are rare. The child of a slave mother is a slave,
and numbers of children are sold in the markets—slaves by
their mothers only. Once sold it is very difficult to free the
slave. But provided the owner is humane, the lot of the slave
is preferable to that of the peasant, who is nothing but a serf.*

---

* It is remarkable how a slave may improve as a slave. It depends, of
course, upon what his condition when free amounted to; but the fact remains that many slaves have risen in slavery, and turned the curse of Ham
into a blessing, the curse they have left to those who have enslaved them.
But to see how greatly our views on this matter have changed, it is only
necessary to recall that Queen Elizabeth held a religious service and
blessed the ships which she sent out to capture slaves; for at that time
slave-trading was associated with missionary enterprise, and it was

If a good price be paid for a slave, avarice prevents most
Moors from ill-treating him. They try to recover the money.
Slavery is a matter of domestic convenience, and it sometimes happens that a good-natured master sets his slave free,
especially if he knows he is going to die—it is a favourite act
of mercy.

The speculation is chiefly with regard to women. If a
black, newly imported, is young, good-looking and physically
sound, she will fetch a good price; and the first time she has
a child, mother and child are sold together, and she fetches
more than she did before, for Moors have a great liking for
a good boy slave brought up in their own household. The
best prices for slaves, especially young women, are given
in Marakish, Fez, and Tetuan. Along the coast, in towns
such as Casa Blanca, there are Moors who know the market
thoroughly, and buy up slaves to sell again, knowing before-
hand exactly where they can place them advantageously.

Slavery is precisely one of those features which form a
stumbling-block in Islam. The law must be accepted by
the Faithful in its entirety, and whatever is according to the
law is lawful. Whether as civilization advances Moslems
and Jews will see that their creeds are not in accordance with
higher civilized ideals is the question. The Jew dropped
slavery long ago, and polygamy, though his creed allows it,
is very rarely practised. Will the Moslem do likewise when
in the course of time he has learnt to know better and to
exercise self-control? The most that can be said at present
is that the Moors are aware that slavery is unpopular with
Europeans, and especially with the English, and they
begin to feel very 'sneaking' about it. They are not at all
anxious to talk on the subject; they assert its religious
sanction; they object to Europeans seeing slaves sold. It is

---

regarded as doing the work of the Lord when the negroes were caught
in West Africa and sold in America.

better for the matter to wear down by degrees rather than to
deal with it wholesale or make it a point for attack. When
Moor has learnt that it is not economic for Moor to eat
Moor, then he may safely be depended upon to free his
slaves and abstain from importing fresh blood.

There are no public buildings which can be visited in
Marakish; but from the outside some of the mosques are
very fine. It is, however, more the grouping of towers,
domes, and doorways which is striking than the actual architecture. The Kutubiya Tower is the pride of Marakish.
Its height must be considerable, and it stands in a large
walled enclosure, its base surrounded with tapering cypress-
trees and olives. The summit of this tower is decorated
with three golden balls of diminishing size, the smallest being
the highest, and about these globes there are many tales.
They were believed to be of pure solid gold, but the discovery
that they were copper gilt was made recently when repairs
became imperative. The tower itself was intended as part
of a large library, and was at one time surrounded by book-
sellers' shops, of which not one is left at the present time.
The library was never finished; only the tower attained com-
pletion, and testifies to what its sister-tower at Rabat might
have been had it been finished.

The Moors in Marakish are fond of books, and may often
be seen reading them in their little shops and at spare
moments; but I seldom saw books in their houses. Once,
as I was buying some goods at a shop, I opened the book
which the trader had just laid down. It was bound in
morocco leather of the rich, soft brick-red colour of the real
Tafilat skin, called in Morocco fillali. The binding was not
in hard boards such as we use, but the leather was thickened
or stiffened slightly. The book itself was written in Arabic
characters, and was, I gathered, a holy book relating to the
Koran, probably a commentary. The trader was not very
well pleased that I touched it. The touch of a Nazarene is

Mr Cavilla photo Tangier.

THE KUTUBÍYA TOWER

defiling; but he knew something of me personally, and made the effort which a Moor will always make to set aside convention and prejudice where individuals are concerned.

My day in Marakish began as soon as it was light. I called down into the patio to the Kaid to feed my horse and mule. My bath was established in a lovely room, covered with arabesques, and with a very fine ceiling. The floor was of tiles and marble, and I could splash to my heart's content. As soon as I was dressed, and had snatched a cup of coffee and a biscuit, we were off through the nearest city gate.

There are several delightful rides when once the rubbish-heaps are passed. Before there was much heat in the sun, I reached a grove or garden of olives, and the pleasure of the quiet shade of these fine old trees in a comparatively treeless country was inexpressible. There is one ride which goes out by Bab Rub to an old kasbah, two miles from the city, and from there I frequently rode across country to Bab Dukalla; the change was very refreshing from the highway, of which I had had so much. The view of the Kutubíya Tower on that side is grand. It rises above the city walls, whose low, horizontal lines give it height. The colouring of the city is enriched by the bright green of the foliage, and to see it glistening with the tarnished gold of the old balls on the top of the ancient tower catching the light makes Marakish look like a city in a dream. As I looked at the great tower, I thought again of the Moorish proverb of the three best things in life—'A horse, a woman, and a book.' But, alas! the fact is, they neither know a good horse nor a good woman, and I very much doubt the value of their books, though I wish they could read mine.

Before leaving Marakish, I went to see the newly-established school of the Jewish Alliance in the Jews' quarter. It was started, in spite of considerable opposition, both from a party among the Jews themselves, who are backward and very

bigoted, and from the Moorish officials. It is evidently very
well managed, and a most commendable undertaking. I was
quite astonished to note the improvement in the children
who attended the school compared with those who were
forbidden to do so by their parents' mistaken conservatism.
But the entire teaching is French, except for a little Hebrew,
and I gathered from some Jews of English origin and
Gibraltans that they felt it as a grievance that there was no
English master provided for their children. I believe that,
were a master given a small stipend to take English classes
in the school, he could at other times make a very good
living by giving lessons in English. There must be plenty
of young English Israelites who would do this, but certainly
some society among their own people ought to secure him
a small stipend in connection with the school. I marvelled
that so little interest was taken in these Barbary Jews by
their co-religionists at home. I experienced much kindness
from them. They were very intelligent and hospitable, and
in such little transactions as I had with them, I found them
perfectly fair and straightforward. They have suffered most
cruelly in the past, but given a helping hand now, I
believe they would rise to become a great people.

I continually heard reference made to the mission of Sir
Charles Euan Smith. It was a piece of English diplomacy
which failed remarkably, and its failure I heard attributed
to various causes. Some people said it was due to want of
skill in the conduct of affairs by the Ambassador; others,
that he failed because he was not supported by the home
authorities; others, that his failure was a triumph of French
intrigue. The Moors plume themselves to this hour in
having discomfited a European Ambassador and frustrated
a scheme which had for its object the taking of their country.
They are only just beginning—those who are most enlightened—to question the wisdom of having rejected the
proposals then made to them.

In point of fact, I believe there is a little truth in each of these views of that signal failure. The Embassy appears to have behaved in an incomprehensible manner; the home authorities can generally be reckoned upon to send an Envoy anywhere, and desert him if the slightest difficulty arise. French intrigue is undoubtedly very active in Morocco, and it would be very grateful and comforting to the Moors to feel they had dared to humiliate a Nazarene. They have no foresight.

I heard it said that had the British Vice-Consuls on the coast, who are merchants, been listened to and supported, they would have been able to effect a good deal more than the Ambassador; and had they been consulted and supported, they could have done much to remedy the bad effect of his failure. This is quite possible. The merchant has his own prestige with the Moors, and knows the phrases in which to address them; but had they been hampered with a retinue of wild young men who practised revolver shooting on the roof at the pet cats of exalted Moslems, even their tact and discretion would have availed very little. Too much care cannot be taken in the selection, not merely of an Envoy, but of every detail of his suite. This brings us to the Diplomatic Service itself, and to that Foreign Office whose somnolence is most regrettable.

People talk of the sights and the smells of the East, but far more remarkable to me are the sounds. It is not merely the difference in the sounds, but the absence of any European sounds to tone them down. Once only, riding in Marakish, I heard an English sound. A bevy of women masquerading as Moors came round a corner, and though I was too far off to hear what they said, their voices were English. There is never the rattle of a tramcar, never the roll of a train, never the rumble of wheels, never the throb of an engine, except on those rare instances I have mentioned in the coast towns, when one starts at the sound of a petroleum machine grinding

corn.   Close to the Bab Dukalla there is a well, and the
rattle of that worn old wooden pulley and cord are part of
the associations of that entry.   Then there is the scuffling
patter of the ambling mule, when the East is in a hurry and
is going by 'express,' the tapping footsteps of the little
donkeys, the measured tread of a stepping charger ; the
soft sandals or bare feet of human beings make hardly any
perceptible sound, but the cushioned, firm tread of a camel is
always distinguishable.   It is almost noiseless, yet never
stealthy, very deliberate and assured.   The sharp rattling
sound of the storks' bills, the shrill cry of the hunting hawk,
the rapid chatter of the blue roller, or the hoot of an owl—
all suddenly obliterated by the choking sobs of a camel.   In
the gutturals of the Arabic there is nothing soft or pleasant,
and the voices are hard and harsh as a rule.   One of the
most dismal sounds on earth is the song of labourers engaged
in building walls.   It has been suggested to me that it was
the same song that Christian slaves were compelled to sing,
and it may be.   It might be the song of the damned, so
harrowing is the discord and the misery.   The cry of the
muezzin is the only musical sound, a weird wailing which
rises and falls on the air.   Of cries in the street there are not
many.   The water-carrier rings a not unmusical bell ; the
baker's boy goes round shouting that his master's oven is hot.
But the yelling at an auction in the street or market is sometimes terrific.

   At most of the public gates and at many street corners
beggars recite passages from the Koran, or call on the name
of some patron saint.   It is a form of soliciting alms which
is more or less aggravating, and they know how to pitch their
voices so as to apply the screw to a nicety.

   'Ah-h-h !   Moulai.   I dr-e-e-e-e-e-s !' yells a wretch, with
a throat and lungs of brass and teeth like a row of hatchets.
Then, dropping his voice to the pit of his stomach, he
hammers out a wise saying of the holy man.   Practice has

made him perfect, for, pass when you will, the pitch of his voice will never vary.

'Ah! Moulai abd el Cadr-r-re!' says an old hag, in a cross and savage tone, abruptly stretching out her lean hand for the expected coin. The level tone of her voice betrays absolute indifference to the saint whose name she invokes, while her eyes eagerly take in the fact that a Nazarene is passing, which is the best chance she has had of late; and if she gets nothing, she spits abruptly, so that the newcomer might mistake the spitting for part of the saint's name drawn out a little too long.

In general, these beggars are a thoroughly bad lot. Sad as their condition may be, their afflictions have for the most part been brought on by their lives; and when by the malice of man, or the malingering in gaol, or from other causes, they add blindness to their worthlessness, they learn a few parrot phrases and assume a sanctimonious air which out-Pecksniffs Pecksniff. Sometimes they rattle away at the Koran as hard as they can go, while a companion or two ejaculates 'A-men''; or they may be slow and impressive, to allow the pearl they have produced to sink into the heart of some passer-by. 'The slave plans, but the Lord completes.' It is not the words which are striking, but the tone of reproof and the air, which would make the fortune of a preacher in Hyde Park. The way they twist their lips and turn their spittle, and the rapidity with which their magazine comes up with a powerful curse when it is wanted, convinces one that religious begging is a profession as distinguished as it is lucrative.

To hear a fellow-creature being beaten, no matter how much he may deserve it, is excruciating; but the thing which broke my spirit and drove me to utter despair was when the Moors played their music. Very early one morning in Morocco city a string band and singers started performing in the house next door. All the instruments were out of tune. They all played as they pleased, and sang what they

chose. Some repeated one note incessantly, others raced to
the extremes of an incomprehensible scale. The tom-toms—
usually a relief—were on this occasion quite irregular, like
the uncertain slamming of a door. What can be the musical
ear of these people? For this frantic noise was a highly
paid orchestra summoned to celebrate the arrival into the
world of a son and heir, or, as the Kaid put it, ' The m'ra
got a cheeker.' I do not know what happened to her, but I
had to leave the house.

Things may befall one in Marakish which are a mingled
privilege and pain. I thought so when a camel laden with
attar of roses gave me a blow by swinging his load against
me in the narrow street, and knocked me on my face into the
middle of a greengrocer's store. As I picked myself up from
the collection of melons and apricots, many of which were
adhering to my person, I found the owner of the stall had
continued his occupation of flicking flies with a palm leaf,
and took no notice whatever of me, not even when I modestly
offered to pay for the inconvenience I had inadvertently
caused. Then, saying ' Allah is great ' and ' Praised be
Allah !' as politely as I could, I withdrew to the street, where
the Kaid, mad with indignation, was shouting shrill curses
at the slowly-retreating camel in the tone and manner of a
cockatoo.

Though there are some commercial travellers who, from all
accounts, thoroughly understand Morocco—in fact, probably
know it better than anyone else—yet there were many complaints that the young men sent out knew nothing of the
business or the language of the country, and took several
years to learn either.

Another point much insisted upon was the difficulty of
getting small orders booked by English houses. The
Germans would snatch at twenty-five, where an Englishman
would want a hundred. The result is that the young men
starting in business, who have to buy carefully, place their

orders in Germany, and, having done so in the day of small
things, will continue to do so when they increase. Another
difficulty is that the travellers travel for one firm and one set
of prices. In a country like Morocco it is difficult to get the
exact article for the exact price. 'Dear me!' exclaimed a
trader, as the commercial traveller left his store, 'I know if
I could go home for twenty-four hours I could get what I
want.' A German will take down the most careful note as
to uses, material, and prices, and get the article *made*. The
Englishman goes away. It struck me that the young commercial traveller had little or no acquaintance with manufactures in general, or the uses to which raw products could
economically be put.

In Marakish certain goods only are sold by certain retailers,
but the merchants import generally. The retailers purchase
in the fondaks what they require; as, for instance, salam-
pores (worn almost exclusively by the Rahamna tribe) are
sold only by certain retailers, who sell nothing else. Each
retail trade is under the control of a man called an amîna.
He has to ascertain the solvency of anyone who wishes to do
business in that trade. He is responsible for any bankruptcy,
therefore he is certain to be careful who is allowed to enter
the trade. If additional taxes are collected, it is his business
to collect them.

The legs and feet of trade in Morocco are the Moorish or
Jewish agents, protected by firms at the coast. They are of
two kinds. The Semsar is an authorized agent or representa-
tive, and he is protected. His protector has to show the
authorities that he has paid import duties to the amount of
1,000 dollars. The ordinary commercial agent is granted a
mohallet. He may be imprisoned, but his goods cannot be
confiscated.

The city was incensed at the claim for compensation put
in by France for the murder of a Frenchman who landed
against Moorish advice on the Riff coast. Then came the

news that Spain was troublesome respecting a boy and
woman stolen from Azíla and taken to the hills. Certainly
in the latter case an indemnity was demanded in a tone
which would never be used towards a European State, also
the punishment of the tribes, without any inquiry as to the
circumstances; and yet the Powers supported such conduct,
England amongst the rest.

The official world was savagely disappointed at failing to
discover the treasure of Ben Doud. His house had been
rapped and punctured and searched, but no trace of his concealed hoard could be discovered, nor would anything he was
made to endure on the road to Tarudant induce him to give
up the secret. At length the spirit of revenge burst out.
Ben Doud was reported to have 'died.' His wives as well
as his concubines and slaves were put up for sale.

The slave-market was crowded, and the bidding for his
cook, a very ugly old black, but a notorious artist, was quite
exciting. She fetched 250 dollars.

The following day, when I went to the market, I was
surprised to find it so crowded that I could only enter with
difficulty. All Marakish was there, including not a few
women. The great officials strutted about and formed
groups, beckoning occasionally to the auctioneers to bring up
one or other of the unfortunate women, who, for the most
part richly dressed, were parading round the market.

To my astonishment, more than one of them was quite
fair. One looked an educated woman, with a French type
of countenance. All seemed to feel their humiliating position
most acutely. The wives were not unveiled, and the favourite
wife did not march round. She remained in a dark passage,
which apparently communicated with a neighbouring house.
Only once she was brought out at the bidding of an old
Moor, who insisted on her veil being lowered that he might
examine her face. This was done for a moment, and I saw
that she was quite fair. She was sold for 432 dollars. It

was stated that Ben Doud had freed many of his slaves, and if so, their being sold again was a disgrace. The horror of the day culminated in my seeing a leper sitting opposite to me afflicted with Naaman's leprosy, which is a particularly contagious kind, and this wretch actually beckoned to the auctioneers to bring the slaves to him that he might examine them, and this he did with his horrible leprous hands, feeling their arms, breasts, and legs, and peering closely into their eyes and teeth. I saw them shudder at his touch.

CHAPTER XXIV

ON leaving Marakish I decided to travel with a caravan to
see what this mode of travelling was like. The caravan consisted of only five camels, the three principal drivers being a
Shereef, who prayed for them all and was a Dacouwah; Abd el
Cadre, who was the rogue of the party; and Alli, a neat little
Arab of regular features, white beard, and good brown eyes,
and the most peculiar voice I ever heard. It had a hard,
rattling, creaking sound, and recalled the old rope and pulley
of the well at Bab Dukalla.

The caravan went on overnight with my heavy baggage,
and I was to catch them up at Jehoody the next day. But
they went on, leaving me with no comforts and hardly any
provisions. I rode after them hard, and just as it was getting
dark, by good luck, discovered them camped some distance
from the track, and threatened that I would charge them
before the British Consul with purloining my property.

The road from Marakish to Mogador is far more interesting than to Mazagan. At one place I should like to have
spent some time. It was volcanic country, and, though very
dry on the surface, I could see plenty of gas-holes, into which
the water must run in the wet season. Hereabouts are the
remains of an old city which was overwhelmed by the

volcano; and, as in most volcanic country, the soil—where there is any and water can be applied—is very fertile. There was the square-headed mountain of the South, recalling Amajuba. The mixture of the ground is remarkable, and I should think that, if precious stones are to be found anywhere, it would be in this district.

That evening we camped at a settlement of Jews beside a running stream, which made music all night. It was a lovely moonlight night; the light of the moon put to shame the ruddy glare of the camp-fire. The stars were as clear as frost overhead, and I could watch the grand outline of that African mountain. Then, trooping stately against the sky, came a caravan of thirty camels. So grand they looked, they might have formed the retinue of the Wise Men of the East following some bright particular star. They came close to us, and passed on again out of sight. The houses of this village were clay structures, with curious clay additions on the roof for keeping grain out of the way of rats and mice. The ground was alive with rats and mice; they lived in crevices and cracks in the ironstone. Some appeared to be like our field-mice; others were much larger, with long fat tails, and some, I think, were voles with white throats and breasts. I thought of the story of the celebrated Lord Mayor, whose only possession brought him such a fortune when presented by the merchant adventurers to the Sovereign of Barbary. There was a great deal here to interest me, and I regretted being obliged to leave.

The next day the camels went off early, and they made light of a road over which our horses could scarcely scramble. I was riding Conrad again, and though he was a hill pony, yet stepping for five hours over loose rocks and boulders tried him a good deal. We had a hot wind from the desert in our faces; then the Kaid's horse cut its fetlock with a stone, and yet I felt the necessity of not giving the caravan another chance of bolting, for they had three hours' start of

us. So we hurried on. At length we came to a deserted
soko called Oolad Omsheba, or Child of the Lion, where we
found the camels.

The Kaid was speechless with wrath, for his horse was
lame ; but, beyond giving him a remedy, I said but little, and
after a cup of tea retired for my mid-day rest to one of the
empty huts and soon fell asleep. My rest was disturbed by
the camel-drivers, who each in turn appeared to come and
look at me. Beyond telling them once to go away, I took
no further notice, for I never do so when natives fuss, knowing that if it were necessary the Kaid would come to me.
Presently, to my annoyance, I heard a rush carpet being
spread just outside, and down on his knees went one of the
drivers, who was a Shereef, and began to pray by groaning
out the name of Allah at regular intervals as though in
physical pain. I made up my mind to engage a donkey at
the next village to carry a few extra provisions, and send on
the caravan.

At twelve o'clock I left the hut to get some luncheon, and
was received with a chorus of 'Amdullilah !' and 'Allah
Arkbah !' from all the camel-drivers, and exclamations of
'Salaama !' The Kaid acted Grand Vizier with unusual
dignity, which caused me to wonder, but I said nothing.

That evening we went on to a small village about two
hours' ride from the soko ; and this move was most necessary,
for there was no food to be bought at the soko, and the
animals had not had a bite since they left the last camp
before sunrise. The village was on a hill above a stream,
and as the people seemed to have nothing to do, I had no
difficulty in hiring a man and a donkey. I wrote a letter
consigning my heavy goods to Mr. Ratto at Mogador, and
gave it the next morning to Alli, the camel-driver. I saw
Alli turn pale under his brown skin—he was a very good-
looking little old Arab—and I nearly asked what was the
matter. But the Kaid stood by looking as wise as an owl,

and, as he said nothing, I made no remark. The Shereef, who did all the praying for the party, had been hard at work on his mat. He was greatly venerated by them all, notwithstanding that he was the slimmest liar imaginable. This holy man came at once and offered me his services, which would 'not cost me any money.' But I told him that I had decided that the caravan should go on without me, and that he was to go with it. I wondered whether they would go. I looked at my watch, which had stopped, and said that in half an hour the camels were to be gone, and in less than that time they rose up and departed. But Alli remained behind.

After I had had my bath and killed a yellow scorpion under my bed, we started, Alli acting as guide because he knew of a good place to rest for the mid-day halt about an hour from the village. As the Kaid knew every inch of the road, this was superfluous, and I suspected a motive. When we reached the olives and the pool Alli gave a loud call, and implored us to go on a little further through the rushes and bushes. He tried to egg his donkey to pass us, but this it was not difficult to prevent. Suddenly I saw ahead into the rocky plain beyond, and there were five camels, and the next moment, under a bush, I saw the Shereef and all the drivers. I swung Conrad round, calling the Kaid, and telling Alli what I thought of him in English as I galloped past. Mooleeta followed me, and the villager on his donkey brought up the rear. At the olive-trees by the pool I pulled up, and, dismounting, said the tent was to be pitched there. I was vexed to think that I had travelled through so much interesting country at a pace which prevented my seeing half of it. I saw that Alli had not intended me to camp, for the camels were on rock, where there would have been no pitching a tent. Presently, however, he appeared, but I told him to go to Mogador and take my letter to Mr. Ratto, and he vanished.

While the tent was being pitched I sat down under an old olive which had been pollarded, and, looking up, I saw the most beautiful and the largest chameleon I have ever met with. He was of a most exquisite green, with lighter markings in patches, like the reverse side of an olive-leaf. He watched me most attentively, moving his position from time to time very cautiously. He laid hold of the branches with his strong, square hands, and, advancing his tail above his head, curled the end of it round a twig in front of him and crawled after it. How long he had lived there, and how many travellers he had taken note of, what his family history might be, I longed to know. Was it the one that Leo saw? —for they live in a wild state to a great age.

The Kaid praised Allah, and said the señorita would be safe from serpents. Leo tells how the chameleon 'killeth the serpent,' and thus describes it: 'The camelion, being of the shape and bigness of a lizard, is a deformed, crooked, and lean creature, hauing a long and slender tail like a mouse, and being of a slowe pace. It is nourished by the clement of ayer, and the sunbeames, at the rising whereof it gapeth, and turneth itselfe up and downe. It changeth the colour according to the varietie of places where it cometh, being sometimes black and sometimes greene, as I myself haue seen it. It is at great enmity with venomous serpents, for when it seeth any lie sleeping under a tree, it presently climbeth up the same tree, and, looking downe vpon the serpent's head, it voideth out of the mouth, as it were, a long threede of spittle with a round drop like a perle hanging at the end, which drop falling wrong, the camelion changeth his place, till it may light directly vpon the serpent's head, by the virtu whereof he presently dyeth. Our African writers haue reported many things concerning the properties and secret qualities of this beast, which at this present I do not well remember.'

He made no attempt to practise dropping 'a perle' on my

head, but hid himself in the thickest part of the old pollard.
Innumerable pigeons and doves of many kinds had come to
drink here, and all through this district I noted the absence
of hawks. I saw a beautiful little bustard about a foot high
exactly the colour of the rocky ground. He ran and hid
between the stones.

Up to this point the mountains had accompanied me,
though we lost the Atlas range the second day after leaving
Marakish. No road is dull which has mountains in sight.
They are doing the work of the world as grandly and un-
ceasingly as the sea. They are like certain great human
natures, who, having passed through a time of agony,
become the steadfast friends and servants of humanity.

There was also at this place a large black-beetle about
2 inches long, with brilliant yellow legs. A goldfinch came,
and, sitting on a twig by my tent, sang for a time. He was
a young bird, and his plumage was not perfect. I had seen
partridges in small coveys on the road, and another sporting
bird, which got up with a loud ' whir-r-r,' like a grouse, but
which, I believe, was a kind of francolin. In the rivers
which I forded coming down on this road there were
always small fish, sometimes 3 or 4 inches long. They
were always coming down-stream. At Marakish fish the
size of herrings were caught in the river, which looked
like young shad, and I wondered whether the shad bred in
the upper reaches of the rivers. The river at Marakish is
fed by the snows of the Atlas. After a hot day a flood comes
down, which drops again before morning. In riding out I
found the river easier to ford in the morning than in the
evening.

I wondered whether there were lakes in the Atlas where
trout would thrive. The Sebou looked as if it might well
be a salmon river, but, so far as I saw, there were no trees
or shade such as fish love for breeding purposes. The Moors
are very fond of calling all fish mullet. When I was on

board ship at Mogador, some very large gurnard were caught, and these they called mullet.

I had not proceeded above 200 yards on my next march when out of the rushes on either side rose up five camels, and in another moment there was Alli one side of me and the Shereef on the other. It was so supremely ridiculous that I should have laughed if the two drivers had not been watching me intently where they jogged along on their little donkeys. I felt sure that even if I galloped they would somehow keep up with me, and it was just the pace I did not want to go. It is only occasionally that I care to gallop, when I am in hurry to reach a given point, or when a certain mental listlessness comes over me.

That evening we camped at an empty soko, where there were some guards of the Sultan in a house on the hill. On the way the conversation had turned on the appointment of a new Kaid to replace one recently dismissed. The people differentiated strongly between their loyalty to the Sultan and their loyalty to Kaids. The former appeared to be part of their religion, but with the Kaids it was a personal affair. A figurehead these people must always have—of their own religion—but Governors are another matter.

As evening came on, travellers swarmed into the soko, and one caravan of thirty camels. When my tent was pitched, I called the Kaid and asked him to tell me what was the matter with Alli and the caravan. At my question the Kaid nearly died with laughter, and then confessed to me that all the drivers expected to be put in gaol at Mogador on account of their conduct at Jehoody in absconding with my baggage. He said that Alli declared he would not go to Mogador, but that the Kaid advised him to do so, rather than return to Marakish, where Hadj Absalom would be ready for him. Abd el Cadre was also in a cruel state of anxiety, having been blamed by all the others. The Kaid, with many explosions of mirth, confessed to me that,

when I had been sleeping at the soko, he went to them and
told them that I was dying, if not already dead, and bid
them go and see for themselves—well knowing that I should
not trouble to speak to them.   They were scared out of their
wits, the more so that the Kaid raved and swore at them,
and promised that they should all suffer the full penalty of
the law.   I interrupted him here to ask why on earth he had
acted thus, but the vexation of independent action on the
part of a caravan was galling to the Kaid, and he had not
yet got over having lamed his horse.   He had so filled them
with panic that Alli exclaimed: ' Let the English take me
now and hang me, for they are a merciful people !   La ' la !
la ! Hadj Absalom will bastinado me first.'   The Kaid said
that truly they should *all* be hanged.   He would see to it
that not one escaped.   Whereupon the Shereef arose, and
took his prayer-carpet and spread it at the back of my hut.
Taking counsel with one another, they agreed that if I did
not die—which seemed only too likely, since I appeared to
be insensible—they must in future take the greatest care of
me, and on no account allow me out of their sight.   Somehow I must be got alive into Mogador.   The note I gave
Alli for the consignment of my baggage was believed by them
to be an order for their arrest.   I told the Kaid that he had
carried his joke quite far enough, that I would not have
them punished any more, and that I wished to see the last
of the camels, and to travel at my leisure.

Hardly was this settled than Alli arrived.   ' Salaama.'   He
had a favour to ask of the señorita.   It was that she would
visit his house in the argan forest on the following day.
I said I would think about it, and he and the Kaid withdrew.

The next morning the Kaid came to tell me that he had
smoothed matters.   He told the drivers that, though they
had assuredly sinned, Allah had been merciful to them, and
no harm had befallen the Englishwoman ; therefore the

English Consul would not be severe upon them if they in
all things did as the Englishwoman desired, and followed
the good advice of Kaid el Hashmy, who knew the English
and the manner in which they acted. Alli sat down by the
Kaid, and said : ' Al Kaid, your whiskers are the same as
mine, and if you will bring the Englishwoman to my house
I will make her a feast.' The feast would be made for me,
and eaten by the Kaid, so I saw that the inducement was
considerable.

Accordingly, the camels having started before daybreak,
we followed them three hours later. We left the main road,
and branched off by a bridle-path along a lovely valley in
the argan forest. A thunderstorm the day before had laid
the dust, and heavy mists concealed the hill-tops, and as the
sun rose higher the warm earth and flowers exhaled a
delicious scent. Blackbirds sang, and once more I heard
my old friend the cuckoo.

The argan-tree is in growth something like an English
yew. Some were still in blossom, others were fruiting, while
from a good number the ripe fruit was falling in quantities. I
saw a gray squirrel like the Canadian chip-munk, but more
than twice the size. This animal, I am told, eats mice.

The track through the forest wound about ; in places the
branches met overhead, and often it was impossible to see
more than a few yards ahead. A part of the valley had been
cleared by a settlement of Jews, who had planted vineyards
and gardens both of fig and olive and cultivated them beautifully, and fenced with stone. They irrigated from the stream
which ran through the valley. Hills clothed with argan-
trees shut in the scene, which was one of enchantment,
owing to the intense light, the evergreen nature of the trees,
and their great age.

After three hours' riding—for we went slowly—we reached
the house of Alli, and my tent was pitched in a stubble-field
under an olive-tree. Before me was a plot of flowering maize,

beyond that an olive-garden, and down a deep vista I could see the distant hills clothed for miles with argan-trees.

After I had rested and had a bath, I lunched, and then Alli came with the Kaid to ask me to visit his wife, bringing a present of wild honey and butter and two loaves of barley bread. These Arabs live in stone-built houses—two or three houses shut in by a high wall. Their wives are veiled, and those families I visited consisted of one wife and two or three children, all strong and healthy. In the courtyard lay a great heap of the argan fruit, and in the houses the women and children were busy breaking the stones to get at the kernels, from which they crushed the celebrated argan-oil.

Alli's wife, a very sweet-looking, elderly woman, whose eldest daughter was a really lovely girl, met me at the threshold of her house. In the centre of the floor a fire was smouldering. A hen was brooding some chickens close to the ashes, and at either end rough planks raised from the floor a few sacks which served for bedding. Some shelves for odds and ends completed the furniture. Immediately opposite the doorway lay a heap of broken argan-stones and a large boulder, and one or two round pebbles for breaking the stones lay beside it. When the argan harvest is over, the fig harvest begins, and then the olive. Besides there is the barley to be sown and gathered, and the maize. Then there is wool-carding and spinning, butter-making and corn-grinding, and the collecting of beeswax. There stood the little mill upon the floor, worn smooth by long use.

What struck me most about these people was their evidently strong family feeling and their affection for one another. Even the sinister-looking Abd el Cadre was a most affectionate father to his little girl, who cried and held out her arms to him, and would not be satisfied unless he carried her, rubbing her little head against his grim counte nance in a most wheedling and caressing manner.

My whole person and appearance was strange to these

women. My hat filled them with wonder. They were surprised that the Englishwoman wore no ornaments, but my
signet-ring, which was gold, was much commented upon.
They told me many times that they were pleased to see me,
and they hoped I would stay with them. Why did I want
to go back to my home ? I had a wish to give something to
Zara, Alli's wife, but I had nothing about me but one precious
safety-pin. This I offered her, showing her how it worked.
She was enchanted with it, and added it immediately to her
many adornments of beautiful old silver brooches and chains.

Zara stroked my cheeks with her hands, and told me with
delicious flattery that I was 'beautiful,' till with a start of
consternation she perceived my gray hair—a sign of ill-luck,
I believe.

After this I went for a walk in the argan forest,

> 'And all within were pathes and allies wide
> With footing worne, and leading inward farre
> Faire harbour that them seemes so in they entered arre.'

The detestable camels had arrived, and I was glad of
them this time, for I was able to extricate a sugar-loaf and
some green tea ; but the Kaid disapproved of the green tea,
so we went with the sugar-loaf to present it to Zara. The
children had already been to my tent, and returned sucking
large lumps, so I knew this present would be acceptable.
I found Zara at work preparing to cook a fowl, and, as it was
dark, she had lighted a rag dipped in argan-oil, and a most
beautiful, clear, steady light it gave, with no unpleasant smell.

After I had been in bed about an hour, and was dozing off
to sleep, the Kaid roused me with the announcement that
a kouskous was coming. I struck a light, and tried to wake
up, but I was desperately sleepy, the air in Morocco being
very conducive to sound sleep.

Then there rolled into my tent two white bundles, which
proved to be Zara and her daughter Tamer, who brought
with them the kouskous. They sat down on the floor and

threw back their veils. I invited them to partake of the kouskous, which, after well-bred hesitation, they did. The two women and the kouskous filled up my tent, so that I found it best to remain where I was strapped in my valise. It was a trial to me to be called upon to eat at that hour of the night, and still greater to see them eat. The approved manner of partaking of kouskous is to squeeze up a handful, roll it into a ball, open the mouth wide, and throw the ball down the throat. Then, to my great regret, they spoke an Arabic of a different dialect to the little I had picked up. They asked me how soon I should leave Morocco, and I told them when I expected to do so. They asked if it was far to England, and I said not very far. Then it seems they expressed a wish to accompany me, and, instead of saying they were welcome, I said, 'In'shallah' (If God wills), which caused them exquisite amusement. My tent interested them, and they almost crawled underneath my bedstead in their deep perplexity at the arrangement of its legs.

At last Alli put in his head and beckoned to them to come away, and with a most friendly leave-taking they departed, and after summoning the Kaid to remove the remainder of the kouskous—which, being cooked with argan-oil instead of half-rotten olive-oil, was really excellent—I was left to sleep in peace.

The following morning we started for Mogador soon after four o'clock; but the road was very rocky and mountainous, and as I purposely rode slowly through the forest, we did not reach Mogador till past ten o'clock.

In the centre of the plain in the valley where Alli lived was a knoll, crowned by the shrine and family residence of Sidi Bulwarri. Once it must have been a palatial mansion, but it is now in a ruinous state, though the descendants live there, and it is customary for the Arabs to bring them offerings. They, in turn, never refuse hospitality to any traveller. Whoever goes there is sure to receive food and refreshment for himself and his animals, and safety for the night. It is nevertheless a gracious act to make some suitable offering in return.

The forest was full of birds in full song. Blackbirds roistered, and there was another fowl with a voice like a very fat flute, who produced most remarkable intervals. The song was uninteresting, but the quality of the voice, though rather heavy, was rich in the extreme. Besides the cuckoo, there was a bird which was even more monotonous, and had not the exhilaration of the one high note. He kept on repeating a sound three times, like a little trumpet blown by a child—pom-pom-pom, pom-pom-pom.

I heard these birds again when I was riding towards Saffi and entered a corner of the argan forest. The argan-tree has to endure a good deal from its youth up. First goats browse it ; then, when it contrives to outtop their reach, the camels nibble it. There are many which have become like bushes trimmed with shears.

The argan-trees died out, and cypress took their place, insignificant and uninteresting. At length we reached the sand-hills, beyond which lay Mogador and the sea. Conrad gave a shout of delight and commenced capering, evidently believing that he had reached Tangiers again.

The view of Mogador from the land side is very lovely, as its old Moorish name of Essueira indicates. It is a clean but not very interesting town, with straight streets, and has many hotels much appreciated by Europeans. The climate in winter is excellent, and there has been some talk of building a sanatorium on the hills.

The population is largely Jewish. The natives are neither so pleasant nor so well-mannered as elsewhere. Education may do something to soften the behaviour of the girls, but at present they struck me as uncivilized and common, and, not being Moors, they go unveiled, and are very bold.

From the value of its products, the trade of Mogador is

held to be the most important on the coast. Gold, ostrich-feathers, gums, skins, oil, and wax, are rich exports, though they do not bulk so largely as the cereals from Casa Blanca and Mazagan.

Owing to the French railway, the trade with Timbuctoo is lost to Mogador, but the Sus country enables it to hold its own, and must eventually render it a very important port. Drought had injured the cereals in Sus, and barley was dear, which would probably increase the cost of transport, just as the price of coal may diminish the profits of railways. But though there are independent owners of camels, the peasants themselves ride transport on their own beasts, and the partial failure of a cereal crop in Sus is of less importance than the failure of demand for their almonds or oil would be. The Italian trade has made a great advance in one year owing to a failure in Italy of both olive and almond crops. Olive-oil is worth £27 a ton in the unrefined state in which it is shipped from Mogador. Eighty-five thousand pounds' worth went to England, and another large export, the precise amount of which I did not learn, went to Italy viâ Marseilles. For almonds there is always a demand, owing to their use in manufactures, such as sweets, and for the oil, used in printing fast colours on calicoes. Germany is a large importer of almonds. Some Germans whom I met told me that they were constantly busy in Germany endeavouring to find new inventions and new processes for turning to fresh account the raw products from Morocco. The Italians do not manage their merchant shipping with the sagacity displayed by the Germans. The freight of goods to Italy is very high, some-times amounting to as much as thirty-five shillings the ton.

At one time British trade suffered severely by the abuse of credit. The manufacturing houses at home were far too ready to give credit to anyone who asked it. Now the system is that they export through their agents, who sell to the merchants, who sell to the shops on three months' credit

20

small parcels of mixed goods. The sales to up-country
Moors are always cash. The merchants have refused to
allow the agents to take small orders of mixed goods direct
from the shops, on the ground that if they did so mercantile
business would be injured. But there is a tendency for
business to become direct between merchants and manufacturers. The business done by the merchants with the
shops on three months' credit is a very good one, making a
return of 10 per cent.

I found that Germans were, at all events temporarily,
rather less active than elsewhere. Though they are often
held up as an example to Englishmen, I cannot always
approve their methods. But their commercial travellers
are always good. German methods of trade achieve for
commerce results resembling those of trades-unionism on
industry. Labour has been taught to regard its interests as
isolated, and the German takes the narrow view that only
German trade is beneficial to Germany. A policy of grab is
as ruinous in commerce as in industry, and the marvel is
considerable that a philosophical and highly educated people
should evolve an empiricism as reckless as the infringement
of banking laws. To get trade away from other people by
any means does not necessarily increase the bulk of exports,
or even their value in favour of those who secure it. The
price paid may prove altogether beyond any working value.
I have known instances of large purchases of produce by
Germans at figures which would prohibit them from export-
ing the goods. The loss may mean not merely bankruptcy
to the firm, but the decline of the original trade, and prove
far from being a substantial gain to Germany or anyone else.
But these matters are slow in coming to light. Reports are
misleading, especially those of shipping and tonnage ; and
when commerce receives a severe blow, such care is taken to
conceal the fact that it takes time for the mischief to declare
itself.

I met Mr. Elias Hatchwell in Mogador, who told me much that was interesting about the Sus province, which is unquestionably the richest province in Morocco.

As regards the gold exported from Mogador, it reaches the coast in the form of native ornaments. It is a very soft, pure gold, and is probably found in the form of dust. From all I heard, I should doubt whether any process yet known would be able to recover it in payable quantities. The natives have their own ways, just as the Chinaman who goes to work with a blanket and a tooth-brush, and realizes a profit which would never be returned upon any machinery. Extraordinary tales were told me of how the Arabs find the gold, all more or less romantic. For example, I was told that it is found by Arabs who travel at night. When a storm of wind has moved a sand-hill, the gold falls to the level of the plain, and the caravan passing by night sees the trace of gold in the moonlight. It can only be seen by moonlight. Then the Arabs take a powder and carefully cover up the gold, and come back next day and fetch it away. These stories always have something which happens ' by night,' and the finder is generally a mysterious person—a ' traveller.' But there is nothing improbable in the sand containing gold, and very likely the places where it is found are known to these Arabs, who have for centuries travelled in all the by-ways of the desert.

The Jews in Mogador have more than one good school, and subscribe for the stipend of a doctor. They also support a hospital. I was struck with the efforts they are making for the improvement and amelioration of their general condition, especially as most of them are extremely poor.

Mogador is most striking seen from the sea, when the steamer makes a magnificent curve in entering the harbour inside the two islands. As I came down the coast when I left Saffi for England, I felt that that sight was one of the most remarkable in Morocco.

Kaid El Hashmy was still very bitterly disposed towards
Abd el Cadre, whose name he never uttered without hasten-
ing to add, ' May God leave him without clothes !' I had
no intention of punishing the ' sin of Jehoody,' as the Kaid
described the bereaving me of provisions. I contented myself
with leaving Mr. Ratto to talk to them as Allah put it into
his heart to do, and with deducting a dollar from their wages
as payment for the villager and his donkey; and this I did
to teach them not to be slippery in their dealings with English
travellers   Then I sent the wife of Abd el Cadre and Zara
presents of figured muslin and a silk scarf for their personal
adornment.

The following morning I departed for Saffi. The road lay
along the beach when the tide served ; when it did not we
had to go inland, sometimes over very steep rocks. The
shore was covered with beautiful shells, pebbles, and agates.
At one place we climbed over limestone rocks, which contained wonderful fossil remains of shells, etc. One evening
late we forded my old friend the Temsift River, which flows
by Marakish. It was full of white fish about a quarter of a
pound weight.

Arrived at Saffi, the Governor assigned me camping-ground
in the prison of the old palace. He gave me two guards for
day and night, and allowed me to make use of one of the
rooms, which was originally part of the State prison, and
now occasionally used either for prisoners or soldiers. The
horses and Mooleeta were stabled in the outer courtyard,
which was closed and barred at night.

The air on this hill-top was delightful, and the week I
spent at Saffi was very pleasant. Mooleeta had lost a shoe,
and jagged her hoof on the journey from Mogador. She
had immensely enjoyed coming from Marakish with a light
pack, and however she was tied up at night, she almost invariably got loose, and I would be called, to see her little
figure silhouetted against the sky-line, with her heels ' knock-

ing holes in the sky.' The night before I came on to Saffi
Moolecta got loose in Mogador. She found two donkeys,
and these she took with her at a smart gallop, their hoofs re-
sounding over the paved streets. They ate whatever they
could find in the market, and Moolecta was out of sorts next
day. The donkeys enjoyed themselves so much that they
lifted up their voices and sang. The maddened inhabitants
opened their bedroom windows and called to the town guard,
who traced the mischief to its source and came to my camp.
I sent the Kaid, but Mooleeta, on seeing him, went gaily off
again, and he returned, feeling his dignity affronted. Therefore I went myself. It was a beautiful clear moonlight night,
and I waited for the cantering hoofs to come round the
corner, and then I called ' Mooleeta !' and she stopped and
walked up to me, rubbing her head against me and looking
very foolish. At Saffi I was thankful for the gate to the
courtyard, but when she went to drink at the fountain she
took the opportunity of a race through the streets, with the
guards after her. Sometimes I went to the end of the square
before the castle and called her, when she always came.
The Moors watched the proceeding, sitting on their heels
and laughing incredulously. I believe they thought there
was magic in it.

> ' " Why does the lamb love Mary so ?"
>   The little children cry.
> " 'Tis Mary loves the lamb, you know,"
>   The teacher did reply.'

CHAPTER XXV

SAFFI was the scene of some severe fighting at the time of
the rebellion after the death of the late Sultan. The Abda
tribe rose, but first some of the headmen came into Saffi and
appealed to the leading merchants to do something to help
them. They said: 'It is not a case of paying taxes, nor even
of paying what we can pay, but even our children's food is
taken from us.' The merchants could not interfere, knowing
that the Kaids who squeezed the people were in their turn
squeezed by the authorities. Then the tribe rebelled.

The Kaid of the district fought a battle with them outside
Saffi, and they took refuge in the saint's house on the hill.
Their strength was considerable, and the Europeans in the
town were in great fear, knowing that at any moment the
feeling might turn against the Christians.

The attack upon the town was planned to take place on a
public holiday. There was feasting going on, and all the
town was given over to pleasure with that zest of enjoyment
which is so marked a feature in the Moorish character. The
extravagance of the harem is in all they do. They are
feminine in their sensitiveness, in their fancy, in their intui-
tion. They are childish in their thoughtlessness and aban-
donment. Just about an hour before sunset a man within the

city was to give the signal to those outside by waving a flag. He was detected in the act and killed on the spot. Immediately the firing commenced. The people in the town ran hither and thither, talking and shouting in consternation and alarm. The rebels within the gates fought with the soldiers, and for some days the struggle went on. In some places the dead bodies lay in heaps; on one spot over 200 men were killed in one day. The Europeans remained passive, and probably saved their lives by so doing. One English merchant insisted upon going to his office as usual, as though nothing was happening, while his wife entertained the ladies to a champagne luncheon. But the town was in the direst jeopardy.

The Kaid of the district, Aissa Ben Omar, had massed all his troops, but the rebels came on in a greater force and fought with the courage of despair. Then Aissa offered terms of peace, and four of the rebel leaders were to come to him to sign the terms. He had four men in readiness with swords, and at a given signal the heads of the four rebel leaders were struck off simultaneously.

That it was an act of supreme treachery no one will deny, an act which no civilized people could readily excuse. Yet, in general opinion at Saffi, Aissa's conduct is condoned as having saved the town from massacre. The certainty that the wholesale massacre of men, women, and children was the alternative is clearly established in the mind of all who knew the situation.

The fighting in the town itself must have been very general. There was fighting at the gates, in the main street, at the sanctuary called Rabat, and on the kasbah hill. On the spot where my tent was pitched a great hole was made, and no one knows how many men were buried there. The order given was, 'Roll them in their haiks and bury them at once.'

Saffi is a place of many legends. The patron saint of Saffi appears from his name to have been a sailor, Mûl Amûd es Swari, signifying 'master of the yard-arm.' When

on the road to Mecca this holy man begged hospitality at an
Arab douar and was refused, and he was told to rest on the
top of a slender pole. Probably his seafaring career had
taught him the trick, for he immediately climbed the pole
and settled himself on the top. The Arabs, filled with
amazement and alarm at his feat, hastened to fetch a bull
and sacrifice it at the foot of the pole, imploring the acrobat
to descend and cease threatening them with divers plagues
and calamities. At length, taking off his shoe, he wound up
by casting it into the air, and made his final condition as
follows: ' Wheresoever this falls you must erect and dedicate
to my memory a fondak for the reception of weary travellers
and pilgrims on the road to Mecca, who, like myself, tired,
hungry, and overtaken by night in a strange land, can find
there refreshment and rest.'

It was from the sanctuary of this saint that the wounded
rebels were dragged by order of Aissa, and shot in the square
immediately before it. Yet the sanctuary is so sacred that
no European may pass down the streets, no Christian foot
defile the precincts.

The palace where I had my quarters was built by the
Sultan who married the daughter of an Irish sergeant in the
Royal Engineers. Sidi Mohammed ben Abd Allah was the
Governor of Saffi, and ruled Morocco well for the space of
thirty-three years. In his reign several treaties were signed
with European States, and Moorish Embassies were sent to
the chief European capitals. He also encouraged education.
He reigned from 1757 to 1790. Much that happened then
would make a good and profitable study for the present
youthful Sultan, who probably knows nothing at all about it.
All that this Sultan did for his country was on strictly
Moslem lines, but in his removal of oppressive Kaids, in his
defence of the country against foreign aggression, and in his
liberality towards learning, he forms an excellent example to
Abdul Azziz.

Opinions differ as to his Irish wife, but for the most part those I asked inclined to think she had but one motive in marrying the Sultan—the gratifying of feminine vanity in hearing herself proclaimed Sultana. Her retribution was severe enough in the form of a son who, without excepting even the infamous Mulai Ismail, was the most cruel Sultan who ever rode beneath the red umbrella. 'According to El Gazad's own expression,' says Meakin, 'his principle was that a Moorish Sultan should keep a continuous stream of blood from the palace gate to the city, that the people might live in awe.' Among the first acts of his reign, the same authority records that ' the breasts of the Basha's wives were squeezed in presses, and his mother was suspended for two whole days over a slow fire with screws on her head.'

There is a legend that the palace was built at the request of the Irish bride, that she might live where she could see the sea. There it stands in ruins, but wonderfully grand, and forming a perfect piece of history. By the permission of the Governor I went over it, and found that it consisted of four parts: First, the palace of the Sultan, where there were noble halls and grand reception-rooms, with beautiful arabesques; then a lady's bower, built in a Portuguese style, with a terrace and little turrets, and a wide view commanding the sea. At the back the palace and the bower were supported by a strong fortress, still used as an arsenal. It was the strongest place I had seen in Morocco, but I was not allowed inside. The part in which I was quartered was the State prison, and below me were the dungeons.

During the lifetime of this Sultana the policy of the Sultan is said to have been favourable to the British, and a mournful interest hangs about the rooms where she lived, full of graceful and exquisite arabesques, equal, it is said, to anything in Spain, of beautiful proportion and simple, graceful lines. Doubtless the terrace, which opens on the roof, was once provided with oleanders, orange-trees, and flowers in

pots, and trellises covered with the passion-flower and the
blue idumea. From the two little turrets—where a person
might sit as in a summer-house, entered by an archway to a
raised platform within—a wide view of the sea and the Bay
of Saffi can be enjoyed. But the terrace is cracked and
threatens to fall; the paint is dim upon the walls; bats,
owls, and hawks fly through the silent, empty shell of what
was once the gilded cage of a Sultana. Down below in the
dust the camels tramp along the road to Marakish, and far
off against the sky a distant sail may now and then be seen,
and sometimes storms of tremendous violence hurl the long
Atlantic rollers into the bay and cast wrecked ships upon
the shore.

It would be impossible to restore the palace. May the
day be long distant when tourists from Mogador swarm
through its crumbling courts and picnic in the deserted
mosque in the great square! The most fitting end would be
a grand explosion in the arsenal at the back, but probably
the powder there is mouldy. I brought away with me two
fledgeling hawks, as companions to another I had rescued
from a boy who was tormenting it in the market. Other
countries have ruins which are treated with respect as in-
cidental to the history of the country; but in Morocco the
grandest things are the ruins, and nothing greater has been
built upon them. Their neglect, even more than their ruin,
impresses one with the fall of an empire which once planned
so greatly in Africa for pleasure, for learning, for civilization.
Decorative as Morocco is, both historically and as a geographical feature, she has had no poet as yet to put her
feeling into song. The romance is not that of Greek classic
or German legend or medieval drama, any more than it is
an eighteenth-century play. Its character is all its own, and
hitherto, because of something wanting in the soul of the
people and in their religion, it has lacked the voice of song,
which alone can hand it down to posterity. Will the day

ever come when a poet will walk in 'his singing robes, with
the laurel round his head, through these old towns, finding
his home and his welcome in every dumb heart and upon
every learned tongue in the Christian world'?

I found that the men who loved Morocco best were not
Moors, but Western people, and perhaps one of them may
do for Morocco something approaching that which Lord
Byron did further east. His poems touched the scenery so
tellingly that they were often in my mind, especially 'The
Corsair,' but also the lines commencing

> 'Know ye the land where the citron and myrtle
> Are emblems of deeds that are done in their clime?'

And yet I thought almost as often of the answer to it, which
puts in a not ungraceful parody the spirit of a not altogether
unjust criticism, which those who write sympathetically of
the East must expect to meet with from the West. As
poetry the lines cannot compare with Lord Byron's, but the
spirit they breathe contains the essence of psychological
fact :

> 'Know'st thou the land where the hardy green thistle,
>   The harebell, the heath, and the woodbine abound?
> Know'st thou the land where the shepherd's shrill whistle
>   Is oft heard in the gloaming so sweetly to sound?

> 'Know'st thou the land of the mountain and flood,
>   Where the pine of the forest for ages hath stood;
> Where the eagle comes forth on the wings of the storm,
>   And its young ones are rocked on the high Cairngorm?

> 'Know'st thou the land where the cold Celtic wave
>   Encircles the mountains its blue waters lave;
> Where the maidens are pure as the waves of the sea,
>   Their footsteps as light and their actions as free?

> ''Tis the land of thy sires, 'tis the home of thy youth!
>   Where first thy young heart glowed with honour and truth;
> Where the wild fire of genius first caught thy young soul,
>   And thy feet and thy fancy roved free from control

'And is there no charm in thine own native earth?
Doth no talisman rest on the place of thy birth?
Are the daughters of Albion less worthy thy care,
Less soft than Medora, less bright than Gulnare?

'Oh, why doth thy fancy still dwell in a clime
Where love leads to madness, and madness to crime;
Where courage itself is more savage than brave;
Where man is a despot and woman a slave?'

In the evening I rode out of Saffi to take tea with Mrs. Russi at her house in the country, and returned with a beautiful bunch of flowers, which she gathered in her garden for me herself, and with a blue roller to add to my young hawks. On riding back in the evening the beauty of Saffi struck me more than ever. Even in the twilight the colours were very strong; much could be left to imagination, and yet the touches of colour were there. The rich brown of the rocky headland was felt rather than seen, contrasting with the gray-blue of the evening sky; the white decision of the houses, with their square lines jutting one above the other, was thrown up by the rich red tone of the earth; the square turrets of the palace, roofed with green tiles, cut the sky-line above the hill; here and there a lighter touch outside the walls suggested in the dim light the soft tone of a plot of barley; while in the near foreground rose up a field of brilliant green maize fenced by huge aloes.

It rapidly grew dark, so dark that Conrad had to find his own way down the rocks. I saw a light flicker here and there, which added to the mystery of the scene; but Saffi is not lighted at night, and as we rode down deeper and deeper the whole town lay in darkness, save for one dim candle, which hung in the great Bab as we rode through. Small wonder was it that the Kaid lost his way in the winding streets which led to the kasbah.

The country round Saffi contributed very largely to the grain supplies sent to England at the time of the Crimean War. In the last century there were immense shipments of

Mr Cavilla Photo Tangiers

THE CAMP OF A CARAVAN

.

cereals, a Danish company under the governorship of
Mohammed XIII. securing exclusive trading rights. As
may be supposed, the Portuguese encouraged the trade at
Saffi, and the town was so famous commercially that in 1639
an English Order of Council directed all ships trading with
Morocco to go first to Saffi.*

In reading these accounts, the full magnitude of what
oppression can do to ruin a country is brought home to one.
The province of Abda, being immediately under the Sultan's
rule, together with that of Dukalla, is very impoverished.
The Rahamna, and especially the Abda tribe, have suffered
from every kind of cruelty, extortion, and oppression. Those
who have not saved themselves by flight are too wretched to
farm with any enterprise. The rapacity of the Kaids is so
frightful that women who are left without husbands have been
known to come into Saffi carrying a load of wood on their
backs to sell it to buy a little food for their children, and the
Sheik has followed them and stayed outside the gate, waiting
to take the few pence from them when they came out. However bitterly the townspeople at Casa Blanca may feel at the
rebellion in which they were sufferers, there was a cause to
be maintained, for which it was more legitimate to fight than
that of the Government which by one means or another
suppressed the rebellion.

The Kaids felt that the youth of the Sultan and his
minority gave them a chance they might not have again for
amassing wealth. Now the fear that their good time may be
drawing to an end makes them worse. The Court officials
have driven them to extremes by the sale of offices, which
here takes place with the most shameless bidding. The
influence of M'nebbi had done nothing so far to discourage
this state of things. He started as a poor man, and to keep
his position and influence he has been obliged to resort to
various expedients for getting money. In a country where

* Budgett Meakin, 'The Land of the Moors.'

local magnates are frequently made Governors, it is very easy
to get one to bid against another. There was a Governor
who had in his province four very wealthy men. They
offered the Sultan a large sum if either of the four were made
Governor. This was the nearest approach to a joint-stock
company which I heard of in Morocco ; but it ended badly,
for the existing Governor immediately offered to double the
sum offered by the four men to retain his governorship, but
he made it a condition that the four men should be under his
jurisdiction. He won the trick and the rubber too, for he
kept his Bashalate and had the men imprisoned, stripping
them by degrees of all they had, reimbursing himself for his
outlay and making a little more besides. Two of the men
died, but the wives went to the Sultan, and after much
supplication obtained the release of the other two, though
not till they were beggared.

The gaols throughout the southern part of Morocco were
crowded. At Mogador the prisoners were said to be dying
at the rate of ten to fifteen per diem. When a man has been
officially robbed, I have heard a Moor say : ' That man is no
more good ; why shouldn't he die now ?' And they certainly
do die, and in what circumstances ! The funerals of prisoners
were frequent. The corpse was wrapped in a coarse shroud
and put in a rough box or open tray. The form, and almost
the features, of the dead could be seen. He was carried
shoulder high by six men, who chanted in a suppressed tone
phrases from the Koran, but there were no religious rites
accorded them. Once I asked why the dead man had been
imprisoned, how long he had been there. Not a creature
could tell me. He was alive, and now he was dead; they
were going to bury him. And no more was said.

But the gaols of the tribes or provinces are very much
worse than those in the large towns or seaports. I met a
man who knew the gaol of Kaid Aissa, and he said it was
crammed, there being at least a thousand prisoners in it. He

could not tell me what the death-rate amounted to, but he said that, as very few were released and they were always putting fresh ones in, a good many must die daily. The prisoners in these provincial gaols have a certain amount of air and light during the daytime, but at night they are, for the most part, put under ground, where there is neither air, light, nor drainage. They get no food except what is supplied them by their friends outside.

I saw a good-looking mare for sale. She had had a foal, and the owner was selling her to find money for the Government. Once I heard of three horses, not of the first class, but good ones. They were sold in Saffi Market for 15 dollars the three. It is not that there is much to sell, but no one has any money to buy with. Those officials who have money do quite a nice little business by buying up slaves and forwarding them elsewhere. In Sus the stealing of women and children for slaves is a business which, like any other, depends on prices. Fatalism is poor comfort, but it helps the people to a stony resignation.

The Order of the Aisaweeya is very strong in Saffi, and they were preparing for their feast. The town is very fanatical, and formerly no Christian would venture to cross the square while the procession of the Aisaweeyas was passing. It was a very bold step of Sidi Aissa ben Omar when he dragged the wounded rebels from the sanctuary of the Rabat and shot them in the market-place. But probably that is really the best way to deal with these people; for in such a case their very fanaticism would quiet them. They would find an excuse for Allah; they would say that Allah did not protect them, because He willed that they should fail.

The Aisaweeya practise thought-reading. I have watched the proceedings at odd times sufficiently to gain a fairly good idea of the whole. The prophet arrives with two or three musicians, who beat tom-toms and play on a weird flute.

He has also a bag of snakes, a little straw, a box of matches, and a well-blunted dagger.

The musicians sit on the ground and start playing. A crowd collects. The snakes crawl out of their bag, and the prophet beats a tom-tom over their heads, and hits them or boxes their ears right and left a few times; probably the noise stupefies them. Then he lights a fire of the straw, and inhales the smoke, making great grimaces to indicate satisfaction. This is supposed to inspire him, and when the spirit has entered into him he fears nothing, and struts and stares before the company, and winds the snakes round his arms and neck. They lay hold of his cheek, and sometimes he puts out a tongue of disgusting size and thickness, and the serpents press their teeth into it, and generally draw a drop of blood, but, as their poison-bags have been removed, he can allow this with impunity. This is the moment of supreme triumph. Who will dare now to question whether he be a true prophet? And with a snake gripped in each hand, to a terrific outburst of music, he marches majestically round the circle. The musicians shout, and the snakes go back into their bag. Then the prophet begins to preach. He tells the people that he can do these wonderful things because his patron saint protects him, and because he trusts in God. His patron saint watches over him and gives him this wonderful power. Meantime the tom-tom goes briskly round for contributions, but it is difficult to make him hurry. He walks up and down, taking stock of his audience, talking in a fervently religious manner, and inhaling fresh whiffs from the straw, which lies smouldering on the ground. Suddenly he declares that he can do still more wonderful things : he can read the thoughts in other people's minds. At this announcement the music bursts out wilder and madder than before, the prophet himself playing the leading tom-tom, dancing, whirling, stamping, and shouting. Each one in the crowd looks on, wondering whose thoughts the prophet has read. Glancing shrewdly round, he selects some old man with a sad face, and, advancing towards him with stealthy steps and an unctuous grin on his face, he makes a few mysterious passes before the old man's face. Then he adjures him in the name of his patron saint, shaking his finger at him. The poor old man becomes bewildered, and is passively led into the centre of the circle. A frightened peasant may well believe that this inspired prophet is a power, and he sinks resignedly upon the ground near the smouldering straw, the bag of snakes, and the musicians, while the prophet, with a loud voice, shouts his fortune to the audience. 'This man,' he begins, 'is one who cries with his heart, but not with his eyes. He is poor and sad, and struggling bitterly to do himself some good, but it does not seem possible to him. He is beaten down and very miserable, and his heart is ready to break. But a better time is in store for him, because he is a true believer, and Moulai Abd el Cader' (here all the crowd kiss their hands reverently) 'has taken care of him, and will send him a good fortune.'

The peasant's face brightens, after being clouded with intense anxiety. He feels it is true, and that he must lose no time in showing his gratitude to Moulai Abd el Cader for his unsuspected care, and for sending his prophet to him. He beckons the latter, and folds both arms round the impostor's neck, whispering to him that he will give him a present of money for Moulai Abd el Cader's sake, that he (the prophet) may give it to the blind and poor in the name of Moulai Abd el Cader. At this the prophet rejoices. He tells the crowd openly what has been whispered to him in secret. He seizes a tom-tom, and bangs and thumps it, flying round and round in madder and madder dances, skipping in the air and descending on one foot. He draws the dagger and stabs himself, but he does not die. He beats the heads of the musicians with the tom-tom as he flies past where they are sitting on the ground. In his frenzy he

21

knocks over some of the audience. He grins, and smirks, and rolls his eyes about, and finally throws himself prone on the ground, and begins to saw at his bare arm with the dagger, but does not succeed in making it bleed. He pretends to force the dagger down his throat. Finally he plants it by the hilt in the ground, and makes believe to throw all his weight on the point. Then he jumps up, and calls to the people to give him three reals (about fourpence half-penny). These people are invited to contribute a real each for the sake of Moulai Abd el Cader, who enables him to do these wonderful things. He shouts and yells, and threatens that he will curse the crowd, and at length a copper comes in. By degrees he gets his three reals, after which he may start telling a story or perform some cheap conjuring trick.

I saw the peasant hurry away. He was going to sell his last sheep to give the money to the prophet for Abd el Cader, in the hope of receiving a hundredfold from Abd el Cader's protection in future. And that rogue of a prophet would take the money and hurry off to cheat someone else elsewhere.

In these entertainments there is nothing really Mohammedan. The snakes, the smoke, the dancing, the stabbing, form a *rechauffé* of many heathen rites and beliefs, each of which might be unravelled and traced to a particular origin. Serpent-worship is a very ancient superstition, and power over serpents has been a much-coveted attribute from very early days. In ancient sculpture the serpent is frequently found as the emblem of eternity, and when people strove to express their ideas—the earliest ideas of the world and of God—in a lisping symbolism, the serpent stood for a power which we at present lack words to define, but which many writers seek to account for by declaring that the prehistoric serpent was 'free from venom, with scales that glittered in the sun like burnished gold,' that it 'walked erect and was probably winged.' In the sculpture in the temple of Osiris

Eve appears offering the fruit to Adam beneath the tree,
and the serpent is standing erect. His was the voice which
tempted the woman.   Animal worship, indeed, flourished
with every variety of superstition throughout Egypt and the
Delta, and Mohammedanism was the strongest protest against
it which has ever been made—the boldest attempt to maintain the simple faith in one omnipotent God.   In the eyes
of the stars and the angels what a decay of ideas is here
reached in this mountebank calling on the name of God,
thumping his tom-tom, and cozening the poor!

It is not easy to understand Moorish sects or orders.   The
Moor will not, as a rule, indulge the Christian with information on this subject.   The Jew is not to be trusted, for if he
be a strict Jew in Barbary, he will say nothing good of
Islam; and if he be not a strict Jew, he loathes and condemns all religious distinctions.   I have heard such a Jew
say that he sees nothing to choose between the Church of
Rome (in Spain; he does not know it elsewhere), the Jews
and their Rabbis, or the Moslems, with their fokis and
imams.

I was fortunate in meeting a good Moslem and having at
hand a sympathetic interpreter.   He told me that Aisaweeyas are the followers of Sidi Mohammed ben Aisa, who
was born in the sixth century of their era at a place near the
Red Sea called Linbore, where there are palm-trees and
fig-trees.   His grandfather is buried there, and his tribe is
therefrom.   The legend is that he went mad and ate his
daughter; 'but,' said the Moslem, 'you must not believe
that; it is figurative.   What really happened was that she
became regenerate.'   As to why the Aisaweeyas eat raw flesh
and dirt, and roll on knives and dance, he maintained a
dignified silence, insisting rather on the saintly life of the
founder of the Order and the books which he had written.
I asked him about the prophet in the market-place, and he
merely remarked: 'People are at liberty to believe them or

21—2

not, as they please. You may believe them, unless you see
some reason for not doing so. It is their way of getting a
living, and why should they not do it as well as anything
else?'

The Order which carries the rosary in the hand is called
the Sidganya, founded by Si Hamed ben Salem in Algiers.
He was a very learned man, and the Order affect learning
and study. Schools are connected with their work, and
there is a celebrated one at the place in Algeria where
Si Hamed is supposed to have received visitations from
Mohammed, who gave him personal directions as to his life
and work. It is not an old Order, having been founded
towards the close of the eighteenth century. They have to
recite a great many prayers, which are merely the repetition
of one simple sentence, such as, 'There is no God but God,'
a hundred or more times in the day.

The Dacaiwas are another modern Order, having been
founded by Ben i Zerouch near Wazan comparatively
recently. His followers are chiefly peasants. One of them
was called Sidi el Arbi, and lived in the mountains. He
proclaimed a holy war against the French, and the Sultan,
who had in consequence to pay a heavy indemnity, ordered
all Dacaiwas to be thrashed wherever they were found.
They pray to God without the intercession of any saints, and
meditate on the attributes of God.

I wanted to know this Moslem's opinion of Senussi. But
he eagerly asserted that in Morocco there was no necessity
for Senussi. As is well known, Senussi lives somewhere in
the region of Tripoli. He has collected a great number of
Moslems round him, and he preaches that it is not lawful
for Moslems to submit to any but a Moslem ruler. He is
undoubtedly a power, and Moslems who do not join him
highly commend his principles, and perhaps assist him.

My birds were a great pleasure to me. The companion-
ship of dumb animals puzzled the Moors, but they indulged

my weakness by bringing me all sorts of strange creatures.
I had to practise catching locusts to feed my birds with,
and every morning I went round the courtyard hunting for
lizards or beetles. For the latter I set traps of pieces of
bread.   There was one beetle who spent several evenings
with me, and took his sport by aiming his person at my
candle.   He would try, and try again, till at last, with a
crash, he went bang through it, and I had to lay down my
pen and hunt for the matches by moonlight.   At last, being
hard up for provisions, I had to sacrifice him to my birds.
He was round, about as big as half a crown, and very black
and shiny.   I also sent the guards out to catch grasshoppers,
which they brought me in their pocket-handkerchiefs.

My Kaid was very clever in picking up the meaning of
English words which he heard me use, and we talked such
a strange mixture of tongues that no other soul could understand us. He talked what he thought was English ; I talked
what I thought was Arabic, and we both talked what we
thought was Spanish.   When I wanted his horse for him to
accompany me, I gave up saying, ' Jibli el owd dirilicht,' for
it struck me that Anglicized the term precisely suited his
marvellous old beast, so I used to say, ' Fetch the derelict
horse,' and the Kaid always brought it at once.

I had a habit of calling Mooleeta ' old lady '—why I cannot
say.   But I used to tell the Kaid I was going ' to feed the
old lady,' and sometimes when Mooleeta was playing her
antics I would inquire, ' Is that the old lady, as usual ?'
From this the Kaid gathered that the term was good English
for all young and intemperate animals.   When I wanted an
extra man, a friend recommended my having a boy to wait
on me ; but the Kaid squashed the idea by calling me aside
and shaking his head.   ' Eteeflah mucho ole lady,' said he,
which in our language meant: ' The lad is too much of a
rascal.'

But the climax of all things was reached when he for good

and all christened the young hawks 'ole ladies.' That
happened the day they all three escaped from their usual
quarters, and gave us both endless trouble in catching and
confining them again, for they ran like mice.　The next
morning, when I was feeding them, a lady came to ask for
me, and I know she was utterly mystified by the Kaid, who
met her with the information, 'Señorita feed 'em ole ladies.'

Mr. Hunot, the English Consul, was extremely kind during
my stay in Saffi, and I found his head-clerk a referee in all
matters of difficulty, especially in the packing of my birds to
go on board ship.　Mr. Hunot showed me a very fine horse
of the pure Abda breed.　It was a lovely animal, but hardly
what we should call a horse at home.　He had some other
very pretty ponies, and I regretted nothing so much as not
being able to accept his kind offer to ride out to his country
house and see his colts; but I daily expected the ship which
was to take me to England, while my Kaid went on with
Conrad and Mooleeta to leave them for me in the care of a
kind friend in Mazagan.

My stay in the kasbah gave me a better insight into the
amazing mismanagement of things military in Morocco, and
also something of prison manners, for a prisoner was chased,
arrested, imprisoned, taken for trial, and condemned, all in
the space of an hour and a half, and the whole affair was a
little spectacle play of considerable interest.

I especially enjoyed my morning rides on the shore.
Starting very early on my last ride in Morocco, I rode out
through the waterport of the old Portuguese fort, among the
quaint old boats with high peaks fore and aft, like the canoe
of the red man, down on to the strip of sand which borders
the bay, and on which at low-tide there is a passage through
some formidable rocks.　Many wrecks have been driven by
gales from the Atlantic and carried right across the bay,
and landed on their beam practically on the dry land itself.
In one year eleven sailing-ships were thus driven by the

winds into Saffi Bay, and the hulks at the foot of the cliff
are a lasting memorial. I found by walking my horse
into the sea that the shore at a certain distance shelved
precipitously, almost like the bank of a river.

The hulks lying there speak volumes—they below, and
the crumbling shrine of old Sidi Boukris above. Soon the
saint's house will fall with all its contents. No one ventures
to pray in the shrine where the old saint sleeps his last sleep,
for the waves have undermined it, and some winter's gale
will finish it, and the saint-house will be gone, with its
generations of bats and owls, and the dust and bones of the
old saint will be carried away by the restless, dissatisfied
waters.

The hulks, plain, honest craft as they once were, recalled
to me those splendid old wooden ships which now do duty
as coaling-vessels in Gibraltar Bay. Only that theirs is an
honoured and useful old age. If the gilding which decorates
their prows is wearing away, and if their graceful masts and
sails are gone, and they may never again race home with
cargoes of fruit or tea, or carry His Majesty's mails, they
still show splendidly beside the vulgar tramp and useful
but prosaic steamship 'liner,' who come to them for coals.
The life of a ship is like the life of a man, and every traveller
must have felt it, most of all in ports such as Saffi Bay.
Probably it was of such stranded hulks and such sealed
ports that Sir Walter Raleigh, the old 'Shepherd of the
Ocean,' was thinking when he lay a prisoner in the Tower,
and which drew from him that touching farewell descriptive
of a sailor who has reached the last port of all: 'When we
reach the port of Death, to which all Winds drive us, and
when by letting fall that fatal Anchor which can never be
weighed again, the Navigation of this life takes end.'

CHAPTER XXVI

A BORDERLAND—FRENCH DIPLOMACY—RESULTS

THE most striking feature in Morocco is that the country was once the heart of an empire which was practically only limited by the power of its Ameers. The rule of Islam is over men, agglomerations of men, not territory; and for this reason in former days boundaries were very loosely considered.

Since the expulsion of the Moors from Spain, and the limiting of their empire on the European side by the narrow line of the sea, they have been gradually crushed out of Tripoli, Algeria, and the desert, and the importance of Morocco to-day is its geo-political position as a narrow strip of Africa between European Governments.

As is historically common to all borderlands, the tide of humanity has surged backwards and forwards. To this day the Moors regard Spain as theirs by right, and they still look forward to the day when they will reconquer the territory on the other side of the Atlas. They are a mixed race, which for centuries has owned no other faith than the militant creed of Islam. To conquer is their right and privilege, and they resent defeat with a bitterness that leaves a long memory behind it.

But there is yet another feature in Morocco which is more singular to the country. Through the narrow Straits of Gibraltar, which the natives call the Rio Grande, and across which they cast longing eyes, there passes the most important sea-borne commerce of the world. It is the 200 miles or so of coast-line from Cape Spartel to Ceuta which renders

Morocco the largest factor in ˙the Near East. There her
boundary touches India and Australia. She holds their
trade, and their connection with the island centre of government, in the palm of her hand—a feeble old hand, a palsied,
diseased hand, a savage hand, so it may seem at present.

After the Straits, the features bearing most influentially
on the country are the rivers and mountains. They are of
relative geographical importance. The rivers offer means of
communication, passing through fertile valleys to the ports
of a long coast-line from the mountains, which provide
natural fortifications, containing considerable mineral wealth,
and furnishing Morocco with a backing of hardy, fair-skinned
mountaineers. This human material, like the mineral wealth,
needs enterprise to develop it. The ore lies, as it were, ' in
the dump,' and the process has yet to be found by which the
human rock may be treated and the true metal passed on to
good use for civilized purposes.

Except the Riffs, who do not appear to have left their
present territory at the bidding of anyone, most of these
turbulent tribes have been deported in sections by victorious
Sultans and planted down at some distance from the scene
of their fighting.* This was done by El Mansûr, who conquered the Arabians in Tripoli, and settled the province of
Dukalla with them, by this means bringing them into sub-
jection. ' For,' says Leo, ' the Arabians out of deserts are
like fishes without water : they had indeede often attempted
to get into the deserts; but the mountains of Atlas, which
were then possessed by the Barbarians, hindred their passage.
Neither had they libertie to passe ouer the plaines, for the
residue of the Barbarians were there planted. Wherefore
their pride being abated they applied themselves unto Hus-
bandrie, having nowhere to repose themselves, but onely in
villages, cottages and tents. And their miserie was so much
the greater, in that they were constrained yeerely to disburse

* See chapter on Azíla.

unto the King of Morocco most ample tribute.'*   The strong
policy of compelling the wandering Arabs to become agriculturists by placing them between mountains garrisoned by
armed foes eventually gave Morocco the peaceful and docile
plainsmen.   But the constant employment of one tribe to
fight another tribe has resulted in divisions and distinctions,
so that the whole of Morocco is parcelled out into tribes
which are more or less prepared to raid each other.   Therefore the turbulence common to border and mountainous
countries is accentuated in Barbary.

The hill tribes are people of race and breeding, being
generally free from the taint of black blood; but the towns,
being easier of communication, are chiefly inhabited by a
mongrel race.   For not only did the corsairs collect slaves
from nearly every land, the females going to the harems and
the males being allotted wives of the country, but Morocco
has long been the sanctuary for those Europeans whose
crimes prevent them from living elsewhere.   It pleased the
humour of the Moors to encourage alliances between fugitives
from justice and the children of fugitives.   But Mulai Ismâil,
the worst of Sultans, established camps where his blackguards
bred half-breeds, whom he felt he could rely upon to gratify
his cruelty better than the more tenderly nurtured Moors.

The land belongs theoretically to the Sultan.   Foreigners
cannot buy it without his consent; but the tribes can sell it
to each other and to rich Moors who are private individuals.
The tribes either pay rent by doing military service or they
pay taxes.   But some tribes neither furnish troops nor pay
taxes; they make presents.

The standing army is a kind of militia, one half of a tribe
serving in turn with the other.   The land held by this
military service is called 'guiche land,' and the soldiers
provided by it furnish the force which collects the taxes
and special contributions under the Kaids as administrators,

* See Leo Africanus, vol. i., p. 140.

and out of which they get good pickings. Only in a few
tribes is military service hereditary. The land which pays
taxes is called 'naiba.' I never found any reliable figures
given me as to how many soldiers even one tribe could
furnish. In the same way, I found all sorts of estimates
given of the population, which might be anything from
4,000,000 to 8,000,000. Besides the forces above mentioned,
there are what we should call volunteers or yeomanry. They
are mounted men, and are only called out in case of need.
They are called 'Nouăıb.'

To any Western Power this population would yield great
wealth. On the plains live a most industrious, docile, and
intelligent peasantry, and on the hills a fighting material
second to none in the world.

Besides the tribesmen, the Sultan has his own bodyguard
—the Mechouari—which serves either on horse or on foot.
These are part of the Court show, and the Grand Vizier is
preceded by them. In addition to this bodyguard, there is
a religious Order of soldiers who are especially ruffianly and
bad. They are called the Abds Bou Khari, or the slaves of
Bou Khari. They regard themselves as the special care of
the celebrated author of a commentary on the Koran. They
are under a devotional rule, and when a recruit joins he
takes an oath of fidelity to his chief on the sacred book of
the saint. A copy of this work accompanies the Kaid upon
all expeditions. It is carried with great pomp in the middle
of the troop, and reposes in its own tent at night. It is
regarded as a talisman, and the success attending their arms
and the valour of the corps are attributed to it.

There were said to be about 3,000 troops in Marakish
when I was there; those which came under Kaid MacClean's
instruction were greatly improved by it. Nor can there be
any doubt that, if he succeeds in carrying out certain reforms,
he will eventually secure for Morocco a very fine army. The
use of artillery for coast defence will be the great difficulty.

It requires finished training on the part of a European to work the machinery of modern guns. But for fortifying the hills no better infantry could be found. Eye-witnesses have told me they stand fire remarkably well, and, given good horses—an easy matter in Morocco—it would be impossible to imagine more dashing cavalry or better scouts. This, in brief, is the geo-political interest of Morocco, which is now harassed by France with a boundary question.

In 1845 a treaty was signed between France and Morocco, in which the boundary between Morocco and Algeria was not expressly defined. The Sultan claimed to exercise authority over a considerable stretch of the Sahara from the Little Atlas south-east. The following is the fourth article of the treaty:

'ART. 4.—Dans le Sahara (désert) il n'y a pas de limite territoriale à établir entre les deux pays puisque la terre ne se laboure pas, et qu'elle sert seulement de passage aux Arabes des deux empires qui viennent y camper pour y trouver les pâturages et les eaux qui leur sont nécessaires. Les deux souverains exerceront de la manière qu'ils l'entendront toute la plénitude de leurs droits sur leurs sujets respectifs dans le Sahara. Et toutefois, si l'un des deux souverains avait à procéder contre ses sujets au moment où ces derniers seraient mêlés avec ceux de l'autre État, il procédera comme il l'entendra sur les siens mais il s'abtiendra avec les sujets de l'autre gouvernement.'

Then follows a list of the various tribes belonging respectively to France and Morocco. Certain villages in the desert were relatively apportioned. Those belonging to France were Ain Sefra, S'fissifa, Attla, Surit, Chellara, El Abiad, and Ben Semgônne. Only two were assigned to Morocco—Figuig and Sche. More remarkable features in a treaty between two countries than the following could scarcely be imagined:

'ART. 6.—Quant au pays qui est au sud des ksour* des deux

* 'Ksour' means an Arab village.

gouvernements, comme il n'y a pas d'eau, qu'il est inhabit-
able, et que c'est le désert proprement dit, la délimitation
serait superflue.

'ART. 7.—Tout individu qui se réfugiera d'un État dans
l'autre ne sera pas rendu au gouvernement qu'il aura quitée
par celui auprès duquel il sera refugié, tant qu'il voudra y
rester. . . . S'il veut rester il se conformera aux lois du
pays et il trouvera protection et garantie pour sa personne et
pour ses biens.'*

That this treaty indicated a distinct policy on the part of
France is proved by the following passage in a letter from
M. Waddington :

' L'absence de limites officielles entre deux états est toujours
au détriment du plus faible. . . . Nous ne devous pas recon-
naître sans nécessité le droit absolu de l'empereur du Maroc
sur les territoires où son autorité n'est le plus souvent que
nominale et que nous pourrions avoir un jour l'occasion de
revendiquer surtout si les études du chemin de fer trans
saharien aboutissaient a des conclusions pratiques.'

The boundary question became so fraught with difficulty
and anxiety to the Moorish Government that efforts were
repeatedly made to induce the French to define the boundary.
In 1877, in 1884, in 1885, and again in 1891, the subject was
raised, but without avail. In the following note by M. de
la Martinière we have the finishing touch :

' C'est la, en effet, la politique que l'on s'est toujours pro-
posée, attirer et capter, fixer et retenir les tribus nomades du
Sud. . . . Notre seul but semble devoir être de nous établir

---

* I quote from M. Jean Hess (*Le Magazin Colonial*, July 15, 1901),
who continues : 'Nous partageons les points connus. Cela nous suffit . . .
mais un jour . . . on s'aperçoit que ce traité donne matière à conflits
entre les deux États. Que le Maroc pour régler ces conflits invoque la
lettre du traité—nous en alléguons l'esprit. Qu'a son tour le Maroc parle
comme nous de l'esprit du traité alors nous pretentions changent, il nous
en faut la lettre. Et quand la lettre et l'esprit sont contre nous, c'est la
force qui est notre argument'

solidement au milieu de ces populations, *de profiter pour cela de l'absence de frontier*, d'enclaver les tribus dont nous avous a craindre la turbulence jusqu'à jour où la question de Maroc se posant d'une manière definitive nous pourrons agir et parler en maîtres.'

Meantime, the education of the French public and of Europe in general, to the idea of the rights of France over Morocco, is proceeded with. In speaking of the extension of British Imperialism, a writer in the *Temps* asks: 'And we, whither can we turn to compass a parallel development?' He calls attention to North Africa as the proper field for the expansion of France.*

'Two-thirds,' he says, 'of what of old used to be called Barbary now belongs to France, and it is a vital necessity for her not to cease thinking of the other third. It in no wise follows that France should have an aggressive policy towards Morocco. All France has to demand of it is to keep the peace on its frontiers, and it will then be allowed to rest in peace.' But the steps taken by France could not by the grossest flattery be described as ' keeping the peace.'

The telegrams which reach Europe as to fighting on the Moorish boundary *come through French channels only ;* and to the general public, which cannot be expected to remember the details of treaties, they frequently convey an impression which does not coincide with facts. For instance, a *Daily Mail* telegram from Paris, dated February 24, 1901, is as follows :

' Over 1,000 Berbers made an attack from the French post of Timmium, but were beaten off, and lost over 100 of their number. Nine Frenchmen were killed and twenty-seven wounded.'

The *Matin* insists on the absolute necessity of watching the Moorish frontier (*sic*) and the Shereefian Court, declaring

---

* The *Times* correspondent, extract from the *Temps*, July 9, 1901.

that the plots against the French occupation of Tuat originate there.

The correspondent of a Spanish paper, telegraphing from Paris on March 10, describes an encounter with rebellious Moorish tribes who attacked Timmium :

'The rebellious tribesmen had sought refuge at Gurara' (on French territory). 'After two volleys had been fired by the French troops the Berbers were dislodged from their position.'

The object of these accounts is transparent; they are intended to show cause why the French should advance further, on the old plea that the Sultan cannot maintain order. A few days later another telegram is published : 'La ghazza venait directement de Tafilet. Ell s'est retirée dans la dune a l'ouest de la Sebka du Gourara.'

A glance at the map shows the distance between Timmium on the lake near Tuat in the Sahara and Tafilat near the Atlas. The French had occupied Igli, which is about half-way, and, indeed, were moving on towards Tafilat, having reached a point within sight of the oases of Tafilat when I was in Marakish. Probably there was fighting among the French tribes at Timmium ; but as the Sultan was unaware of any rebellion, and as the publication of the telegrams was immediately followed by another French advance, the object was clearly to show cause to Europe why France should advance, on the old plea that the Sultan cannot maintain order, and that France represents civilization.

The French have also backed one Moorish tribe against another. Both the El Mehaia and the Beni 'guil are Moorish tribes, but the French laid a claim before the Sultan on behalf of the Mehaia on account of cattle raided by the Beni 'guil. The matter had no connection with foreign affairs, and French interference was declined by the Sultan.

The recent attempts to obtain a frontier south of Ain Sefra will probably result in fixing the limits of Algeria within a few miles of Tafilat. The accompanying map gives the original boundary of Algeria in a dotted line, where it was generally believed to be at the date (1888) of the publication in Paris of a well-known map. In the corner of this map of Morocco another small map gave a portion of Europe with North Africa, and here, as though by the gift of prophecy, the missing boundary line cuts through Tafilat.

The murder of a French subject who landed on the Riff coast contrary to orders was made the occasion of an ultimatum, with a demand for indemnity enforced by men-of-war in Mazagan Harbour. Moors, it is implied, are bad neighbours. The patience and endurance of France will be exhausted, and she will be compelled to put in an army and annex the country.

Even the *Times* assists in preparing the mind of Europe for the final *coup*. The sad state of Morocco is harped upon. The correspondent from Tangiers telegraphs to the ' *Thunderer* ' in the same key with missionary reports. Dark Morocco must be tarred and tarred again. That Morocco must ultimately become French territory has even been propounded in a leading monthly review, and a proposal appeared in the *Spectator* that Spain should take over Morocco. The British public is thrilled with the tales of outrage, torture, gaols, missionary devotion, the freeing of grateful slaves, etc. At Tangiers a small party of Europeans actively favour French annexation. The Moors, they say, are devoid of all sense of gratitude. Whatever kindness is shown them they ascribe to selfish motives. There is no moral fibre whatever in the people. They are avaricious, and their rule of life is to get all they can for themselves, no matter how. They will not act together on any ground except religion, which is a deeply ignorant fanaticism, etc.

These representations, whether true or exaggerated, refer to an Oriental people which was ruled much as it is to-day long before we came to be even a small nation. They neither justify our imposing an alien rule, nor do they prove Morocco to be past hope. The late Sultan had a policy not dissimilar to that of Mehemet Ali when Egypt was no better than Morocco is to-day. It was 'the transformation of a barbarous province into a State formed on a civilized model, with trained armies and fleets, with treasure to fall back upon, a vigorous head, and a definite policy not lacking in grandeur.'* But France is alive to such possibilities, and Europe has so little wish for a revival of Islam power that the Christian Governments unite in harassing the Sultan. The promotion of trade would mean the introduction of inventions, which would be followed by the same rush of civilization which it introduces elsewhere, and none of the Powers wishes to see Morocco rich and self-confident. A hundred years ago our prisons in Christian England were in some respects worse than the Moorish gaols. A woman was liable to be hanged for stealing a pair of boots. Our whole criminal code was a mass of cruelty. Our notions of sanitation were on a par with those in Morocco to-day. Even towards the middle of the century the poverty and immorality of the peasants,† the cruelty practised under the Poor Laws, the greed and avarice of the manufacturers, would be incredible if it were not supported by irrefutable evidence.

The result of my ride was that I corrected many things told me in Tangiers. Considering their history, the Moors are very good natives. They are industrious, persevering, and enduring, but they break down in office. Not even their keen appreciation of justice in others makes them just to one another.

In spite of the loud talk about maintaining the *status quo*, France is actively undermining the Sultan's authority with any tool which comes to hand, from Jew pedlars to the

* 'England and France in the Mediterranean'
† See *Times*, July 6, 1801 · 'A blacksmith near Beverley lately sold his wife to a neighbouring bachelor, and delivered her in the customary manner on such occasions, with a halter round her neck, at the Market Cross.'

22

dummy Shereefs of Wazan. Algerians, as French protégés, Moors bribed into French service, all can be used as instruments for flouting and annoying Moorish authorities and damaging the Sultan's prestige. Even the peaceful agency of the Jewish Alliance, whose headquarters are in Paris, is encouraged to spread the language and influence of France in Morocco.

The part which the Alliance plays in the matter is not very creditable. Paris has shown itself to the Jews as strongly imbued with anti-Semitism. But the whole French nation has condoned the treatment meted out under a show of legal justice to a solitary Jew, whose misfortune it was to serve France as a soldier, a treatment so barbarous in its details, so questionable in its principles, as to render it comparable only to the procedure of an Oriental State. With this before their eyes, the Alliance goes willingly to play the game of France, which will result in placing some millions of Jews under French rule. I visited some of the schools of the Alliance, and I found French teachers trained, as all the Alliance teachers are, at the University belonging to the Alliance in Paris, and the French language used as a medium of instruction. On one occasion I asked the children a few questions myself; on another I suggested that the teacher should ask them a few geographical questions. The first question asked was, 'What are the names of the French colonies?' and when this had been answered correctly, it was followed by, 'Tell me the names of the English colonies.' But there was silence, and at last 'India' and 'Brazil' were given as our sole colonies (sic). Yet the children had a very good notion of French history (English they 'had not commenced'), and their arithmetic was remarkably good.

In Tangiers an English teacher holds an English class in the school of the Alliance. The London Board of the Jewish Alliance raised a sum of money in London for the relief of the Jews in Morocco after the Spanish-Moorish War of 1860.

It was found that a surplus remained, and it was decided that the interest of the sum should be assigned to the payment of an English master at one Jewish Alliance school. It was explained to me that the use of French as the medium of instruction was 'regulated by the official language of the country and by diplomatic usage.'

I met many Jews who were British subjects, and they were very bitter upon the language question. One man told me that no child of his should be brought up to be French, and that they should not attend the schools. When he could afford it, he would try and send them home. I think it amounts to a hardship, and the influential Jews in England would do well to direct their attention to the matter.

The Comité de Tanger de l'Alliance Française, which is quite distinct from the Jewish Alliance, has a school in Tangiers where upwards of forty children, divided into two classes, are instructed under a young Algerian Moslem. There is a Moorish teacher who gives instruction in the Mohammedan religion, and a monitor who takes the younger or less advanced children. The school was started upon the pretence that it was to supply the want of the Algerian subjects settled in Tangiers; but I was assured on good authority that there are not half a dozen Algerian children in Tangiers. At the distribution of prizes by the French Ambassador, which took place when this school had been in existence a year, M. Benghabrit, an Algerian who is on the staff of the French Legation in Tangiers, made the following remarks :

' Vous n'ignorez pas, que si nous recevons dans cette école quelques élèves marocains désireux de s'instruire elle a été surtout fondée pour inculquer aux jeunes musulmans algériens eloignée de leur pays, avec l'enseignement de la langue française des sentiments d'amour et de reconnaissance pour la France.'

Another point upon which French influence was continually

playing was the railway between Fez and Tangiers, which should connect at the border with the Algerian line. It would suit France very well if such a railway were built with English or German capital, for, holding the other end in her hands, she would exercise enormous control, and be able to draw whatever produce she could get from Morocco into Algiers, to the ruining of the coastal trade and the weakening of European influence.

But railways form a branch of economics which can only go into a country safely hand-in-hand with other developments, and in a new country require a place in the administration. The ventilation of such schemes, with the addition of a tunnel under the Straits, is merely a part of the distinct educational policy of France.

France has never proved herself a good neighbour, and a boundary policy is nothing new. It was part of Napoleon's strategy. We meet it in Siam. It is so old that the royal arms of Scotland bear to this day a tressure of fleur-de-lis, signifying an alliance between the King of France and the early Stewarts—a policy which was only dropped when Louis failed to give his promised support to Prince Charles Edward, an omission which the Highlanders avenged on the Heights of Abraham.

As she spreads out in Africa, she will carry her boundary policy with her. There are Spanish towns on the Moorish coast, and it would be easy to find a *casus belli* with respect to Ceuta, which is the Botany Bay of Spain, and start a war which would win instant popularity with all the Moors. No Power could hold any coast town with France in possession of the hinterland, and her command of the Straits would reverse the balance of power in Europe.

Morocco would enrich France enormously. The great desert trade in the hands of a country which has always shut out other nations, combined with the territorial wealth of the borderland itself, would mean an increase in armaments.

French pamphlets referring to Morocco allude to India. Then, given the opportunity, who can deny that some new Napoleon may arise 'to shame the world again'?

This mere boundary question actually provides every element for which men and nations will fight, every chance for contention. The religious Orders, if rightly handled, will induce Moslem to strike Moslem. Trade, where it finds itself worsted, looks to military support. Our Empire has lately found a link binding strong men together in a determination similar to the thirst of native tribes for equitable government.

Napoleon's scheme of empire was the forming of military bases, the arming of conquered people, and the turning of them upon fresh conquests. We possess now one-sixth of the habitable globe, and can weigh the value of French designs. Looking back to the empire which Napoleon sought and lost, and out upon the empire which we won, but did not seek, we can count the cost of French ambition.

> 'Thanks for that lesson ; it will teach
>   To after-warriors more
> Than high philosophy can preach,
>   And vainly preach'd before.
>
> 'The triumph and the vanity,
>   The rapture of the strife,
> The earthquake voice of victory,
>   To thee the breath of life ;
> The sword, the sceptre, and that sway
> Which man seemed made but to obey,
>   Wherewith renown was rife'

It is the memory of the Napoleonic military glory which acts as a madness upon France. She has not the genius for governing other nations, neither has she the power to colonize nor the necessity for so doing. The temperament of her people is too closely akin to that of the dark races not to be affected by contact with barbarians. But she can arm native tribes with modern weapons. In spite of her

high culture, and, what is even more deplorable, in spite of
the many great men whose spiritual minds have been revealed
to us in a literature second to none, the mass of the people is
only capable of responding to the fanfare of trumpets, to
gaudy display, and blood, such as delighted their grandfathers, with whom the teaching of philosophy and religion
alike failed, and is wrapped under the same spell

> 'That led them to adore
> Those pagod things of sable sway,
> With fronts of brass and feet of clay.'

Against an Imperialism born of a lust whose gratification
requires a Timour for its agent, humanity will rise at last.
But the real loss will be the loss of France to civilization, and
the blow under which she will sink will be delivered by her
own hand. From outside, the corrupting influence of countries
she will try to make her own will turn within, and gnaw
like a cancer through her national life. It is customary to
censure England for her unsympathetic rule in India; but it
is precisely because of its 'unsympathetic' (sic) nature that
it can rule at all a people composed of various races and
different creeds, but alike in being semi-civilized in the
mass.

What Spain and Portugal could do we have seen, and we
know the power which eventually broke their sway was not
a force to be compared with the arrow that flies by day, but
another more subtle but surer agency resembling the pestilence which walks in the darkness, and which crept home
into their blood and spread like a leprosy, corrupting national
morals and degrading public and official life.

France, which could not be subjugated by a European
State, may shatter herself in Africa. She is the last Power
which should touch the East. It requires the cold, resolute,
dogged North to control the childish, passionate, feeble
East.

Considering the enormous influence of French thought and sentiment on Europe, no one can see her embark in Imperial responsibilities which she has not the numerical strength to grasp without anxiety and regret. The course she is pursuing is calculated to jeopardize the entire peace of Europe; and for this Great Britain is to blame, above all other Powers, for the carelessness with which she has allowed her prestige in the Near East to be obscured.

The Germans whom I met were all anti-British. They were well alive to the display of bad officership in the Transvaal; but naturally they were most impressed with the advance of France in the Mediterranean, which one of them told me was improving exactly at the rate of Great Britain's decline. 'Your days of Nelson are past,' he said, as he handed me a German newspaper containing this sentence: 'It is quite certain that on the shores of the Mediterranean, where the most vital destinies of mankind have been decided from the earliest times, an important shifting of the conditions decisive for the results of a naval war have taken place to the advantage of France and the prejudice of England.'

CHAPTER XXVII

SALE OF 'PROTECTION'—AMERICAN DIPLOMACY—AMERICAN
CITIZENSHIP — CONSULAR APPOINTMENTS — THE CON-
SULAR SERVICE—IMPROVING THE PORTS—CIVIL COURTS
— M'NEBBI'S DISGRACE — ORIENTAL POLITICS — WHO
GOVERNS US—THE AIM OF TRUE CIVILIZATION

IT is held that British law, the result of action taken in
moments of pre-eminent sanity, protects a man against the
enemy, his neighbour, and himself. In Morocco protection
has to be sought by the native under the treaties and statutes
of foreign States, and its uses and abuses form the chief con-
troversy in the country. There are places where it is better
kept out of the conversation, because men now occupying
good positions have dabbled in the sale of protection, much
as men in the South dabbled in I.D.B.

I was glad to find that British merchants consider it
discreditable to sell protection. The large firms take no
payments whatever; although, considering the trouble frequently entailed, it would be quite fair for the native to pay
something for a privilege which enriches him. Besides, the
custom of the country admits of ' presents.'

The Americans (but I believe especially the Germans)
indulge freely in the sale of protection. In trade, where a
man competes in business with similar enterprise, he can
afford to undersell if he can make a profit by levying a poll-
tax on his agents. His business provides him with the
opportunity, because the number of protected agents which a

merchant may employ depends on the extent of his business, and is limited according to the terms of the treaty; and so anxious are the Moors to obtain protection that they will pay any price and submit to any terms. I heard of only one instance where an abuse was attributed to an Englishman, and the opinion rules even among Moors that the British authorities were backward in granting protection, and slack in doing anything to advance the interests of British trade, or even of those Moors whose interests were associated with it.

An instance of corrupt practice and its bearing on trade was given me as follows· There was a man (not a British subject) who went to a number of small traders and bribed them to let him pass all their goods in his name. A very moderate capital laid out in bribes was thus sufficient to show the authorities that he was a merchant of some substance. Consequently, as it is imperative that the agents employed by large merchants should be protected, protections were granted to this man to the number of thirty. These he disposed of to peasants, who at any time will pay their last farthing to get protection. He granted them protection upon their handing him a document to the effect that they owed him so much money. As soon as the natives had sown and gathered a few good crops under the shelter of the protection and were getting a little fat, the man sold the Protection certificate to the Bashaw or Kaid, who instantly destroyed it and pressed the claims. Many of the peasants were thus robbed of everything they had and imprisoned; some even died in prison.

To the Legations belongs the sordid and ungrateful business of acting in the capacity of Sheriff's officers for coercing the Sultan into making his subjects pay their debts. It touches the administration, and is a great opportunity for effecting reforms meanly thrown away. It is a low and degrading business which Great Britain scarcely manages to swallow.

In all matters affecting Morocco under the present treaties the person to be approached is the Sultan. The proceedings are similar to those of the old woman who wanted to get her recalcitrant pig home from market. It is useless to go direct to the pig; in fact, no merchant can do so. He must first find his Consul, and get the Consul to move the Legation. The Legation has to approach Sidi Mohammed Torres, till the last person of all is reached. But a show of force has to be made. Not till the butcher threatens to kill the ox will matters be set in motion.

The abuses incident to this mode of debt recovery are vast. Whoever has a claim against a Moor gets his Consul to correspond with the Moorish authorities, which results when sufficient claims have been collected, in a mission to the Court, and His Shereefian Majesty is threatened by a naval demonstration. In this the British err, being averse from taking the only measures open to them, failing to see through lack of business acumen that with a people like the Moors the first article of commerce, the payment of debt and the keeping of contracts, must be enforced, or the state of the country will become far worse even than it is at present. Insecurity of contract is the worst state that any country can get into.

But the settlement of claims has a very odious side. It was very forcibly brought home to me, because at the time I was at Tangiers the American Consul was preparing to go on a mission to the Court of the Sultan for the settlement of claims said to amount to a very large sum, principally due to American Jews. Some excitement was caused at Tangiers by the arrival of a United States man-of-war, in which it was said the Consul would proceed down the coast on his way to Morocco city. That the mission intended to start was, I believe, quite true, for I heard on the best authority that their mules were waiting for them at Mazagan. The mission was to consist of the Consul, Mr. Gummere, a young Syrian who acted as interpreter, and an American subject who was born a German Jew, a Mr. Nathan, known among missionaries as 'Brother Nathan.' I first heard of him conducting prayer-meetings in the soko, in the pay of an English society, and he appears to have distinguished himself in the field of missionary work. Whether he went as private chaplain to the Consul or not I cannot say. At interviews with Sidi Mohammed Torres he played the delicate rôle of interpreter, and as the American Consul is said not to understand a word of Arabic, doubtless it was a comfort to him to be able to rely on such a support as the missionary could offer in matters of so complex and awkward a character.

When I heard the booming of the man-of-war's guns and thought of all that lay behind the show of force, and of the means used to drive home the settlement of claims, I hoped with all my soul that every care would be taken that this great Western Power would not use her strength against the helpless peasantry in a doubtful cause. The finished excellence of the ship was there, the hand of a great Republic was knocking at the door, but behind it all I seemed to see the prison and the lash, and the famished children of a ruined village.

Then appeared the following singular telegram in the *Standard*, and expectation in Tangiers rose on the tips of its toes:

'[*Central News Telegram.*]

'WASHINGTON, *March* 22.

'Mr. Secretary Hay has decided that the time has come for forcing the dispute with Morocco to an issue. Advices were received at the State Department to-day to the effect that the Moroccan Minister for Foreign Affairs had, on behalf of the Grand Vizier, tendered a formal apology for his insolent attitude towards Consul-General Gummere.

'This, however, was considered altogether inadequate, and Mr. Hay to-day cabled Mr. Gummere to that effect. Consequently, in accordance with the course of action previously decided upon, the Consul-General will go on board the United States cruiser *New York*, now at Tangier, and proceed on her to Mazagan. At the latter port he will disembark, and travel thence, without any escort whatsoever, to the capital There he will personally present to the Sultan a demand for an official apology by the Moroccan Government for resisting the demand of the United States Government for the collection of the indemnities due for the murder of American citizens.

'Consul-General Gummere has also been instructed to notify the Moroccan Government that any attempt to remove the Court for the purpose of avoiding a meeting with him will be regarded as a deliberate affront to the United States. Mr. Gummere will sail for Tangier on his risky mission on Monday next. It is confidently believed here that Morocco will now comply with the American demands.'

The above affords an instance of how strangely things are misrepresented in the press. The telegram implies that the collection of indemnities due for the murder of American citizens was part of the object of the mission. Nothing of the kind was suggested in Tangiers. In June in the previous year an American citizen, who drew his revolver on a Moorish crowd, was killed. The United States asked for the moderate indemnity of 5,000 dollars, which the Sultan paid immediately, adding of his own accord, ' I am very sorry for the deed, and I will punish the doer.'

The Central News telegram also speaks of insolence on the part of the Grand Vizier. If there was any such insolence, it must have been offered in private, and it was a pity the news of it should be published from Washington. The only correspondence in which the Grand Vizier took part appears to be the answer given to the American Consul's offer to go up to Morocco city. The Grand Vizier replied that the Court was likely to move, and any claims which the American Consul had could be settled by the Minister for Foreign Affairs at Tangiers. But as the American Consul still pressed his visit, the Sultan consented to receive him, and appointed the middle of April for the visit.

The *New York* was a beautiful ship, and I hoped to obtain permission to visit her, when suddenly she sailed for the East. Hurrying into the town to find out what had caused

this abrupt departure in the wrong direction, I heard that
the Consul had received a cable from Washington to the
effect that he was to remain at Tangiers and await further
instructions; while almost simultaneously the Admiral was
cabled to proceed to the East.

The reasons for the postponement of the mission were not
made public during my stay in Morocco; but I heard that
there was great consternation among a certain class of Jews,
and that all the efforts of the missionary, Mr. Nathan, were
expended in vain attempts to comfort and reassure them.
Some of the claims were of very long standing, and a former
Consul, Colonel Mathews, had struck them off the consular
books. It may have been fortunate that the mission did not
start; for even if they took the unusual precaution in diplomatic affairs, a missionary as interpreter and to ask a blessing
on every inch of the road, the affair bears the stamp of a
diplomatic blunder on the face of it. The Americans, so
shrewd in finance, do not shine as diplomatists, and when the
great ship scuttled out of Tangiers Bay in the wrong direction
the Moors laughed. There had been a vulgar display of force,
and nothing came of it. The reason given for the failure of
the mission was the mud on the roads; but I was preparing
to start on a much longer ride myself, and as I packed my
new valise I remembered a song in which some wit described
the Americans and their diplomacy:

> ' They're the most go-ahead people that ever were seen,
> For, look ! they invented the sewing-machine ;
> And now, to beat that, the untiring elves,
> They've invented a question that'll sew up themselves.'

And certainly the countenances of the members of the
mission who did not sail in the *New York* exactly expressed
that they felt ' sewn up.'

In connection with the above incidents it is necessary to
remember the keen anxiety displayed by Jews, German as
well as Moorish, to obtain American citizenship and trade

in Morocco under the protection of the American flag. The benefits of foreign nationality have been thus described: ' Subjects of friendly nations are exempt from all taxes or impositions, from military service on land or sea, from forced loans, and from all extraordinary contributions,'* which proves that an immense advantage accrues to the Moorish Jew who obtains the citizenship of another State. From being trampled upon by Moors he becomes able to trample upon them; nor is he likely to miss an opportunity. He takes the status of ' a foreigner ' in the land of his birth, and the same authority already quoted gives the further advantages of being a foreigner in Morocco as follows : ' To the foreign consular officials also is reserved the settlement of all dis- putes and claims among foreigners without native inter- vention, and so are all charges or claims brought by Moors against foreigners, each consular official trying those of his own nationality. Moors charged by foreigners are, on the other hand, to be tried by the native courts, foreign officials having the right to be present. Moorish claims must be made through the Moorish authorities.'

American citizenship can be obtained after five years' residence in America. Many Jews emigrate to America from Morocco for this object, though Brazil attracts the greater number of genuine emigrants. But there was at one time a practice made by certain Jews of obtaining American citizenship by trickery. They applied personally for the privilege during a short visit to America. It was never difficult to find a co-religionist of the same name, and answering to the description given to the lawyer, to come up whenever called for. A short three months spent in the States would settle the matter, and thus a man who had not been absent six months from his own country received the legal status of American citizenship.

It is said that the trick was discovered and laid bare

* Budgett Meakin, 'The Moorish Empire.'

owing to a man having an enemy in Morocco. This enemy
employed a friend in America to watch the case from the
application to the granting of citizenship. The Jew had
lent his enemy money, and when he went to claim it, the
other denied the existence of the bond, adding significantly
that it would be wise to say nothing further about it, or the
fraud perpetrated to obtain American citizenship should be
laid bare. The Jew, perhaps unwisely, pressed for the payment of his bond, and eventually the threatened exposure
was made. It led to the implication of some lawyers, who
were privy to the working of what amounted to a considerable business, in which they made a good deal of money.

How unequal the Moorish Government would be to lay
down lines on which commerce might be engineered is
testified by their failure to suppress usury.

They forbade payment of interest as contrary to their
religion. But the Jews were equal to the case, and merely
altered their terms. The peasant who wants to borrow
twenty dollars to pay taxes, or buy seed-corn, or get his son
out of prison, goes to the Jew. The Jew says: ' Very well;
we will lend you twenty dollars for six months on a bill
drawn up for fifty.' The peasant has no choice but to agree.
Perhaps at the end of the six months twenty dollars have
been repaid. The Jew then says: ' I will renew the bond
for the rest at double the amount.' Therefore the bond
starts afresh at sixty dollars instead of fifty, and the peasant
has already paid twenty, though he only borrowed twenty.
If at the end of a year the whole sixty dollars are not paid
off, the bond is renewed again, and, as before, the amount is
doubled. This goes on till the Jew believes the man's whole
stock is involved. Then he produces his documents and
presses for the payment of his claims.

It is vain to look to the Moors for reform. There is no
patriotism in the country to foster the spirit which enables
men to subordinate private advancement and other con-

siderations to the welfare of the country. Reform implies the existence somewhere of a compact body capable of sinking differences and of trusting each other, and in Morocco every man goes armed against his neighbour. Trade cannot and does not advance where there is no security. But a modicum of security might be achieved under treaties with a foreign Power.

It affords a comment on the absence of systematic trained thinking on commercial subjects that no other means for developing trade have been devised except the use of native agents, which effects practically no improvement in the Moors. Granting that Nature has made the Moors covetous and slippery, we must rest the more upon treaties rendering intercourse statutory, yet which shall be capable of amendment to suit the ever-changing circumstance and opportunity of commerce. No moral lectures addressed by Lord Salisbury to His Shereefian Majesty, the promptings of benevolent people at home, will have any further result than to be gracefully and politely received in public and laughed at in private. They will form a 'cracker' at a feast. But if the conviction could be driven home that money could be made by releasing the peasants and freeing trade substantial reforms, according to modern standards, would follow.

British diplomacy in Morocco furnishes a remarkable instance of intellectual dry-rot. It is difficult for the British public at home to picture official Englishmen allying themselves with the policy of 'maintaining the *status quo*' in Morocco. If the *status quo* has any meaning at all, it signifies the existence of a cruel and rapacious band of officials called the Shereefian Court, who rob and oppress the poor, cheat the foreign merchants whenever they can, and defraud the Sultan. In full knowledge of the acuteness of this position, with the bitter cry of these suffering people in their ears, the Western Powers callously pursue their course, using Morocco as a pawn in the game of politics, while their representatives are open to more than suspicion of practice which, to say the least, is sharp.

The British Consul represents the largest share of commerce, and Morocco requires to be relegated to the class of subjects which should be treated as part of the commercial interests of the Empire. Whether we, in common with France, choose to regard it as a border question because it touches the highway which is the backbone of our Empire, or whether we merely regard it with a view to the Manchester cotton interests, what is required is that there should be a distinct commercial policy. There should be such a policy for the whole world. Nowhere ought the commercial interests of Great Britain to suffer the slightest danger or neglect. Commerce is the surest way to a *modus vivendi* with any people. But we have yet to discover a commercial policy. Had our interests been maintained in South Africa, the cruel misgovernment, the wild ambitions, built on the misapprehension that Great Britain did not care, would never have led to the late war. It is time we inquired, 'Who frames our foreign policy? Who shapes the views of our statesmen?'

The Consular Service is underpaid; but it is frequently remarked that the best Consuls are the Vice-Consuls, who are generally speaking merchants, and are not paid at all. Their knowledge of business enables them to direct operations intelligently. But that is no excuse for underpaying men who have no other means of support.

It would be interesting to know the system of Consular appointments. There appears to be no competitive examination, and no preliminary course of instruction is considered necessary. But a man may obtain a Consulate or Vice-Consulate because his father was an official, or because his brother is at Court, or because his mother knows 'somebody at the Foreign Office.' It is not even necessary that the man should be English. He may be German (as, I believe,

23

is the case in Rome). He need not even be a European; a half-breed will do to represent British merchants, if he is only nominally white.

'The further you get from the Legations, the better you will find things,' I was told. And this is true so far that the mismanagement and confusion in the docks and warehouses, and the obstacles placed in the way of landing both passengers and cargo (in spite of the fact that Tangiers offers a very fair natural harbour), are not merely without parallel on the Moorish coast, but probably exceed anything to be found in the rest of the world. So far as our prestige is concerned, a Moor who was talking politics with me implied that France was exacting, but the 'English Sultan did not mind if people did not do all they promised.'

Methods are resorted to in a country like Morocco which are simply expedient, and lie outside the ordinary working of commerce.* I found that merchants charged thieves before the Port Captain, who accepted the word of the shippers, and for reasons it is unnecessary to enter upon took care that the thieves were duly punished. The justification which is put forward for these practices is the indifference of the Consul.

There is a rift between the merchants and the service which is supposed to safeguard their interests, and an impatience at censorship and control on one side, and on

---

* A Moor was caught red-handed on board a steamer, with a hook in his hand, with which he was forcing open a case. The mate watched him, and he was taken to the Consulate. The agent for the shipping company went in person and made the charge. The Consul said, 'What witness have you? Did you see him steal?' The ship was preparing to sail, but the mate was sent for, and gave his evidence. 'Yes,' said the Consul, 'that is all very well, but now you must go to the Bashaw. I cannot judge a Moor.' The Captain said the ship must sail. The Consul said: 'I think you had better go to the Governor.' The ship was obliged to sail, and consequently the thief was released. It might be expected that a Consul would have taken the prosecution in hand himself upon the recorded evidence of the ship's officers.

the other an absence of sympathy. It is only fair to remember that social feeling in England draws a line between
commercial and official life; and in such a case as the Consular Service the division may be accentuated owing to the
want of unity between the Legation (Political) and the Consular (Commercial) Services. In point of fact it is difficult
to see any real difference, but it is made and it is felt. We
are a commercial people. Our diplomacy must be a commercial diplomacy, and the feeling gathers strength that the
success of other nations may be due to the fact that they give
their merchants more consideration diplomatically.

The endurance of the merchants is not entirely commendable. The ass, we know, is a patient animal, but others get
over the ground quicker, all the quicker for being well treated.
Now and again a merchant complains, and a little drama
ensues between Moorish cunning, Consular compliancy, and
the aroused British trader.

'The whole Consular Service requires overhauling as
much as the War Office,' said a merchant, smarting under a
recent rebuff. 'There should be a commercial *attaché* to the
Legation, chosen because of his thorough knowledge of commercial affairs.' Such a man would be difficult to find, but
not impossible, if the entire service and its policy were
changed. In commerce and war there is a singular resemblance in the methods which may be employed; and if in
such a case as Morocco the several branches of the Legation,
the Consular Service, and the unpaid Vice-Consuls and clerks,
could unite and be treated all together and upon the same
terms as one service, there would develop a future and the
right men would follow. It is the long lane walled in down
which no man of ability will travel. In commerce men
require to be no less enterprising, no less bold, no less
patient, no less enduring, than in war. In both there is the
same need of a permanent base, and a staff thoroughly
equipped and responsible to the country. 'As a wilderness,'

says Mahan of war, ' gives place to civilization, as means of
communication multiply, as roads are opened, rivers bridged,
the operations of war become easier, more rapid, more extensive; but the principles to which they must be conformed
remain the same.' If we replace the word 'war' by
' commerce ' the passage reads equally well.

Such drastic remedies as ' clearing away wholesale, root
and branch,' all Moorish officials would be very impolitic.
Reforms, instead of aiming at the Court, should have commenced upon the seaboard, using the coastal towns as bases,
and advancing as opportunity offered. Granting the doubtful
point of the Sultan's capability of grasping reform, it is clear
that his difficulty would be to control his officials ; and if we
insist on treaties which touch on the administration, we
cannot be sure that his Kaids will administer according to
the treaties thirty miles inland. The improvements at the
ports might have been effected by paying over to the Sultan
and the officials a liberal share of the increased earnings.
The opportunity offered by Protection should have been
grasped, and an agreement based on an annual payment to
the Kaid of the district and the Governor of the town
whereby no inhabitant should be imprisoned in the port
without the consent of the British Consul on the spot. The
Consul should have been given the assistance of a capable
paid secretary to attend the Bashaw's Court and proffer
advice. His qualifications should include a University
degree, a membership of the English Bar, a knowledge of
mercantile law, and a fluency in native Arabic. The port
officials should collect all dues and taxes under British
supervision.

At first the Moors would have required pressure to keep to
such terms, but as time went on and they experienced the
advantages of law, order, flourishing trade and agriculture,
security, good roads and sanitation, and found that their
religion and law were unassailed, they would have been

anxious to extend the system, and a body of trained officials would have been gradually formed, growing richer on improved administration.

In Marakish the Moors were ready to grant any terms asked by Great Britain, and sound diplomacy would have taken advantage of this and asked precisely as much as could be certainly enforced. With so flagrant an abuse as the advance to the oases of Tafilat, France could have offered no valid objection to our creating what would amount to treaty ports for the security of our trade on the seaboard, especially in consideration of the infinitely larger interests of Great Britain. The Moors would have accepted and tolerated the Christians as assistants and advisers, knowing that they were physically incapable of withstanding France; and as the dollars came in, with now and then a bonus, and as they found small-pox and plague less violent, and that their condition contrasted favourably with those ports which were not treaty ports, factions and intrigues—the curse of Islam—would wear out, and even Mahdis come to be regarded as bores and impossible people.

The chief objection to such a policy would be the danger of imitating too closely what has been done elsewhere. Our Empire has taught us the difficulty of environment, and how perilous it is to import a law or institution from one province of the Empire into another. A thing which may be as bad as possible in one country may be the best arrangement possible elsewhere, and the reason is that environment assists or repudiates the digestion of the law. The mistake which missionaries and philanthropists make is in singling out features and ignoring their environment. They go into a country and lay hold of something which shocks one side of their disposition, and straightway they return to Exeter Hall and raise a howl of virtuous indignation.

It is difficult to define the effect of philanthropic or religious feeling upon political issues. Those who exalt their

ideals of life into flimsy transcendentalism which admits
nothing practical, and sets no limits to an exaltation of perfection as unnatural as it is impossible, are at total variance
with all the world.   The fretful plaints of these people tend
to sharpen and aggravate circumstances in proportion as
possibility has been misconstrued by them.   But is it,
after all, due to religion, this modern political doctrine which
obscures the use of peace and war, substitutes hollow cant
for sound argument, a whining threnody on humanity for
able criticism, and feigns pious horror and righteous scorn of
a civilization promoted by the natural means of commercial
enterprise and trade ?   There is a peace party which benefits
by living under the protection of a strong navy and army,
which some people would be glad to see deported to an
island where their defence would depend solely on themselves.   There are believers in 'universal humanity' and the
general 'brotherhood of man' who ignore the training of
history, the teaching of science, the divisions of races and
languages, the grouping into classes, the advancement by
form and custom, the instruction of men and nations by the
constant struggle for existence implied by earning our daily
bread, and the energetic determination to be justly ruled—in
a word, all that makes human life human ; who pose as lovers
of humanity and are yet at variance with all that is real and
best in human nature.

The business of successful government is a compromise.
Even in this pattern kingdom it cannot be said that we get
further than an approximation, and in the provinces of our
Empire the choice often lies between two evils.   Our rule at
its best is one of modification.   An endeavour has to be
made to ascertain what tribal government, what religious
form, what industry or trade, what national custom, there
may be upon which we can graft new forms.

The semi - republican government of the tribes might
offer great opportunities, but to introduce mixed tribunals,

as some people have advocated, would prove an unmixed
evil.   This scheme included the appointment by each of the
Great Powers in rotation of a judge for the civil courts.
This would be no development, and would emphasize at
once all the evils of the Legations.   But the state of the
civil courts is deplorable.   There was a Moor who had a
case against a Jew, and, as he feared the Jew would win it,
he presented the judge who was to try the case with a
beautiful mirror.   The Jew heard of this, so just before the
case came on he sent the judge a very fine mule.   The
Moor conducted his case himself, and commenced with a
long and eloquent speech, full of metaphor, and concluded
by telling the judge that the justice of his cause was as
clear as the beautiful mirror he had given him.   'That is
very true,' said the judge, 'but since then a mule came
along and smashed that mirror.'

Some of the merchants who had ceased to trouble the
Consul approached the Moors themselves with certain suggestions concerning the state of the ports.   It may have cost
them money; if so, the speculation was a fair one.   Fruit
and potatoes were a point in exports, and the freeing of the
coastal ports for cereals another, and such improvement of
the landing as an increase of lighters and the provision of
three tug-boats, to be used wherever the merchants required
them; these were the chief features of interest in M'nebbi's
mission to St. James's.

But it can scarcely be credited that any European Government would hazard the tying up of commercial facilities
with internal reforms.   It was no case of any reform movement at all, though it may have been a bold stroke on the
part of M'nebbi to pose as a reformer, in order to secure the
sympathy of England.   Instead of utilizing her merchants
and pressing for reforms at the ports which she could have
supervised and supported very cheaply, England insisted
upon prison and fiscal reform in the interior, ignoring the

total absence of any reliable native administrators. The
Howard Association bustled into the press with 'a communication from the Foreign Office . . . reporting that
reforms in the administration of Moorish prisons are to be
carried out immediately.' A lenient scheme for taxation
was also formulated. The Kaids were no longer to collect
the taxes; special appointments were to be made—to be
checked by inspectors—and receipts were to be given for all
taxes paid.

The state of affairs in Morocco became fairly kaleidoscopic.
Sid Fedool Gharnit intrigued for the downfall of M'nebbi,
and when the Envoy reached Mazagan, on his return from
St. James's, no guns boomed a salute, and the Governor
handed him a letter from the Sultan informing him that he
was no longer Minister for War, and must consider himself
under arrest and remain in Mazagan.

With characteristic energy M'nebbi walked out of the
Governor's camp that night, mounted a horse, and rode
straight to Marakish, accomplishing the journey in an in-
credibly short time. The entrance to the palace from
M'nebbi's residence had been closed and sealed. But
either struck by the rapidity and daring of his Minister,
or curious to hear the latest news from Europe, the Sultan
received him for a conference of some hours' duration, and
reinstated him as Minister for War.

Sid Gharnit, backed by the religious order of the Tayeb,
held his ground. The charges against M'nebbi were
numerous. He was accused of withholding in part the
treasure of Hadj Moktar, the late Grand Vizier, instead of
handing it over to the Sultan. This he explained by showing how the money had been spent in the Sultan's service in
Europe, and a ship, laden like a Noah's Ark, was even then
at Mazagan containing lions and wild beasts, besides pianos,
automobile cars, reaping and threshing machines, and other
'toys.' The next important charge against M'nebbi was

that he had acted without consulting the Sultan, and this charge was, in a measure, well founded. But it is customary for Ministers in Morocco to act without referring details to the Sultan.

M'nebbi fought with all his natural courage. The reforms he had promised were proceeded with. Letters were posted permitting the exportation of fruit and potatoes. The agreement was ratified as to the tug-boats and certain improvements in the port of Mogador. These items, together with the coastal export of cereals, appeared to pass with little or no comment in Marakish.

It was very different, however, when the Umanas were appointed to collect the taxes, and the Kaids saw their chance of gain vanishing. With the country people the news was received with satisfaction, approaching enthusiasm, especially in the oppressed district of Rahamna. The point on which events finally turned was whether the Sultan would leave Marakish for Fez, and place himself practically in the hands of the mosque and the Wazan influence. But wherever he goes he is surrounded by religious fanatics (a Sultan would scarcely be acceptable were he not personally somewhat fanatic), and his mind fed with the lying reports of conspirators, in a land where the intelligence of all men is effeminated by intrigue.

Among the loyal and peaceful tribes the new system of taxation was gradually applied, but with the strange result that the authorities in charge of enforcing the reforms did their best to contravene every point, so that in many places the new system became totally discredited—a disappointment to some, a byword and a laughing-stock to others.

No one stopped to consider what India would be were the natives expected to carry out reforms unaided by British administrators.

It was an occasion for testing the reality of the Sultan's goodness, and the soundness of his views, his Christian ideas, and, above all, his power to govern. The occasion showed us a despot annoyed on the old score of money reported to be purloined from his treasury—money obtained by customary oppression—issuing fiats with the delicious inconsequence of a Nebuchadnezzar. Finding that to fail in carrying out the reforms promised would discredit him in European eyes, he summoned the Kaids, and in M'nebbi's presence addressed them collectively, speaking with great dignity and severity, ordering them to cease from oppression and not allow themselves to be squeezed.

It was a romantic and beautiful spectacle, the young Sultan posing as a reformer, in his simple flowing white drapery, with all his Oriental dignity and charm of manner, and the subtle gift, which is so common to highly religious natures everywhere, of assuming the rôle of a counsel of perfection exactly according to the standpoint of the most influential spectators. The stage effect was admirable, and the bare fact was concealed completely that the Sultan was actually playing for the maintenance of his throne by securing British sympathy, and probably prompted by others, who saw if he were squeezed out of existence they must go with him. It was just a significant touch that, of the many Western inventions the Sultan is desirous to introduce into his country, machine-guns and arms of precision were prominent, and apparently appreciated by the Moors.

But a hint from the outer world as to reforms damped the intrigue against M'nebbi. The Sultan, is after all, an autocrat who disposes of the lives of his people as seems good to his holy judgment. Some Sultans have been more cruel than others, while a few have been almost capable of benevolent rule under pressure of some leading idea or fear of some strong adversary. Reform therefore became the fashionable topic in the Shereefian Court. Taken as a preventative against the French, it might have gone the length of turning out the Moors on Fridays in top-hats and black coats. The Sultan's progress to Rabat was glorious. He paid for all the provisions on the way, which might have been necessary, seeing that the country was suffering from a slight famine, and he paid out of his own treasury with money which, like all the funds of his lavish expenditure, is drawn together by cruelty and oppression.

But he was on the top of the wave, having sent a strong army before him into the north, the country of the Wazans and the hill tribes, on the excellent excuse afforded him by the Spanish demand for punishment. Thus he would not fear rousing the fanaticism of the mosque by his many inventions, or the intrigue of the enemies of his house, while he aired his smattering of civilized notions on the seaboard at Rabat.

It will be interesting to see how he will reconcile his notions of reform with the fact of his own autocracy when he is brought into collision with the hill tribes, whose tendencies are republican. Village communities, governed by councils and resting upon custom and tradition, may well reject the rigid law of the Koran as expounded in the commentaries. The worst of our problems in India is a mere flea-bite compared to Sultanate reform in Morocco.

But the Oriental knows more than the Christian about politics. While we are boggling about the morals of politics, the Oriental long ago disposed of any such question. It has always been possible for them to obey the voice of humanity, dictating what things they ought to do. But it is their nature to say, 'I go, sir,' and remain where they are. They will tolerate Abdul Azziz and his reform as long as they think he is only saying, 'I go, sir.' But were he to attempt to 'go,' with him it would fare worse than with M'nebbi, for the rôle of this 'engaging young man' would terminate in a long nap after a cup of coffee.

In M'nebbi's disgrace there is something pathetic. At

the time of writing he is no longer Grand Vizier, and in the East disgrace is seldom retrieved. The man who was shown London, and who promised in the heart of the Empire reforms which to his dazzled eyes seemed easy then, came back to find these reforms turned against him as arguments pleasing to the fanatical party and providing France with a ready weapon against a strong Grand Vizier.

Like many other natives, he may believe that England was right in the main, but what idea he may form of her methods we had better not inquire, especially if the strictures of the philanthropists, who made the conditions too hard for him, and then blamed him for his disgrace, reach his ears. They pointed to his low origin, to his merciless treatment of adversaries as he carved his way to power and influence, and implied that he was no reformer, that one Grand Vizier was the same as another, and that he had 'vested interests in keeping things as they are.'

The precise position of the Consular Service is similar to a Permanent Staff to the Legation, and part of the Consular business is to act as Information Bureau to the Foreign Office. Apparently it is a fraction of the institution by which we are really governed—namely, the Permanent Staff —and the source of our foreign policy, the Intelligence Department.

The members of the Permanent Staff in the departments cannot be haled before the public. No names are publicly affixed to the advice they tender. No one knows how much they suppress or pigeon-hole, or what use is made of the information they possess. They act with an eye to a possible change of the Ministry, and if they sometimes prevent extreme action, it is useless to look to them for reform. A compact band of small men, with minds cramped by office routine, strongly imbued with the importance of tradition and red tape, they must perforce cling to their stools, seeing that only in very rare instances would they have the ability

to succeed in trades or professions. How can we expect
from them a grand commercial Imperial policy ?

The theory of German rule is that the Emperor reigns
and the Ministers do his will. People differ as to whether
Russia is an autocracy or a bureaucracy, but no one doubts
the unity and continuity of her policy. Republics are
supposed to express the will of the people. We believe that
our people are led by the superior wisdom of our rulers.
The country believes in Cabinets, and if things go wrong
the Cabinet is knocked down and built up again. But the
Ministers depend on the Permanent Staff, being most of
them wholly ignorant of the departments which they are
supposed to direct ; and were the Cabinet, which is only a
committee, to be abolished, the affairs of the country would
continue to be run by the Permanent Staff. It is the Permanent Staff, not the Privy Council, to which Ministers look
for advice as to their policy.

The children of this world make to themselves friends
as prudential considerations dictate, and though people at
home may be slow in realizing the unpalatable truth, there
is a population in the world which has learnt the fact that
' it does not pay to be British.' British subjects suffer
because they are British, and British authorities permit it
with callous indifference. This treachery—this want of
frank friendship and definite aim—has lost us loyal support,
and converted wavering friends into decided foes, nor has
it conciliated a single enemy. ' Perfide Albion ' is not a
meaningless term. We are perfidious to those who are
most loyal to us. There is nothing manly, there is nothing
gentlemanly, in this policy. It is shifty and threadbare and
abject—down at the heels and shabby. It lives on expedients. We even go to war as if we were a State bankrupt in all things but the lives of brave men. Our Government cannot even get drunk like gentlemen, but must ' send
round the corner for two pennyworth of gin ' at a time.

And the heavy score which mounts up at this entertainment of petty flashes is paid at last by the much-enduring
commerce and industry of the country.

One more instance of Western diplomacy (*sic*) came under
my notice. In Azila a woman and a boy of the lowest class
of Spaniards were stolen by a hill tribe and taken away to
the mountains. As they were Spanish, Spain took a lofty
attitude, demanded a huge indemnity and the punishment
of the tribes. She was only able to do this with the consent
of the Powers. About the same time that her man-of-war
sailed from Cadiz with sealed orders, a Spanish convict who
escaped from Ceuta stabbed a Moorish peasant at Tetuan.
But no indemnity was asked and no punishment threatened
for this crime. Under European compulsion, the Sultan had
no choice but to fit out an army to carry fire and sword
through the tribe and to ‘ squeeze ’ the indemnity out of the
unfortunate peasants. There was no demand for inquiry.
Spaniards generally in Morocco are a low and criminal class,
and it is at least open to surmise that the captives, if they
were not stolen with the connivance of townspeople, probably friends or relatives, found themselves in a congenial
situation as dancers to the tribe.*

Such strange things happen in Morocco that it would be
interesting to know who the parties were most closely concerned in the affair and what money changed hands over it.
Outwardly all we know is that Spain was praised for her
action, and by no one more cordially than Great Britain in
the columns of the *Times*. What the Moors thought is not
reported. So at last the Powers were united—united in
backing Spain.

It was a beautiful instance of unity. All Christianity
joined hands ; not even the Czar of Russia or the President

* The Moorish Government, on October 31, paid to the Spanish
Minister at Tangiers an indemnity of 30,000 dollars for the abduction
of the Spanish captives by the Kabyles, together with a further sum of
1,600 dollars as compensation for the parents.

of the United States held back. 'The representatives of all the Powers supported Spain.' And this unity was not to obtain a single reform. It was to secure the payment of an indemnity to a needy, greedy, corrupt old country, and the wholesale murder of a mountain tribe for a single action far less criminal than thousands which take place every night in Paris, London, and Madrid.

Could Western diplomacy have found no higher common ground of accord and assent? Here the East, weakened as it is by the simple savagery of Africa, offered a chance for the solution of problems which render the Mediterranean a sea of danger, by the political extension of those commercial laws which are the best basis of understanding between all people, and whose promulgation in the councils of the world is the natural aim of true civilization.

THE END

BILLING AND SONS, LTD., PRINTERS, GUILDFORD

www.ingramcontent.com/pod-product-compliance
Lightning Source LLC
LaVergne TN
LVHW012206040326
832903LV00003B/151